FINANCIAL
FEMINIST

OVERCOME THE PATRIARCHY'S
BULLSH*T TO MASTER YOUR MONEY
AND BUILD A LIFE YOU LOVE

FINANCIAL FEMINIST

TORI DUNLAP

DEYST.

An Imprint of WILLIAM MORROW

DEYST.

This book is designed to provide readers with a general overview
of financial markets and how they work. It is not designed to be
a definitive investment guide or to take the place of advice from
a qualified financial planner or other professional. Given the risk
involved in investing of almost any kind, there is no guarantee that
the investment methods suggested in this book will be profitable.
Thus, neither the publisher nor the author assume liability of any
kind for any losses that may be sustained as a result of applying
the methods suggested in this book, and any such liability is
hereby expressly disclaimed.

FINANCIAL FEMINIST. Copyright © 2022 by Victori Media LLC.
All rights reserved. Printed in the United States of America.
No part of this book may be used or reproduced in any manner
whatsoever without written permission except in the case of
brief quotations embodied in critical articles and reviews.
For information, address HarperCollins Publishers,
195 Broadway, New York, NY 10007.

HarperCollins books may be purchased for educational, business,
or sales promotional use. For information, please email the
Special Markets Department at SPsales@harpercollins.com.

FIRST EDITION

Designed by Alison Bloomer
Illustrations © OneLineStock, samuii, derplan13, Qbertstudio,
Victoria, Simple Line/stock.adobe.com
Author photograph © Sarah Wolfe

Library of Congress Cataloging-in-Publication Data
has been applied for.

ISBN 978-0-06-326026-9

22 23 24 25 26 LSC 10 9 8 7 6 5 4 3 2 1

For Mom and Dad.
None of this is possible without you.
Sorry about the curse words.

CONTENTS

INTRODUCTION

I WAS ABOUT TO BECOME UNEMPLOYED, AND I HAD NEVER FELT BETTER.

IN LATE 2017, I decided to leave my first stable job out of college as a social media marketer for another position. I had ignored all the red flags during the interview process and took the job anyway. Big mistake.

After only a week, my boss called me into her office. I'd barely had a chance to memorize the code to the bathroom, let alone work out how the company operated—but as I sat in her office taking notes, she told me to my face how she was worried that she would regret hiring me.

I spent the next ten weeks crying almost every day, panicked at the thought of looming termination. On Christmas Day, I had to excuse myself from my family dinner to stare at my computer screen with complete dread, finishing up a project that I was told would determine my fate at the company. I felt completely powerless—she had made me feel scared and small.

If you picked up this book already knowing a bit of my story, the last words you'd use to describe me are "scared and small." As the founder and CEO of the financial education company Her First $100K, I've spoken in front of thousands of people; currently host a chart-topping business podcast; and am regularly featured, in bright lipstick and a leather jacket, on platforms like the *New York Times* and the *Today* show. I don't do scared or small. But during that time in a toxic job, I felt deeply ashamed and paralyzed, with my anxiety at an all-time high.

Then I checked my bank account.

For the past two years, I had diligently saved a portion of my paycheck for an emergency fund. I was slowly growing my first $100K, the personal origin story of the company I started on the side. This money's job was to sit patiently and wait: for a flat tire, an unexpected medical bill—or a toxic job. I realized I didn't have to spend another day at that job because I had *options*.

So, on a chilly day in January, I got to (politely) say "fuck off" to a bad situation. I walked out the door standing a little straighter, smiling for the first time in months. I was in control, as opposed to being controlled. It felt *good*.

This is the feeling I want for every woman.

I was lucky enough to have parents who gave me a financial education. I saw my dad routinely call our cable company to negotiate our bill. I saw my mom balance the checkbook on the thirteenth and twenty-first of every month (using software from the 1800s). They taught me how to be a smart saver, how to use a credit card responsibly, and how to use money as a tool to build a life you love. We worked together—my parents carefully saved and I had three jobs while in school—so that I could graduate debt-free from college. They didn't grow up with much, so they were committed to providing both an emotionally and financially stable life for me.

And because I didn't know any different, I thought this was the case for everyone. I thought everyone had this kind of stability and guidance. But as I grew older—graduated high school and went to college—I realized that financial education was a luxury only those with access to financial resources could pass on to their families. Having a financial education was a privilege. Being a cisgender, straight, able-bodied white woman with a middle-class upbringing was a privilege.

And with that privilege came responsibility.

I graduated from college in 2016, five months before Donald Trump was elected. As I came into womanhood—learning how to navigate my life and career in a society rooted in systemic oppression—I was deciding on the person I wanted to be and what I stood for. I began to unpack my own privilege and wanted to use that privilege to help others. It was the push twenty-two-year-old me needed to build something larger than herself. And so I founded Her First $100K to fight financial inequality by giving women actionable resources to better their money.

Nothing inspires me more than to see a woman standing in her own power. It's my favorite fucking thing. But when I entered the workforce as an adult, I saw sexism everywhere, to the point where women were so beaten down that they doubted their own power. I watched friends get paid less than they were worth. I saw women of color continually get passed over for opportunities. I learned that women hold the majority of debt in America and that they invest less of their money for retirement than men, though we live seven years longer.

A financial foundation provides choices. Small yet impactful choices, like the ability to take a revitalizing vacation, purchase little luxuries without guilt, or donate to causes you believe in. And Big Life Stuff choices, like starting a business, having children, or retiring early. And most important, the choice to exit toxic situations, like leaving an emotionally abusive relationship or an anxiety-inducing job.

Back in 2017, when I felt powerless and scared in a toxic situation, my bank account was the answer. My financial foundation meant I had options.

We live in a patriarchal world—a system that aids and abets inequality. In this system that has gatekept financial information and tools from marginalized groups, it is an act of protest to be financially independent. It is an act of protest to overcome negative beliefs about money in order to save, pay off debt, invest, and find fulfilling work. It is an act of protest to prioritize rest instead of hustle, abundance rather than scarcity, and generosity in place of stockpiling. In a world that actively works to keep us playing small, it is an act of protest to be stable, content, and powerful.

It's deeply important to acknowledge that there's only so much of our financial experience we can control. Personal finance is about 20 percent personal choice and 80 percent circumstantial. Yet historically, money experts' advice has suggested that if you're broke, in debt, or financially struggling, it's entirely your fault.

We cannot discuss personal finance, money, or economics without discussing systemic oppression. Outside forces—including but not limited to racism; ableism; homophobia; recession; natural disaster; and lack of access to health care, paid leave, or child support—are much to blame for why you might be struggling financially.

Financial feminism doesn't hand-wave away these structural problems in pursuit of individual women's success. This book does not solve inequality. It does not solve (or support) capitalism. It's not "I did it, so you can do it too!" inspiration porn or a pedestal for hustle culture. Rather, *it's a survival guide*. While we work to change the system that currently exists, we must navigate it to the best of our ability. We still have to pay our rent, buy groceries, and take care of ourselves.

A financial feminist is someone who embraces the power they already possess in order to help themselves—and those around them—to reach financial equality. Once you are taken care of—are stable, content, and thriving—you will not only have a full cup but also be able to fill others' cups too.

I've seen how financial feminism changes women's lives through my work with Her First $100K. Danielle, a woman who approached me outside of an art museum in Florence, rescued herself and her daughter from her abusive husband, started her own business, and was on her *Eat Pray Love* trip to Italy. Moji, who had always felt scared to negotiate her pay, now asks for her worth and asserts herself as a Black woman in the largely white industry that she works in. Lizz went from having to take a second antidepressant because of her demanding nine-to-five to owning her own tech company; she now makes $60,000 more than she made in her former job and feels more confident than ever.

This book is yours. I give you full permission to highlight, scribble in the margins, and dog-ear the hell out of it. Note passages that make you feel a certain way, homework that you want to come back to, and quotes that stand out to you. Throughout the pages, I will encourage reflection and to-dos, so make sure you have a Google Doc open or a notebook close by. We also have accompanying resources, tips, and guides at herfirst100k .com/book-resources—these are included with the purchase of your book, so please use them!

This book is intended to be read slowly over multiple sit-downs and will work best for you if you actually implement change. Do not try to read this all the way through in one sitting; you will get overwhelmed and never pick it up again. Give yourself grace and take breaks. In the same vein, please do not be a passive reader. Use the material to actually make changes in your life. It may be tempting to skip sections, especially if you're financially struggling right now and you're just trying to find a quick fix. But I intentionally wrote this book in the order it is written to help you to see a shift in your relationship with money in the long term, so please read it sequentially.

Woven throughout the book are interviews with experts and stories from the Her First $100K community. I did this for a few reasons: First, I wanted to showcase and amplify different perspectives, especially from marginalized groups. During moments of vulnerability (like learning about money!), it adds a layer of comfort and inspiration when someone shares an experience that might be similar to yours. And second, I'm not the be-all and end-all authority on everything, so I brought in some other experts to help.

Financial feminism is best summed up in one of my favorite quotes: "When you have all you need, build a longer table, not a higher fence." The mission of financial feminism is to do everything in your power to create a sturdy, beautiful table for yourself, and then invite others to it, rather than gatekeeping that abundance. And when everyone at the table is nourished, we start to tear down the fences others have built. When we are taken care of, only then can we work to change the system that disenfranchises so many. This book is here to give you the tools to help you navigate your financial life, so that when you are financially stable and financially well, we can fight against the system together.

Welcome to my table, Financial Feminists. Let's dig in.

FINANCIAL FEMINIST

CHAPTER 1

THE EMOTIONS OF MONEY

I COULDN'T GET HER TO JUST QUIT HER FUCKING JOB.

Kristine is my best friend and my absolute favorite person in the entire world. We've traveled to a half dozen countries together, we've been in a car with each other for at least five hundred hours (we once tried to calculate it), and we feel each other's wins and losses like they're our own. We met at my first job out of school—a job that I fled after a year and a half because of its insane toxicity and hellish culture.

This particular evening, she was calling to complain about yet another horror story, because while I had gotten out, she hadn't. After seven years at the same company, she was still dealing with the same bullshit.

While I tried to stay present and listen, one thought kept going through my mind: "I just need to convince her to leave. That will make her so much happier."

You probably know this scenario well. A friend calls, complaining about a problem, and you *know* that you could fix it. You could give them a detailed, step-by-step PowerPoint of what they should do now, because you want them to be okay and to feel less pain. But guess what? That's not what your friend is coming to you for—at least not yet. They're not coming for an action plan. They just need someone to rant to, someone who will listen, someone who can empathize and tell them, "Man, that sucks, I'm sorry. Let's work through it."

Right now Kristine is not calling me for a solution; she's calling to emotionally process her shitty situation at work, because that's the first, most necessary step.

The same thing happened when I started coaching women about money.

When I first began my work as a money educator, I immediately dove into my favorite thing: actionable advice. With good intentions, I thought that offering guidance around goal setting, budgeting, and investment strategies would be enough for success—and we'll get to all those things later, I promise. But after our sessions, my clients quickly reverted to old habits: mindless spending, negative self-talk, and analysis paralysis. We hadn't processed the root of their problems with money, because I just wanted to help them as quickly as possible. All the strategies I gave them to fix their financial issues ended up being temporary solutions to a much larger problem. It was then I realized: if we want to create lasting financial change, we have to do some emotional unpacking first. (Kristine and I have now learned to ask each other, "Do you want advice right now, or do you just need to process some shit?")

It's going to be tempting to skip this chapter. I completely understand that the last thing you want to delve into is "yOuR EMOtiONs aROuND mOnEY," but it's the most necessary part of the process of feeling financially confident. You can't start to change your money narratives until you get honest about where they originated. I can't teach you how to set financial goals if you haven't understood how your money hang-ups will affect you. It's like trying to compete on *The Great British Bake Off* without having a recipe in mind: you're just going to burn some stuff and also have a soggy bottom, and then judge Paul Hollywood will turn his crystal-blue eyes on you with disdain. (No handshake for you!) As shame researcher, professor, and all-around queen of my life Dr. Brené Brown says (she's going to be quoted so much in this chapter!), "If you don't name your emotions and feel them, they will eat you alive."

Money is psychological. I'll repeat it: money is psychological. Our financial decisions are directly impacted by our mind-sets and how we're feeling in a certain moment, and in turn these financial decisions directly impact our longer-term outcomes. We feel positive and negative emotions about every single aspect of money, whether it's debt, investing, or our income. I've done a lot of work to understand how my emotions and financial decisions interact—and I *still* spent countless pandemic nights looking at T-shirts I wanted to buy but didn't need (Madewell, there's something in your water, I swear to fucking God), replacing five unburned candles with new ones for no rational reason, and browsing Zillow for houses I can't afford in places I'll never move to. And then I promptly felt like shit because that jasmine candle was *obviously* the reason I couldn't afford my dream $4.3 million New Orleans shotgun-style house with the massive garden and wraparound porch. This shit never fully goes away—even I, a money expert, sometimes allow my emotional state to dictate my financial choices. I know I'm not alone. Think back on the last month and the kinds of money decisions you made—both the ones you're proud of and the ones you're not. How many were influenced, even subtly, by your mental or emotional state? I'm willing to bet almost all of them.

Your thoughts, feelings, and mind-set dictate your daily relationship with money.

It goes beyond spending and day-to-day finances; our emotions are in play for larger financial decisions too, even in the way we view money or the people with it. No one is immune. When I was twenty-two, I felt like I needed to buy a house that I wasn't emotionally or financially ready to own, because I felt the shame of being a renter and "throwing away money." My clients have so many stories like this: feeling guilt for hiring a housekeeper (despite having a disability), not checking their student loan balance because they're scared of what they'll find, and the all-too-common one: losing out on millions of dollars because they fear the idea of investing or of negotiating for a higher salary. And for most of my clients—and most likely for you, if you're reading this—avoiding money issues altogether might be a response to the emotions that come up. The prospect of studying, understanding, and executing financial tasks is intimidating and overwhelming, so we avoid them.

Women who *have* worked to learn more about investing, negotiating, paying off debt, saving money, and so on must often handle a double-edged sword, because the patriarchy punishes us for trying to improve our situations. Some examples include calling us "ungrateful" when we ask for the salary we deserve, actively gatekeeping information about the stock market, or shaming us for spending money on things that make our lives better.

Our feelings about money are intentionally weaponized. There are predatory companies taking advantage of our lack of education—store credit cards pretending to be reward cards, "Get rich tomorrow off this hot stock!" scams, multilevel marketing companies, and private student loans come to mind. These companies use our fears and insecurities to make money, in the same way that magazines, beauty companies, and the diet industry have historically done. Women consume their offerings in an attempt to feel less shame for not looking like we "should."

Alexis Rockley

POSITIVE PSYCHOLOGY COACH AND AUTHOR OF *Find Your F*ckyeah*

Shame is a social, fear-based, universal emotion—something that all of us experience, and regularly.

We hate talking about our shame; it's up there on the list of Topics That Make Strangers Uncomfortable at Boring Parties. I wish we would, though, because shame's control over us gets stronger the less we talk about it.

According to experts such as the famous shame researcher Dr. Brené Brown and author and clinical psychologist Mary Lamia, shame is rooted in our fear of disconnection. It's a very painful, predictive kind of negative emotion: *If I do not meet society's expectations, then I will become isolated from and rejected by others.*

You'll recognize it as that familiar "I'm not enough" or "I'm too much" feeling—an excruciating sense of unworthiness, the painful twinge of feeling unwanted or being unacceptable. Shame is that out-of-control feeling we experience whenever we're worried that something undesirable about us has been—or is about to be—exposed.

And who wants to be exposed?! We humans are a famously social species who crave connection and support; of course, we want to avoid isolation at all costs! It's what makes shame such a powerful source of motivation in our lives.

Shame, like all emotions, *exists to motivate us.*

As far as we can tell, shame, like its fellow negative emotions, serves a crucial evolutionary purpose: to keep us alive and in relationship with others. Shame is so uncomfortable that it *interrupts* our positive emotions and *redirects our attention* to the source of our shame. In other words, shame is just a signal; it's our brain's version of ringing an alarm, like, "Hey! Pay attention! Make sure you don't do anything that will get us shunned!"

But if shame is just a message from our brain, why do so many studies find that shame is highly correlated with violence, aggression, bullying, depression, addiction, and eating disorders?

Because we haven't been taught to experience our feelings like they're messages from our brain.

We're taught almost nothing about our negative emotions, except to be afraid of them, to shut them down, and we confuse them with *who we are.*

The result? Shame affects us in ways entirely opposite to what it evolved for. Instead of helping us stay connected to others, shame makes us shrink, self-isolate, and shut down. Rather than motivating us to reevaluate the "social norms" that people project onto us (and decide whether we even want to align with those expectations), shame makes us obsessed with those so-called norms, manifesting in all kinds of self-censorship.

In this way, shame's first demand is conformity. Ashamed, we believe we must look, think, have, choose, and act identically to everyone else in power. Familiar with the pain of rejection, and desperate to avoid its sting again, we align ourselves with the status quo: no risk-taking, no standing out. It's too dangerous. And if we can't conform? Then we see no other option than to shrink, minimize, and downplay all the ways that we deviate from that norm.

Shame traps us with comparison bait, leading to that familiar "I'm not _____ enough" spiral. It's why an innocently mindless, twenty-minute social media scroll leads to rethinking every single one of our career choices, like: *What, they're in Tulum now? How is it possible they look this good on-camera at all times? Honestly, how the hell do they afford this many vacations a year? What do they have figured out that I don't?*

Shame's comparison bait seems innocent enough—*I'm just gathering inspiration! I just want to find out what so-and-so is up to!*—but leaves us feeling like failures every time.

Shame's second demand is perfection, rendering success totally unattainable. Acknowledging that we're capable of outgrowing ignorance and learning from our mistakes shouldn't ordinarily trigger a full-on identity crisis. But when we take shame's humility bait ("Who do I think I am to _____?"), we drag ourselves into a pit of self-loathing that's hard to escape.

Humility bait is why people (and especially women) avoid saying anything that would imply we might want to be rich: *Who am I to admit that money is a priority for me, instead of something more… noble?* It's the reason we'd rather share an embarrassing sex story with coworkers than discuss differences in our salaries: *What if I make them uncomfortable? It's impolite to talk about money…*

Shame's humility bait seems innocent enough—*I'm just being realistic! I don't want to impose by asking too many questions!*— but it leaves us feeling (inaccurately) alone in our struggles and trapped in ignorance, afraid to admit what we don't know.

Shame convinces us to judge ourselves through a lens of perfection and conformity because it talks to us in the first person—I, me, my, mine, myself—and speaks in our voice. But when you confuse shame's emotional alarm (*I feel disconnected from money, what do I want to do about that?*) with who you are (*I'll never get my shit together, I'm just bad with money*), you've been tricked into believing the discomfort you feel is evidence that you're failing.

Let me be clear: The pain of rejection is *real*. The physical and emotional toll that widespread social rejection (marginalization) has on us is *real*. Shame is a powerful motivator, an evolutionary form of protection, and nothing to be embarrassed about feeling. (Ask me about the shame we feel about being ashamed; it's a meta mess.)

But! And! You don't have to subject yourself to shame's private torture. You are not alone. Perfection does not exist, and conformity is not an admirable goal. You deserve to be seen, supported, and connected while you outgrow your lack of knowledge and learn from your mistakes. Each of us is trying to figure out how to be a person in this body, with this brain, with these resources, in this society, at this time in history, on this planet. We're a mess, but we're doing our best.

To reframe shame from a crushing emotional burden to a simple message from your brain, start here: Reach out and connect with someone else. Partner up with others who want to learn what you want to learn, who are willing to admit what they don't know, who will celebrate one another's differences and acknowledge our intersectional needs. The community that Tori and her team have built seems like a good place to start, eh? *winks aggressively*

Shame can be one of the most destructive of our negative emotions, especially if we don't know what it's trying to tell us. A recent study stated that we women are also more likely to experience shame, "in part due to societal and cultural standards placed upon women that create negative self-evaluations in women when those standards are not met." It doesn't help us correct behavior in a useful manner, but rather causes us to spiral out.

It's these cycles of shame that keep us from bettering our financial foundation. We don't log in to our financial accounts because we're too scared of what we'll find. We feel ashamed for not understanding what a 401(k) is, so we don't ask. We feel guilty asking for a raise, since maybe we "haven't earned it."

From Brené Brown's work, we know that there is an antidote to shame: vulnerability. Facing the unknown, doing something that feels uncomfortable and new, allowing ourselves to admit that we don't have all the answers—it's one of the bravest things we can do. So, throughout this chapter—and throughout this entire book—I ask for your vulnerability. I ask for your trust in my guidance, even when it might be scary or overwhelming, and I ask that you put trust in yourself. This is a judgment-free, shame-free zone where you can feel safe to be a little bit financially and emotionally naked. (This book is financial strip poker, y'all. And I'm *pushes her chips into the center* all in.)

So, in the spirit of vulnerability, we're going to focus now on the emotional side of money—good, bad, and ugly—and how we can use more of our money to bring us joy, comfort, and stability. And we're going to frame the most common of those financial emotions—shame and judgment—in what I call the Five Patriarchal Narratives. These are common stories or mind-sets that keep you from becoming financially educated, stable, and confident; the hoops you have to jump through in order to assemble your financial foundation.

As you're going through these narratives, think about times you found yourself succumbing to them, and if they've affected your relationship with money. Because here's the thing: when we talk about the emotional side of money, we're also talking about its political and social sides. Your emotions didn't come from nowhere, but from a long history of patriarchy drilling these messages into you.

Without further ado . . .

narrative #1
YOU SHOULD KNOW "HOW TO MONEY"

VARIATIONS INCLUDE: "Why didn't I know this sooner? I'm such an idiot," "This should be easier for me to understand—am I stupid?" and "Everyone else seems to know what they're doing, why don't I?"

Oh, if I had a nickel for every time a woman in my community said, "Sorry for the stupid question . . ."

We are expected to be financially capable, but no one has taught us. Unless you had family to teach you (a privilege I had) or *maybe* a high school class called How to Use Quicken from 1992, you're in the dark. When I interviewed my friend Tiffany "The Budgetnista" Aliche on my podcast, *Financial Feminist*, she said, "No one breaks their leg and then thinks to themselves, 'Why can't I set my own bone?' So why do we feel that way with money?" Instead of offering ourselves grace and space to learn something new, we beat ourselves up, as if our not knowing (yet) is a failure in and of itself. Weirdly, when it comes to our financial education, we set different expectations for ourselves that are impossible to live up to. We didn't come out of the womb expecting to know how to speak Italian or play the tuba, so why do we expect to know how to avoid debt and how to pick stocks?

Now, regardless of your gender identity, this narrative exists. Society expects *everyone* to magically be good with money. But for men, this expectation comes with education.

On the other hand, the system was not built for women or anyone who isn't a straight, cisgender white man. (This is the thesis of my entire book, really.) On average, women are less likely than men to know about different financial practices. Men are taught about money in a way that women aren't, starting in childhood. This continues into adulthood. Golf courses, whiskey bars, and online message boards are chock-full of men trading stock tips, discussing their annual bonuses, and sharing real estate theories. It's socially acceptable—nay, *encouraged*—for men to discuss money and pursue wealth. Women could not have a credit card in their own name without a male cosigner until 1974. Women couldn't get a business loan without a male cosigner until fourteen years later. And even now, in the twenty-first century, men make the majority of the wealth-building financial decisions in heteronormative relationships. There are thousands of other examples. The system does not consider us and then shames us when we fail to understand.

When we as women are told to just be magically good with money—even though no one taught us—we are then scared to ask questions for fear of seeming dumb or naive. That fear doesn't come from nowhere. Many of the prominent financial experts we've turned to have reinforced and reminded and redrilled those emotions into us. The people we've trusted to give us good information that should set us up for success have instead made us feel stupid and small. An example: On her show, financial advisor Suze Orman once yelled at a divorced mother of three who was caring for an aging parent and had almost $250,000 in student loans from medical school to "tell [your children] the situation you have gotten yourself into. Let them see the reality of when you are irresponsible with facing the truth—what it can cause."

So, when we tally up systemic oppression, lack of education, and shame, *of course* we haven't been successful with our money. *Of course* we have all of these negative emotions tied to it.

Learning anything takes practice, time, and vulnerability. It's scary to do something for the first time, knowing you're going to be bad at it. It's Bambi learning to walk, all sprawling limbs and face-planting on the ice. Learning something new takes so much patience and, overall, kindness to ourselves. As Brené Brown says, "Feeling unsure and uncertain is the foundation of courage."

With financial education and knowledge about why shame is happening, that shame turns to anger at the unjust systems that cause it in the first place. Once we turn shame into anger, we can turn anger in action. And turning shame into action can be a powerful fucking thing.

narrative #2
TALKING ABOUT MONEY IS IMPOLITE

NO DOUBT YOU'VE HEARD THIS ONE. This narrative starts when we are children and continues into adulthood. Asking people how much they make, what their net worth is, how much they paid for something—it's "tacky" and must be avoided at all costs.

We are more likely to talk about any other uncomfortable topic—sex, death, politics, religion—before we'll bring up the subject of money. We will literally get naked with someone before we will ask them what they earned last year. At the societal level, we're led to feel that having a conversation about money is not only incredibly intimate but insanely invasive.

My not-so-conspiracy conspiracy theory: the system has perpetuated this narrative as a way to continue to control us.

The patriarchy profits off our silence. If it can convince us that "talking about money is gauche," then we stay underpaid and overworked. Not talking about money means we don't know that our coworker with the same experience is making 20 percent more. Not talking about money means that we feel deeply ashamed about our debt, thinking we're the only ones who are struggling. Not talking about money means not being financially transparent with our partner before marriage. There are countless examples of how this narrative hurts us: our earning potential, our net worth, our goals, our relationships.

The avoidance of money conversations can be a symptom of yet another narrative: we believe our net worth is our self-worth. Caitlin Zaloom, an anthropologist at New York University, hit the nail on the head when she said, "Your value as a human being is somehow made material in your pay and in your accounts." If you believe your inherent value is material, it will be deeply uncomfortable to be vulnerable and discuss money.

If this book gets you to do anything, let it encourage you to talk about money. Incorporating financial transparency into your life is one of the biggest ways we can not only change our personal situations but also create systemic change. We'll talk more about how and why to talk about money throughout the book.

narrative #3
YOU'LL BE RICH IF YOU JUST WORK HARD!

WE'VE ALL HEARD THIS ONE, and it is the ultimate shame tactic. The expectation is: work hard, save money, don't go into debt, and then you will be a millionaire. Not only is this narrative incredibly hurtful—especially when you're hustling your ass off—but it fails to acknowledge systemic oppression, generational poverty, discrimination, and other forces beyond our individual control. The single mom who works two jobs but can't seem to make ends meet doesn't need to work harder—she needs financial/societal support·and systemic change.

Of course, the American Dream, "pull yourself up by your bootstraps" narrative isn't new. The Puritans, who set sail to the English colonies in the early seventeenth century, believed that those who worked hard deserved more than those who were lazy, and that only those who worked hard prospered, revealing God's favor. The narrative is also rooted in racism: white landowners believed it was their mastery over the "lazier races" that was being rewarded with wealth and land. Ironically, the iconic image of the American Dream as we know it—a young couple standing proudly in front of their new home surrounded by a white picket fence—is largely the result of (white) soldiers' newfound ability to buy houses, financed through the GI Bill enacted by Congress near the end of the Second World War. In other words, government assistance, but only for white people. Yet the myth oozed into our culture, was woven into the ultimate American tapestry: "Just work hard, good things will come!"

Even worse, the primary pushers of this narrative are the very people we've turned to for advice around money. (See traditional personal financial experts like D*ve R*msey or Suze Orman.) "If you're working on paying off debt, the only time you should see the inside of a restaurant is if you're working there" is a real thing D*ve R*msey tweeted.

On the surface, we know this narrative is bullshit. We feel its bullshittery in our very bones. Yet this narrative still makes us question ourselves and our self-worth (much like those moments before I go to sleep, when I think, *Yeah, but what if I meet Timothée Chalamet, and he* doesn't *think I'm hot?*).

We are being gaslit. We are being lied to and then accused of being lazy and/or crazy. "Am I working hard enough?" "Should I take on more hours?" You can see how this is a slippery slope psychologically. You may (and should) scoff at this narrative, but it doesn't mean it won't affect you. It seeps in, whether we like it or not.

"Hard work = wealth built" isn't an accurate equation. There are so many more complicated factors that go into building wealth—some within our control but most outside of it. We must improve the things we can control and then work to change the systemic issues at a societal level.

narrative #4
UNLESS YOU'RE A MAN, WANTING MONEY IS "SELFISH"

THE CRAZY PART of shame and judgment around money is that women feel it not only when they're learning the ropes but also after they're successful. Even when we've built wealth, even when we've paid off our debts and are counting our investment returns, we *still* feel shame. But now it's feeling shame for doing *too* well. We feel guilty about how we're perceived when we're doing well largely as a result of social conditioning when we were children: "don't stand out," "put others first," and so on.

I'm a fucking internationally recognized financial expert, and *I* feel this shame. When I started building my own wealth, when my business grew to six figures and then seven figures, when I paid off my debt . . . I felt ashamed. Sometimes that shame was internally induced: I would feel ashamed that I wasn't struggling when so many others were, ashamed that being financially comfortable must mean I wasn't donating enough. That internal shame was the result of our culture's messaging about women with money, but the trolls that swarmed my social media mentions, making assumptions about my story, just reinforced that I was *supposed* to feel ashamed for having money.

We tend to think of women as caring, maternal, and self-sacrificing, and over and over again, studies do find that correlation. For example, a study published in the journal *Nature Human Behaviour* in 2017 found that women's brains exhibited a greater response when sharing money, while in men, the same part of the brain showed more activity when they kept the cash for themselves. It's a conclusion I'm proud of: I'm glad that women default to being caring. But like so much of being a woman, this is something conditioned into us. This default nature of giving and selflessness is an expectation of our gender.

Now, let me preface that by saying that donating your money and your time is *hugely* important, especially if you have the means to. Feminism that isn't intersectional, that doesn't help others and work to change systemic inequality, is not feminism. But we need to call out the different expectations for men when it comes to altruism. As women, we are *presumed* to neglect our own wants and interests to give back, and, let me tell you, men aren't. It's not conditioned into them like it is into us.

Beginning in childhood, boys are typically given toys that teach innovation, creativity, and self-reliance—things like Legos and trucks, things to build and create. And what are girls given? Dolls. Easy-Bake Ovens. Bridal veils. Before we can even speak, we're told that our value to society is not our own ingenuity but rather how we can serve and belong to others. A literal child is given another "child" to caretake. In a study about children's toys, psychology professor Judith Elaine Blakemore found that "girls' toys were associated with physical attractiveness, nurturing, and domestic skill, whereas boys' toys were rated as violent, competitive, exciting, and somewhat dangerous. The toys rated as most likely to be educational were typically categorized as neutral or moderately masculine."

As we age, this socialization continues. According to Dr. Mariko Chang, an expert on wealth inequality, "Girls, as they are growing up, are not socialized to feel that it's okay for them to have ambition about creating wealth, not the way it is for little boys. They're encouraged to take on roles that let them take care of other people." The result is that women are overrepresented in jobs such as nursing and teaching, or they perform unpaid domestic labor—important jobs that our economy devalues precisely because they are performed predominately by women. Beyond "traditional gender roles" that used to keep women in the home, we actually assign those gender roles to specific kinds of work and then pay people who do those jobs less than people who do other work. In our capitalist society, this conditioned tendency toward caregiving, sadly, punishes us financially.

For me, the message, over and over again, was that declaring I wanted to be rich wasn't socially acceptable. It was okay for men to spend their hard-earned money on vacations or a nice watch—but the question to me and other women was always: "But how are you prioritizing others?" It's like blowing out the candles on your own birthday cake and being told you're an asshole for not wishing for a cure for cancer. Even though it's your day, your cake, and your wish—you're expected to wish for world peace and then are shamed if you don't. Society doesn't expect that of men.

What happens, then, when a woman becomes financially independent? When she uses her wealth to better not only others' lives but also her own? The patriarchy realizes that when a woman gains the knowledge to build wealth, soon it will have no control over her life or decisions. Her financial independence is a threat to the status quo. So, the patriarchy demands we tax ourselves. It weaponizes our altruism. Recent research suggests that women are expected to behave altruistically and, given that they disproportionately occupy societal roles involving caregiving and subservience, are punished for deviating from that norm to a much greater extent than men are. Thus, women may internalize altruism as their instinctive response, even at their own expense.

As a result, we can't or won't say we want money for our own benefit—it has to be in service to others, whether that's through philanthropy or for our families, coworkers, or staff. My friend and fellow money expert Paula Pant explained it like this:

> Women are taught that our labor should be free (or labor should be poorly compensated) and that there's somehow nobility in that. If we do have to justify charging people, we often have to explain how it will not just help ourselves but help others. I can't make a statement such as "I charge X" without also saying, "I charge X in order to give my employees a better wage." Women's earnings have to come with an explanation. I think this messaging, in terms of how we earn, also gets translated into how we spend. Whatever money we make, we're supposed to spend it on other people. Even if you bought the fanciest stroller, no one is going to call that frivolous because you're at least buying it for someone else. However, if you buy a pair of jeans, that's somehow different.

I know that sometimes resentment of wealth comes from a well-intentioned place—in a time of rampant inequality, celebrations of wealth can feel gross—but I reject the notion that women should be the ones to face most of that backlash. If one of the causes of inequality is men getting to be rich individualists who force everyone else to do the caring, support, and redistribution of resources, women finally "gaining" that right doesn't change anything. We need to challenge men's gender roles in the process, or we'll be left with a society of individualistic assholes where no one cares about anyone. Financial feminism isn't just about a woman's right to decide what she does with her money, without the current socialized pressure to exist in service of others. It's also about each of us demanding that the people who have access to the most money (i.e., men) actually *start* thinking about their existence in service of others.

As we work toward bridging the inequality gap, what if becoming financially stable was an answer? What if a step toward making the world a better place is to ensure that marginalized people have options and time to rest and the ability to buy beautiful things—and, yes, have money to give to others?

There is nothing wrong with a woman wanting money for any reason that doesn't harm other people. Any criticism of what a woman does with her money reads as especially ridiculous when it's directed not just at discretionary spending but also at expenditures involving safety, healthy housing, and the ability to leave toxic situations, whether at home or at work. Which leads me to . . .

narrative #5
"MONEY CAN'T BUY YOU HAPPINESS" (AKA "WANTING MONEY IS EVIL")

THE OLD ADAGE "Money can't buy you happiness" is bullshit. The general sentiment may be true: buying things is not where you should turn for contentment. But at its core, the statement is false. It's meant to keep you powerless, unpaid, overworked, and financially unstable.

Anxiety regarding money-related issues has been at or near the top of the American Psychological Association's *Stress in*

America survey every year since it began in 2007. Overall in 2022, two-thirds of all Americans reported feeling stressed about money. But among men and women between the ages of eighteen and forty-three, financial worries affected *four in five* poll respondents. (That's 82 percent of those age eighteen through twenty-five, and 81 percent of those age twenty-six through forty-three.) When you're poor or financially stressed, the words "money can't buy you happiness" is the most gaslight-y thing someone can say. Just as our finances are affected by our emotions, so are our emotions affected by our finances. And these emotions can stem from the kind of poverty where you don't know where your next meal is coming from, from being in a financially abusive relationship, from carrying crippling student debt. Being broke and financially unstable fucking sucks.

Studies about our brains "on poverty" show that lack of resources negatively affect our cognition, stress levels, and decision-making. Recently, a landmark study even suggested that giving poor mothers a cash stipend during the first year of their babies' lives literally improves their children's cognitive development. And we know from research that higher incomes are correlated with higher well-being (there's debate around the threshold this stops, but the point still stands). So, when someone says, "Well, money can't buy you happiness," you think, *Umm*, wanna bet, *motherfucker?!* Because not only does money provide you with your basic human needs such as safety and healthy food, but also it gives you the ability to rest, to nourish your body and mind, and to leave bad situations. Money can buy stability and choice, and *that* is happiness.

Inherently, money is not valuable. I don't want a photo of Ben Franklin on a stack of some government-issued paper. I want choices. I want what money can buy me. For millions of American women, the dream of wealth is a dream of freedom, because it's money that provides us with options when our government and society fail to. Freedom from a toxic relationship or client or situation. (I can't tell you how many of my clients have told me that this is their primary goal.) Freedom to move into a bigger apartment so that each child in the family can have their own room. Freedom to spend more time with your aging parents. Freedom to start the business you've always dreamed of. Freedom to travel the country in a souped-up school bus. Or, like one of my first coaching clients, the freedom to waltz into a Whole Foods and buy the fanciest cheese she could find for her weekly charcuterie nights—without thinking twice.

"Money can't buy you happiness" is what the patriarchy says when you show interest in becoming financially educated, when you start gaining power. It's meant to keep you playing financially small: accepting the first offer without negotiating your pay, allowing your male partner to invest for you, not getting a better-paying job for fear of being labeled a "job hopper." But, really, the patriarchy is happy when you conform, when it can control you—so it keeps you in homeostasis, playing small.

The patriarchy's worst nightmare is you being uncontrollable. Its worst nightmare is that these narratives no longer affect you. Its worst nightmare is you standing in your power, advocating for yourself and others. (I've always loved being the patriarchy's worst nightmare.)

You might be asking, "But, Tori, why do I need to know these narratives to figure out my money?"

The majority of money habits are actually formed by age seven. Yes, seven years old. By second grade, you have largely established how you will view and manage money as you move through life. Researchers found that even children as young as five could reliably report their feelings about money.

A word from
Dr. Brad Klontz
FINANCIAL PSYCHOLOGIST AND AUTHOR

After I finished my doctorate in clinical psychology, I owed $100,000 in student loan debt. I saw a friend of mine make $100,000 trading stocks in one year, and I thought that was a brilliant strategy. He knew nothing about the stock market. I knew nothing about the stock market either, so I thought I could do that too. I sold what I had of value and started day trading with it. I did great for a few months, and then the tech bubble burst (just to give you a sense of how old I am), and I just watched it all melt away. I thought, *Oh my God, why would I do something so dumb?* That's when I got interested in financial psychology and decided to dive into the science.

In trying to develop a treatment program for people with money issues, I developed a money belief scale, because nothing existed. I say sort of tongue in cheek that it took me something like a couple of months to become the world's leading expert in financial psychology, mainly because psychologists didn't want to talk about money. These are the four categories of beliefs (or what I call "money scripts") that came out of that:

The first script is **money avoidance**. Money avoiders think rich people are greedy, money corrupts, and there's virtue in living with less money. This is a really common belief in lower socioeconomic groups. Ironically, you *do* want to be wealthy, but you repel wealth because if you do start to make money, then you feel like you're drifting away from your friends and family. Or you might sense (or imagine) resentment on the part of people you'd been close to. In effect, your newly acquired financial stability becomes a wedge between you and them. This stirs up a lot of anxiety, and you feel bad, so you subconsciously (or maybe even quite consciously) make a series of poor decisions until you wind up right where you started. That's a common pattern with those trying to climb the ladder. So, money avoidance is associated with lower income, lower net worth, and a whole host of self-destructive financial behaviors.

The second one is **money worship**. This is where you think that having more stuff, more money, is going to solve all your problems and make you happy. It's not necessarily negative or positive—but people who believe those things strongly have less income, less net worth, and more credit card debt.

Number three is **money status**. I would basically call it the "keeping up with the Joneses" effect. Your self-worth equals your net worth. Money status seekers might say something like, "I won't buy something unless it's new," or "I'll never buy anything unless it's considered the best," or "If people asked me how much money I made, I'd probably tell them I make more than I actually do." Whatever the outward display of wealth is, it's associated with terrible financial outcomes. It is the one money script that's associated with socioeconomic status in childhood. People who grew up poor are more vulnerable to this.

The fourth category is **money vigilance**. It's good that there's a good one, right? These beliefs are "I'd be a nervous wreck if I didn't have money saved for an emergency," or "If someone asked me how much money I made, I'd probably tell them I make less than I actually do."

In the studies we conduct at Creighton University, we identify something we call "financial flashpoint experiences": these are experiences that lead directly to your money scripts, which predict your financial behaviors and your financial outcomes. Then your financial behaviors lead to more financial flashpoint experiences, which reinforce your beliefs. It's a cognitive triangle, basically. Flashpoint experiences can be identified by asking questions such as: What three things did your parents teach you about money? What three things did your dad teach you? What is your most painful money memory? Your most joyful? It is so important to do a deep dive and emerge with the answers.

I interviewed my parents about these too. I asked, "Mom, what was it like for you growing up around money? How did you feel about it?" It's good to do a deeper dive than just your own upbringing. What was your parents' upbringing? They are leaking those emotions into you even if you never hear the stories or understand the trauma that's getting passed down to you. Many people are traumatized around money, and growing up in poverty is just chronic trauma around money. It explains your beliefs, and your beliefs predict your behaviors.

Your beliefs are your childlike mind trying to make sense of money and what has happened to you. As a child, you can't see the whole picture. Maybe you see your parents fighting about money, and you happen to be rich. Then you go to your friend's house for dinner, and his parents are poor, but they communicate well. You might be left with the impression that having money damages a marriage. That's how the childlike mind works. Then you spend the rest of your life repelling money because that's the conclusion you arrived at. It's really powerful stuff, and much of it is subconscious.

Historical and generational trauma around money have far-reaching consequences. It's a huge leg up if your parents went to college, for example, because they can teach you how to get into college and how to thrive in college. Sometimes there's a lack of trust in established institutions: I see a lot of times with people of color that they are much more anxious about investing because they have an entire experience of society hurting them. There's a reaction to that because they're worried that they're going to get taken advantage of again.

I recommend that people learn to become more open to conversations about money. You can google what to do to improve your financial life, but how do I get you to actually follow through? How do I get you to integrate what you learn? How does this become part of you where you feel good about it, and so you don't sabotage yourself later on? If you don't handle this stuff, you might attain some temporary success but then sabotage it.

Weirdly enough, this should offer some relief, right? It should release some self-blame, realizing that so much of our behavior, our mistakes, our perceptions, are ingrained without us even remembering how—just like those patriarchal myths you know but can't remember where you first heard. Yet, naturally, we blame ourselves for the bullshit we feel around money. We think, *The reason I'm not good with money is I just can't save*, or *I don't want money, because people who have it are awful.*

Psychologists like Dr. Klontz believe that how you saw your parents handle money creates a sort of "money imprint" that guides your behavior unless you actively work to change it. So, your money mind-set is linked to the behaviors you saw your parents exhibit when managing their own money. How did your parents or your family discuss money? Were you like me, with parents who were committed to smart financial habits, to being frugal, and to educating their kids about money? Or, more commonly, was money a source of familial stress or concern? Was money not even discussed, leaving you in the dark about concepts like debt or saving?

We have to find the root of these emotions in order to process them. In order to do this, we have to go back to our childhoods. (Yep, it's gonna feel a li'l like therapy.) As Dame/World's Best Grandma Julie Andrews sings, we have to start at the very beginning. (I've heard it's a very good place to start.)

One of my favorite exercises in financial coaching sessions is journaling through a first money memory. It will change the way you view your money, allowing you to explore your financial hang-ups and showcasing how you can start to fortify your financial foundation. Grab a notebook or open a Google doc, light that candle you don't remember buying, and let's dive in. (If you want to have your notes all in one place, there is also room at the end of the chapter to write the homework in the book itself.)

#1

WHAT IS YOUR FIRST MONEY MEMORY?

WHAT IS THE FIRST TIME that you consciously remember thinking about money? About saving money? About spending money?

Here's mine. I'm a complete theater nerd. I grew up performing in plays and musicals, and was a theater major in college. When I was about four years old, I really wanted to see a local production of *Annie*, but my parents told me I'd need to save for the ticket. I found an empty Altoids tin, and for a solid two months, I would religiously put pennies and quarters I found on the street or got from running a lemonade stand that summer in it. When the day finally came to see the show, I had *maybe* $5— when tickets actually cost around $25.

I was so excited to see *Annie* that I lost sleep over it the night before and was giddy the whole way to the theater, until we were pulling up to park. I realized *I had forgotten my tin with all my money at home*. The drama wasn't on the stage that day, it was in the car. How could I have been so stupid to leave my money tin—the only money to my four-year-old name—at home? I started bawling in the back seat, thinking I couldn't get into the show anymore (somehow utterly convinced that my few dollars in coins was enough to buy me a ticket). Realizing what was happening, my mom reassured me kindly that she would cover the cost of my ticket (which was the plan the whole time). The practice wasn't about the actual money saved—especially as a four-year-old with no real income source—but rather the exercise of saving for something you wanted.

When I reflect on that money memory, I see it as a positive: I learned the value of saving for something I wanted. When I conduct this exercise with clients, however, their money memories tend to be more negative. One client's first memory was watching her parents fight about a credit card statement, while another's first memory of money was realizing that her family didn't have enough of it.

As you're writing down your first money memory, don't just focus on the facts of the story. How did it make you feel, in the moment and afterward? Are there positive or negative emotions associated with your memory?

Once you've written down your first money memory and done some reflection, consider this prompt:

#2

HOW DOES YOUR FIRST MONEY MEMORY DICTATE YOUR RELATIONSHIP WITH MONEY NOW?

I CAN LOOK BACK on my first money memory and think, *That makes total sense now.* I learned how to save money at a very young age. I knew that if I couldn't afford something, I couldn't buy it. This money mantra was ingrained in me as I got older, through more serious conversations in high school about utilizing credit cards, for example. And I learned that you avoided going into unnecessary, costly debt by having savings first. That education directly dictates the relationship I currently have with money.

That doesn't mean it's all roses. Reading further into this and other money memories from childhood, I've come to realize that my parents valued stability over risk and instilled that in me. I'm thankful that my dad's nine-to-five job—complete with a 401(k) and health benefits—plus my mom's hard work as a homemaker gave me a stable upbringing. But when it came time for me to seriously consider becoming a full-time entrepreneur, that stability > risk way of life kept me playing it safe in a corporate job for longer than made sense for me. So, when I was deciding if I should quit, it was one of the most terrifying decisions of my life. My parents told me point-blank, "You should do everything you can to keep your job," even though I had money in the bank and momentum in my business. Even positive memories surrounding money leave their mark and can impact future choices about money.

What if you have a traumatic first money memory? What if you saw your parents struggle financially, and so you've gone in the completely opposite direction, into hoarding money? Or maybe your parents were so frugal that you can't help but spend money willy-nilly now that you're in charge?

Once you've made that connection between your first money memory and your current relationship with money, you're ready to move on to the third prompt.

#3
HOW DO YOU WANT TO CHANGE YOUR RELATIONSHIP WITH MONEY?

WHEN I FIRST STARTED money coaching, I worked with a client who was saving 90 to 95 percent of her income *every month*. That's impressive—but also a red flag. Almost no one can, or should, save 90 percent of his or her income. When I asked her why she was saving so much, I discovered that it was her financial trauma. Growing up poor caused her to be so financially strict with herself. Instead of feeling financially stable, confident in her choices, and like she could ease off the gas, she was asking me to coach her because *she thought she wasn't saving enough*. She felt guilty for spending anything—even the absolutely necessary expenses that made up the bulk of the 5 to 10 percent.

Her saving that much money was incredible, but it was also neither sustainable nor, frankly, joyful. I want you to have a balance. I want you to be able to enjoy the money you have now *and* build your savings for the future. So together, she and I worked to devise a plan where she could feel financially stable and continue saving, while also enjoying her money guilt free.

So, I ask you: How do you want this relationship to grow and evolve? Do you want to start saving more of your money? Do you want to see money as abundant rather than scarce? Have you largely viewed money or people who have money as evil or bad, just by virtue of having it? Is that something that you want to adjust?

#4
HOW ARE YOU GOING TO MAKE THAT CHANGE HAPPEN?

WHAT ARE THE ACTIONABLE THINGS that you're going to do to change your relationship with money? How are you going to make the change happen?

A goal without a plan is just a wish. It sounds so obvious, but nothing about your relationship with money changes unless you make changes. There is no "I'm a financial genius" button to push. You have to take action.

A great place to start is bettering your relationship with money by investing your time and energy into educational resources, such as reading this book (hi!), taking notes, and doing the homework. Listen to podcasts. Have conversations about money with your friends. Open a savings account or an IRA. Write down all of your debts. Rework your budget with a critical eye. Actually look at your credit card statement. We'll talk more about all of this in later chapters, as well as learn how to maintain a financial self-care practice.

For our final money journal prompt, I'm going to ask you to close your eyes. Well, read the question first, *then* close your eyes.

#5

WHAT WILL YOUR LIFE LOOK LIKE IF YOU CHANGE YOUR RELATIONSHIP WITH MONEY?

IF YOU CHANGE your relationship with money, what will a typical day in your future look like? How will your life have been altered? How will your mind-set have changed?

This was one of the biggest reasons I was able to hit my $100K goal in 2019 at age twenty-five. Three years before, I saw very clearly how that $100K would change my life. It wasn't just a random number I picked out of thin air; I calculated that having $100K would free me to quit my job and pursue running my business full-time.

It meant my entire day would change. I wouldn't have to wake up at six thirty in the morning, commute to work, then sit at a desk for eight-plus hours and make somebody else rich. It meant I didn't have to submit PTO (paid time off) requests when I wanted to take a vacation. It meant that I could do what I wanted to do every day. It meant that I was not only my own boss but also the head of a company where I got to make all the decisions and change women's lives along the way.

To answer this question for yourself, I need you to get really specific. We're gonna do some visualization, baby. Wax poetic with me here.

Imagine: What does it feel like, every day, to not be in debt anymore? What does it feel like to wake up every day knowing that your investments made money for you while you slept? What does it feel like to finally have enough money that you're covered for emergencies *and* able to take a much-needed vacation? How is your life different? How is your mind-set different? How is your mental health different? What options open up to you now that you have that financial foundation?

How does your life change because you've changed your relationship with money?

Changing our mind-set means overcoming those negative beliefs about money that were learned at a young age. If we want our relationship with money to change, we have to get to the root of it—right down to where that shit starts.

Once we can start to unpack our money memories, our inherent biases, and the narratives we've been believing, we can begin to release that shame and judgment. We can start focusing on what we can do *right now* to change our relationship with money.

We can contemplate, dream, and fantasize about what our life looks like when we are in control, when we've moved through, processed, and come to terms with the negative bullshit that we've been carrying about money for our entire lives.

This is the other side of our emotions around money. Instead of shame, judgment, stress, and fear, we can feel pride, awe, hope, and joy.

My money has opened up the most joyful opportunities for me: I'm currently writing this chapter at an Airbnb in the middle of France, where I've taken myself on a two-month writer's retreat. Eating kilos of cheese and drinking Burgundy ("write drunk, edit sober," right HarperCollins?!), walking midday through the garden, taking a well-deserved nap when I need a break from writing—while my multi-seven-figure business makes me and my team money in the background. THIS is what money can buy. Stability, options, and a life you fucking love. It opens up every possibility for you, every comfort, every small luxury. It makes unexpected expenses—like a flat tire or the cost of attending a wedding or the one-too-many-drinks Uber at the end of the night—nothing more than momentary inconveniences. It's the definition of the word *ease.*

Money, and the choices it's provided, has brought me so much joy. And even more powerfully, it's given me confidence. I see the same thing in every story from Her First $100K community members. Like Deanna, who negotiated a 6 percent salary increase and a wellness budget for her first job out of college. Or Anna, who, as an eighteen-year-old new mother, used to dig behind her couch cushions for change and who now just bought a car, in cash, for her daughter's sweet sixteen. Or Terry, a first-generation Latinx American who just hit $100K in her 401(k) and is now focused on building generational wealth for her five-year-old child.

This is the feeling I want every woman on this planet to have.

A word from
Cinneah El-Amin
FOUNDER OF FLYNANCED, A DEBT-FREE TRAVEL AND
WEALTH-BUILDING PLATFORM

One of the biggest money lessons I was taught was that money is taboo, that we shouldn't be talking about how much we make or how much we have. That narrative is something that I still fight against.

Another money narrative I inherited is the scarcity mind-set. I'm fighting against this idea I learned growing up and having my nervous system getting used to scarcity around money. When I think about my journey, from when I was literally living paycheck to paycheck, even though I was making good money, to now—it's a lifetime of habits and mind-sets that I'm working against.

Money is such a part of our psyche. It takes time to really develop new mind-sets, new ideas around our money. So, I extend myself grace when I have those moments when I feel like I'm slipping into old patterns, like I'm back in that space that I once was. I'm giving myself the grace.

As a Black woman, money has been a key to help me unlock some of the parts of myself that I feel like I was afraid to really let shine: traveling more often, living in an expensive city that I absolutely love, choosing not to live with my parents—being able to have independence in that way and being able to have a choice when it comes to building my career.

I see wealth as the ability to have options now and to be able to pass on those options to other people. All my foremothers would have already had children by now. Womanhood was so defined by being a mother for them, and it wasn't always because they chose to but because that was the expectation. Being a financially stable woman is being able to say what womanhood looks like to me. It's allowing me to navigate the world and society differently. I don't feel scarcity anymore when it comes to my money. I don't feel scarcity when it comes to dating and finding a partner.

I feel freedom of choice most when it comes to being able to experience travel in a way that's spiritually transformative. This is something that has been totally unlocked since I've become financially stable. This idea that I could literally pack up my life and just decide I'm going to go to Mexico. I want to go to Mexico because I can and I want to, so I'm going to do it!

I attribute all those things to just having more financial stability. That has been the key that has brought me so much joy in my twenties. When I think about the choices that I make, when I think about my horizon and where my life is going, I have a lot of happiness. I don't think that would be possible if I was still struggling to make ends meet, if I was living paycheck to paycheck.

Financial stability opened up my ability to access things that just make my life easier. I can do my own laundry at home. I can hire a personal trainer. I can work with a nutritionist—things that literally are improving my health and well-being. Before I was financially stable, I had so much money that was going toward just paying off debt and staying afloat. Having more surplus in my budget allows me to make those choices by asking *What will make me feel best at this moment?* I don't have to rely on a partner. I don't have to rely on a parent. I don't have to rely on anyone to get the joy that I want out of life. Especially now.

HOMEWORK

1. ACKNOWLEDGE WHICH MONEY BELIEFS ARE CURRENTLY IN YOUR HEAD

Write down the shame statement that is loudest in your head and then practice self-compassion by switching it up:

"I'm not _____ enough."

"I *am* _____ enough."

Try coming up with one or two more affirmations to pair with the one above. Write them on a notecard and tape it to your mirror, leave it in your car, or use it as a bookmark.

_____

_____

_____

_____

_____

_____

_____

_____

_____

_____

_____

_____

_____

_____

_____

_____

2. THE NARRATIVES

Have you been internalizing the Five Patriarchal Narratives? In what ways have they been impacting your money behaviors? Journal about the following:

NARRATIVE #1: You should know "how to money."

_____

_____

_____

_____

_____

_____

_____

_____

_____

_____

_____

NARRATIVE #2: Talking about money is impolite.

_____

_____

_____

_____

_____

_____

_____

_____

_____

_____

_____

NARRATIVE #3: You'll be rich if you just work hard!

_____

_____

_____

_____

_____

_____

_____

_____

_____

_____

_____

_____

_____

NARRATIVE #4: Unless you're a man, wanting money is "selfish."

_____

_____

_____

_____

_____

_____

_____

_____

_____

_____

_____

_____

NARRATIVE #5: "Money can't buy you happiness."

_____
_____
_____
_____
_____
_____
_____
_____
_____
_____
_____
_____

3. FIRST MONEY MEMORY

Let's journal about your first money memory, if you haven't already.

What is your first money memory?

_____
_____
_____
_____
_____
_____
_____
_____
_____
_____

How does your first money memory dictate your
relationship with money now?

_____

_____

_____

_____

_____

_____

_____

_____

_____

_____

_____

_____

_____

How do you want your relationship with money to change?

_____

_____

_____

_____

_____

_____

_____

_____

_____

_____

_____

_____

_____

_____

How are you going to make that change happen?

_____
_____
_____
_____
_____
_____
_____
_____
_____
_____
_____
_____
_____
_____
_____
_____
_____
_____
_____
_____
_____
_____
_____
_____
_____

What will your life look like if you change your relationship with money?

_____

_____

_____

_____

_____

_____

_____

_____

_____

_____

_____

_____

_____

_____

_____

_____

_____

_____

_____

_____

_____

_____

_____

_____

_____

_____

_____

CHAPTER 2

SPENDING

ALLOW ME TO LET YOU IN ON A LITTLE EXPERIMENT I'VE BEEN CONDUCTING OVER THE PAST FEW YEARS.

When I first got started on my own money journey, trying to find personal finance guidance that wasn't written during the fucking Salem witch trials, I would google something harmless, like "financial advice for women." And over and over again, I saw the most interesting thing.

Financial advice addressed to men would tell them to invest in the stock market, negotiate their salaries, and buy real estate. It would give not only specific financial tasks but also ones that were focused on building wealth and making more money. All great advice!

But here's the whammy: the paragraphs of "advice" geared toward women were littered with thinly veiled misogyny. (You're gonna see that as an unfortunate recurring theme of this book.) If women were taught anything about money, it was day-to-day finances: managing the household budget, grocery shopping, coupon clipping, spending less. The gender-specific advice I found around money and wealth was always tied to spending: we went to the mall too frequently, and our purses and lattes and manicures were the reason we weren't building wealth. If I sent Timothée Chalamet a DM every time I read the phrase "designer handbag" used in a condescending way, he'd have blocked me a *long* time ago.

It wasn't about making more but about spending less. It was always framed like this: "Women, you're not rich because you spend frivolously." Recent research looked at three hundred financial "how-to" articles and found that 90 percent of the pieces aimed at women were centered around saving money. Two-thirds of the articles reviewed labeled women as excessive spenders. Advice for men: "Here are five hot stocks right now." Advice for women: "Here are five dinners you can make for under $5."

The solution is always to clip coupons, spend less (or not at all), and budget meticulously. Track every fucking penny. Deprivation is the answer. Even in the twenty-first century, this is the narrative: Men, build wealth by making strategic, long-term financial decisions that actually make a difference. Women, that Dior purse ain't it, you cow.

The real kicker here is that the spending power of women drives the majority of the economy. We've been marketed to since we were young girls, a constant narrative to get us to spend money. The world is built for boys and men to play in with little consequence, but stores and malls are designed entirely to tempt the impulse dollars of young women. Women are the most marketed to but then are shamed for spending!

We've established how the patriarchy wants us to play small, take up less space, and fall in line. Nowhere is this clearer than in regard to our spending, where there's rampant misogyny under the guise of "advice" that ignores the escalating burdens of "necessary" expenses (needs) in order to shame us for purchases that bring us joy.

To be sure, we all—women and otherwise—have necessary expenses. We all have to spend money on housing, food, and transportation, so it's not a bad idea to think about cutting those costs when we can. Yet for most women and marginalized people, that's easier said than done. Early in my personal finance journey, I remember reading a bunch of articles about how to be more frugal. One of the most common advice tropes I saw: to bike to and from work to save money. ("It's healthier too!") While that sounds idyllic (just put the baguette in my front basket, *oui, merci!*), the reality is much harsher. It gets dark at five in the afternoon for four-plus months of the year. As a woman, it's riskier to my safety to bike or walk in the dark alone. In addition, the people who'd benefit most from cutting transportation costs probably aren't making enough money to live in the expensive city centers where jobs are concentrated, making that daily biking distance completely unreasonable.

Other examples include the cost of living in LGBTQ+-friendly locations (typically major cities, where everything is more expensive); for disabled people, the additional cost of homes modified to comply with the Americans with Disabilities Act (ADA) of 1990; and the higher-interest mortgages that many Black families have to pay because of bias from lenders. Most marginalized people have to spend money to get around problems that cisgender white men created but never have to think about. We're spending our hard-earned money to solve problems created by a society that treats us as an afterthought.

Necessary expenses aside, it's additionally frustrating to encounter financial advice that treats discretionary spending as frivolous when those expenses aren't always free choices. A common example of something that forces women to spend more money is the pressure to look perfect. There is the expectation that a woman's natural state requires adornment to reach a minimal standard, whereas men need only tuck in their shirts. While hosting the Golden Globe Awards alongside Amy Poehler, Tina Fey delivered what's both one of my favorite jokes and harshest truths: "Steve Carell's *Foxcatcher* look took two hours to put on, including his hairstyling and makeup. Just for comparison, it took me three hours today to prepare for my role as 'human woman.'"

Let's talk about every single thing, every additional cost, that went into making me presentable for this book's cover shoot. The basic necessities—clothes, accessories, and shoes—alone cost hundreds. But I also needed a supportive bra (which, as my big-titted ladies know, is going to set you back at least $50). I needed hair and makeup on the day of the shoot, but also a trip to the salon for a cut-and-color, a facial, and an eyebrow threading in the days beforehand. Not to mention the time this kind of prep took: getting my hair cut and colored ALONE ate up four hours.

You can argue that all of this was a choice, but it sure didn't feel like it. Most women know there are financial and career repercussions for failing to look "acceptable." My book might not sell well. I might lose media or speaking opportunities. The patriarchy says we're wasting money on makeup and nice clothes, then tells us we look "tired" or "unprofessional" when we don't. We're spending our hard-earned money and time on the bare minimum it takes to show up "professional"—and then being shamed for it and called "frivolous"—but if we listen to that advice and don't put on makeup, we're then less likely to win respect. A fucking massive double standard. And we know this double standard is even worse for women of color, especially Black women. According to a recent survey, white people (especially white women) show explicit bias toward Black women's textured hair, rating it as "less beautiful, less attractive, and less professional" than smooth hair.

Criticism of women's grooming-related spending is even more infuriating, because we're charged more than men for essentially the same products and services. This discriminatory practice has earned the nickname "pink tax." According to a study commissioned by the New York City Department of Consumer Affairs, products marketed toward women and girls cost an average of 7 percent more than those geared toward men and boys. On average, that adds up to women having to spend $1,300 more a year than men spend on the same products. For some products, like razors, women may pay 20 percent more than men do, and—get ready to laugh (or scream)—tampons are taxed as "luxury items" instead of necessities that go untaxed.

This is why the emphasis on cutting down spending is so unfair. Maintaining your appearance, a necessity for advancement; hailing a taxi to make sure you get home safe at night; living in a more expensive but low-crime area—those expenses are a bigger financial burden than the damn lattes. The reason you're not rich has nothing to do with the lattes. As we know from the last chapter, it has to do with systemic oppression, lack of education, our economy's devaluation of certain kinds of labor, and societal narratives about what we can or cannot do.

With all that said, I'm not suggesting that spending—and controlling it—has nothing to do with personal finance. I mean, this book has a whole chapter about it. What I have a problem with is the entire culture of cutting women down to size.

I remember getting a call from my friend Victoria ahead of her bridal shower. She had bought a designer dress she felt beautiful in for the occasion, but she was calling me almost in tears, anxious that people—especially on social media—would judge her for having purchased such an expensive garment. *Should I return it?* she thought. *Should I buy something cheaper? Was it stupid to spend that much money on a dress?*

This anxiety around being judged for a purchase—especially one deemed "frivolous"—is deeply valid because, as women, we're supposed to justify our purchases. Victoria felt like she had to either explain that she was going to repurpose the dress for multiple occasions or say that she got it on sale.

That's when I asked her what she thought the reaction would be if Max, her fiancé, had purchased himself a Rolex watch for the wedding. You can almost picture what the comment section on his Instagram would look like ("Cool watch, bro! You must be doing well for yourself") in contrast with hers ("You spent *what* on a dress?!? So shallow!").

"I really considered returning the dress and getting something else," Victoria admitted. "But I thought, *No. I worked hard to buy it for myself. I want to wear it. I feel beautiful in it.*" And she did—she looked beautiful, owned her choice, and didn't look back.

Spending money, whether on wants or needs, is not a bad thing. I want to repeat that: spending money is not a bad thing! The classic question "Are you a saver or a spender?" is meant to make savers feel good and spenders feel ashamed—when, in fact, that question is bullshit. Lemme let you in on a li'l secret: we are all spenders (yes, even me, who could easily win a gold medal in Olympic Saving). All the money I save *will eventually get spent,* just maybe not this second. An emergency fund to cover my flat tire, a down payment fund for (you guessed it) a down payment, and retirement savings for a Croatian vacation with my hot, much-younger Pilates instructor Luca (yes, that is my real-life retirement plan, more about Hot Luca later)—all of this will be spent. It just might not be for a decade or two.

Paula Pant

FINANCIAL EXPERT AND FOUNDER OF AFFORD ANYTHING

In traditional personal finance advice, when experts discuss discretionary spending, the examples that they cite are disproportionately woman focused. I am guilty of this myself. They'll advise, "Don't spend money on handbags, clothes, manicures, and martinis." But wait a second! Why don't they ever seem to talk about golf clubs? Or box seats at a football game? It's this very gendered advice. We don't write articles about men spending money on power tools or Xbox games, but we write about how we view women's spending choices as this frivolous thing.

I read an article years ago detailing an exchange between the Duke and Duchess of Cambridge. William and Kate were at some symposium learning about emerging technologies, and someone had this technology where if you're watching TV, you can buy whatever's on the screen, like a movie character's outfit or furniture. The prince looked over at his wife and was like, "Oh, you know what? That's trouble. You're just going to want to buy clothing." She snapped back, "Well, you just keep wanting to buy helicopters." That's the thing: in these conversations about spending, no one ever points to things that are stereotypically male or masculine as being irresponsible purchases. [Tori note: Women spending money is an easy punch line and I hate it.]

When people say that something is frivolous, they're casting judgment on it. They're stating that they don't place the same value on that item. That statement is often made without regard to the person who made the "frivolous decision," without regard to whether that decision was made intentionally or thoughtlessly. That's the differentiating factor that I try to teach people about. If you reflected thoughtfully on your finances and the things your money makes available to you and said, "I value X more than any other alternative," then awesome! You've done that inner work and soul-searching, and you've decided that this thing is what matters most to you! Great! It doesn't matter what that thing is—it could be a handbag, it could be weed, I don't care! Whatever you believe matters to you is allowed to matter to you. If you've really put that thought into it, if it's intentional, deliberate, conscious, then it's not frivolous.

Using money as a powerful tool to build a life we love means spending money. The chocolate croissant I would buy at Pike Place Market in Seattle when I was working at my first job. Taking the most nourishing solo trip to Hawaii during the hardest period of my life. Stocking up on Christmas candles at T.J. Maxx. My first designer item, a pair of Dolce & Gabbana sunglasses that look *fucking amazing*, purchased on a recent trip to Paris. No. Better. Feeling.

For most financial experts, a chapter about spending would be to convince you to do less of it, full stop. Suze Orman has the lovely quote that "you are peeing $1 million down the drain as you are drinking that coffee." Australian real estate mogul Tim Gurner says that the reason you can't afford to buy a house is because you're spending too much money on avocado toast. What's the theme here? They are both profiting off your *shame* and trying to get you to use this negative emotion as fuel for your financial success.

But it doesn't work. It's like a diet. And research shows that 98 percent of diets fail in the long run, and that banning entire food groups only causes people to relapse. The more you tell me I can't have fried chicken, the more I will want fried chicken. The more you tell me I can't spend money, the more I will want to spend money. It's not about "willpower"; it's literal psychology.

I am never ever *ever* going to tell you to not buy something you really want. That's just not how I roll—both because it's not helpful and because I like buying things that I love! It's neither sustainable nor joyful, to deprive ourselves. We can find a way to get you that thing; it's just going to involve learning healthy spending.

And the key to healthy spending? Mindfulness. You work so fucking hard for your money, and I want it to give you the best return on investment (ROI) possible. I want you to be so in love with your purchases and your spending decisions. I want you to use money as the tool it was intended to be, to give you a life you love.

You don't have to stop spending money. You just need to stop spending money on shit you don't care about.

Spending money on shit you don't care about takes many forms. Buying a coffee just to have an excuse to get out of the office. Impulsively clicking Add to Cart via an Instagram ad from a skin-care company for $35 wrinkle-preventing stickers (yes, a real thing I did). Going to an expensive museum on your vacation to Rome even though you're not a museum person, because that's what you're "supposed to do." These are wastes of money—not because you're spending but because they don't align with your interests and values.

One of my goals is to *help you make intentional purchases that make you feel like you're building the life that you want with your money,* as opposed to feeling like your money is controlling you. If you find yourself spending money on things that you don't truly love, it's time to make different choices.

Let's use our money as a tool and as a resource and glean as much joy out of it as we can.

Ramit Sethi

AUTHOR AND FOUNDER OF I WILL TEACH YOU TO BE RICH

When I ask people, "What is your 'Rich Life'?" the most common answer I hear is "I want to do what I want when I want." I'll usually respond with "Okay, that sounds great. So, what do you want?" Silence.

What's really going on here is that most of us have never spent even twenty minutes truly articulating what our Rich Life is. If anything, we have articulated what we don't want to do. "I don't want to drive a big truck," or "I don't want to have to be working past seven o'clock at night."

When I ask that question, I'm looking for vivid, rich details. When they say things like "I want to travel!" I ask, "Where do you want to go? What seat on the airplane are you choosing? What do you want to eat for your first dinner in Italy? Who do you want to take with you?" Tell me about that. It's no surprise that most people are not living their Rich Life or even pursuing it if they haven't articulated those details. Those vivid details are what make up a Rich Life.

Most of our relationship with money is based on restriction, guilt, and anxiety. You see this everywhere, particularly in common money-saving advice such as cutting back on lattes. The concept this advice is driving at is that you should take on all the individual burdens of personal finance. In a way, I agree—we *should* take personal responsibility—but it ignores systemic issues.

I think there's a different way to look at money. Instead of restriction, guilt, and anxiety, it can be joy, adventure, and generosity. When you internalize this, you can start to be comfortable with guilt-free spending. "I'm going to get one massage per month guilt free," or "I'm going to tip 30 percent guilt free." On the other hand, "I'm going to downsize my car because it's not important to me to have a new car," also guilt free. That is a beautiful place to arrive at with your money: consciously spending on the things you love and not on the things you don't. What keeps people from embracing their Rich Life is asking $3 questions rather than asking $30,000 questions that will actually make a more substantial impact. Questions such as "How can I make more money?" and "How can I automate my savings and investing so I don't have to think about it?" These are $30,000 questions.

There are a few big wins in your financial life where, if you get them right, you never have to worry about lattes or appetizers ever again. Those big wins include finding a great job and being compensated fairly, learning the basics of personal finance, and investing and saving automatically.

A Rich Life is your ideal life. It's one where you look around at your finances, your relationships, your ordinary Tuesday, and you say, "Wow, this is the kind of life that I want to be living." A Rich Life can be wearing a $1,000 cashmere sweater. It can be picking up your daughter from school at three in the afternoon. It can be having a rule that says you tip at least 30 percent or donate at least 15 percent. It can be as small as buying whatever you want at the grocery store without looking at the price.

Your Rich Life is yours—it's not mine, it's not anybody else's. Not your parents', not your friends'. To me, the most beautiful part is that you can design your Rich Life to fit you like a handmade glove.

So, you're probably wondering: How do you determine the things you truly care about? How do you strike a balance between spending all your money and meeting your financial goals? How do you start spending mindfully, as opposed to the never-ending Add to Cart dance? As Ramit puts it, how can you start living your Rich Life?

Introducing . . .
THE MONEY DIARY

PERHAPS YOU'VE READ those online money diaries on Refinery29, in which contributors from all sorts of backgrounds log every single expenditure they made for one week. Well, we're taking it up a notch.

For one month, you're going to write down everything you spend money on and how much it costs. We're talking about both necessities and discretionary expenses. We're even talking about things that are automated or electronic, such as the electric bill or a Netflix subscription.

But just writing down what we've purchased and how much it costs doesn't get to the root of *why* we're spending and how our emotions fueled each spending decision. So, I've added two transformational steps: you're also going to write down *why* you made the purchase and how it made you *feel*.

For example:

WHAT/HOW MUCH: Starbucks, $4.50 mocha

WHY: Went to meet a friend

FEELINGS: ☺

I sound like a broken record at this point, but we know that our emotions and mental space have a massive impact on our spending. Being mindful of our thoughts, how our body feels, and what emotions we're currently feeling are all important in analyzing spending habits, both when we're making a purchase and after. Even the accountability of knowing you will have to write down something you bought will force you to check in with yourself.

When you're filling out the "Why" and "Feelings" parts of the money diary, consider all the circumstances surrounding the purchase. Did that $4.50 mocha make you happy because it was delicious? Or was it merely okay, but it allowed you to catch up with a friend you haven't seen in a while?

Notice that the "Feelings" section doesn't have to be anything more than an emoji. We want to make this practice sustainable, and writing a full Ph.D. dissertation every time you buy something is very hard to continue for an entire month. Keep it simple, keep it honest.

Considering the circumstances around each purchase is even more important for essential expenses, where it's easy to stop at "I need to eat" or "I need somewhere to live" as your Why. Think about why you shop at *this* particular grocery store or why you paying *this* rent for *this* apartment or house. As we've talked about, your necessary and discretionary expenses can be blurred, but since they affect each other, we're going to analyze them both.

The most important part? *Fill out your money diary without judgment.* You're simply an anthropologist digging into your own life. *Huh! I bought that pair of shoes I didn't need or want because my boss made me feel like shit today! Interestiiiiiiing!*

We're not beating ourselves up. We're not shaming ourselves for our purchases. We're simply *observing* ourselves in our natural habitat. This practice is a great way to figure out exactly where your money goes and what your emotional triggers are: Are you spending your hard-earned cash on things that matter to you? Or spending out of frustration? Boredom? Convenience?

We want your money to have the greatest return on investment—in both saving *and* spending. We're Marie Kondo-ing our money: if it doesn't spark joy, we're not buying it, leaving us room to either save that money OR buy something that *will* spark joy.

You worked fucking hard for your money. I don't want your hard-earned cash going to shit that you barely remember buying or experiences that leave you feeling ambivalent. I want it to bring you the most joy possible.

Keeping a money diary can seem time consuming on your first go, but once you've got the system set up, it's a breeze to quickly jot down your purchases.

So, your homework is to start money diary-ing *today*.

Flip to the back pages of your handwritten day planner, or open a fresh Google doc or sheet, or click the Notes app on your phone. There's no "right" method. Do what works for you. Remember, we want this to become a sustainable habit, so if you hate spreadsheets, don't use them!

Again, this shouldn't be long; we want to keep it short and sweet.

Then we're going to commit to continuing this practice for at least a few weeks—preferably a full month. I know that might feel like a long time, but in order to see the patterns in your purchases and spending habits, a few days simply aren't enough of a sample.

After a month, once the money diary is complete, we need to review it.

We start by looking at our necessary expenses. These include: rent/housing, groceries, transportation, health care, car insurance, and so forth—basically, any payment you have to make either to stay alive or so that no one comes after you.

What we want to do here is look at the "want" side of our needs. As we've discussed, the line between wants and needs is blurred. Is going to the fancy health food store and buying its more expensive produce a "need"—because, well, a girl's gotta eat—or a "want," because you could shop at Kroger instead? Or are monthly massages a luxurious "want" or something that you "need" for your health?

This is where I tell you that *I can't tell you*. I don't know your life, don't know your circumstances. Every person's life and values are different.

Kieryn Wang

FOUNDER OF ALMOSTCONSULTING

I was at rock fucking bottom in 2018. I had lost my main client, and I didn't know how I was going to get income. I had one or maybe one and a half months' worth of emergency funds. I didn't know how much I needed to live. That was a huge, huge deal for me. I was living month to month, hoping I was making enough money and hoping I was spending less than I was making.

One money misconception I had was that if I didn't look at my bank account, then it would all work out. I would tell myself, "Keep spending the way you're spending and keep earning the way you're earning"—which was not enough. "Be okay with it and hope that the universe will give you money if you need it."

I signed up for money coaching with Tori with desperate energy. I didn't know what to do.

Completing a money diary was a mind-set changer for me. I'll admit that I hated it a little at first because it was a lot of accountability at once. But money diary–ing forced me to sit down and see how I was spending money. The exercise is based around emotions, which is what I love most about the structure. It focuses on how you feel about the money you're spending. I was able to recognize that when I'm stressed, I tend to spend money on this, or when I'm sad, I buy food or weed. I understood how much money I needed in a month to survive, which is important to know.

I am a huge advocate of pattern recognition and finding beams of behavior out of patterns, but being woefully neglectful about the information surrounding money hindered my desire to learn about my money patterns and habits. There was shame in my avoidance. I think finally having my spending patterns laid out in front of me opened my eyes. I couldn't avoid that level of accountability of seeing what I spend on a daily basis.

I think the biggest thing is removing yourself and looking at your spending as a third party. Take a step back and evaluate as if it were someone else's. I found more insight that way rather than judging myself for how I was spending my money.

When you do your diary, take it seriously. When you take the time to understand who you are financially, you're set up for success in the future. You don't have to worry. It's the front-end work that you do to make the rest of your life easier.

Here's the tip I can give you: if you're feeling like you need to justify something to *yourself*, not to others (because fuck anyone else's opinions about your money), it might be time to reevaluate that thing. Are you saying that these fancy groceries are absolutely necessary to your life, yet you're throwing away all the produce because you eat out a lot? Are you signed up for a gym membership "for your health" but haven't set foot in there in weeks? Are you justifying paying an insane amount in rent by rationalizing that your area is expensive, when, in fact, you know you would derive as much joy and safety living somewhere else? Be honest with yourself and reflect on your purchases in an unbiased way. And please remember: we've often been conditioned to feel the need to justify, because our spending has been labeled as frivolous. This wants-versus-needs conversation isn't that.

n reviewing your necessary purchases, there might be some money you can save by negotiating. Things such as your rent (especially if the landlord is about to increase it!) are actually negotiable.

At the beginning of 2020, my landlord mentioned that she planned to raise my rent. But, of course, the COVID-19 pandemic happened. It was the perfect time to send an email to advocate for my rent to stay the same. Here's the actual email I sent in December 2020:

Hey landlord,

Hope you're doing well and hanging in there!

I have loved my last two years in the apartment and would love to continue with at least a 6-month lease. You had mentioned you planned to increase the rent, and I would like to discuss keeping my rent the same for our lease renewal.

1) Rents across Seattle have been steadily decreasing [I then linked to an article about this decrease]. Seattle rent prices have decreased 14 percent from March to October and have only continued to decrease in the past 2 months.

2) I have been a dependable tenant, paying my rent in full and on time every month (even during the pandemic), and will continue to be dependable even as the pandemic continues to affect the economy.

I love living here and would love to continue to; a rent increase, however, would keep me from doing so, as rents in other condos/apartments have significantly decreased and are offering new tenant bonuses.

Let me know your thoughts, I would love to work together with you to find a solution!

Thanks,

Tori

I not only bring in data that showcases why my rent shouldn't increase, but I remind her that I'm reliable, clean, and easy to work with. (Landlords hate having to find new tenants!) And it worked: my rent stayed the same, and I got the exact lease terms I wanted. You can use this script and adapt it for other expenses, such as your internet or phone service. Call up customer service and say the following:

> Hello, [name], how are you? I'm doing great, thank you for asking. I'm having an issue, and I would love for you to help me. I saw that [name of a competing company] is offering a lower rate for my same plan; I'd love to discuss any discounts or promotions you could offer. As a [student, five-year customer, reliable customer who pays on time, and so on], I'd really love to continue being a loyal, valued customer. What can you do for me?

Here is an alternative script: "I'm currently going through a tough financial period due to [give the reason, be it a job loss, COVID related, or another medical issue]."

And then, if they say it's not possible, ask again: "I want to have a great customer experience today with [company name]. What can you do for me?"

Always be polite, state your problem clearly, and use data to back up your ask. (More about negotiating in chapter 6!)

When I work with clients, we look at their discretionary spending through the lenses of the Three Value Categories.

These are not the things that you *need* in your life. These are the things that you *want* in your life. These are the three areas in your life that bring you the most joy and would provide you with the best return on happiness investment (ROHI).

My three:

1. **travel;**

2. **food out; and**

3. **nesting (items such as plants, décor, and a Roomba).**

Those are my three priorities, which means that almost all my discretionary spending goes to #friendmoons (the honeymoon-style trips I take with Kristine every year), eating out, and buying all my plant babies.

The things I'm not buying as much are the things that I don't like as much, such as coffee, clothes, and makeup. I do purchase those things, but they're not what I'm spending the *majority* of my discretionary money on. Again, we don't want to stop spending money, we just have to stop spending money on things that we only kind of like or that we don't care about at all. Spend money according to what you value and what you care about deeply. This strategy allowed me to save my first $100K, and with no deprivation, no shame, and no negotiating with myself. I didn't stop spending my money; instead, I focused on value-based spending.

Personal finance is personal. My Value Categories might look different from yours, and that's what we want! Too many financial experts try to tell you there's *one way* to do things, and that's just not true. We're creating a plan that works for you: your wants, your needs, and your goals.

If you haven't started to do so already, reflect on your Three Value Categories and write them down. If you're not sure where to start, take a look at your money diary to determine not only where the majority of your money went but also what gave you the most joy.

When reviewing your money diary as a whole, the question is "What am I willing to spend less on so I can spend more somewhere else?" I would rather you use the majority of your money in the areas that you *actually love and give a shit about*. You're picking the things that you really love and then allowing yourself to spend more freely in those categories. Here's my favorite example: a client of mine once said that one of her Value Categories was vintage clothes—not only buying them but spending money to have the pieces refurbished and custom fit to her body. And I was like, "Great!" That could be a whole Value Category if you want it to be.

But be careful. In my work with the Her First $100K community, I've seen some very fluid lines. It's very easy to say that *everything you spend money on brings you joy* or to make your Value Categories so broad that everything can fit. For example, "entertainment" is not specific enough, because suddenly concert tickets and drinks out and skydiving and restaurants and an Italian road trip and seeing a movie and Cirque du Soleil tickets in Vegas are all "entertainment." Another one I see often is "shopping"—again, so broad that you can justify almost anything under the shopping umbrella.

We make these Value Categories to promote healthy, thoughtful, guilt-free spending that we can balance with thoughtful saving. Therefore, we can't make every single thing that we spend our discretionary money on a value category. So, you're picking the things that you really love and then allowing yourself to spend more freely in those categories.

Paula Pant

FOUNDER OF AFFORD ANYTHING

I came up with the concept of Afford Anything when I was traveling. A lot of my friends who I knew made significantly more money than me would often say, "I would love to travel, but I can't afford it," which confused me. I saw them spending money all the time: they lived in really nice apartments, they drove really nice cars, they went out and ran up huge bar tabs every weekend. So, I tapped into my judgment-free zone and started asking questions. They obviously *could* afford to travel, but instead they were spending that money in other ways.

These friends were obviously in pain from thinking they didn't have the money to travel, so that's where the concept of Afford Anything came to me. It was the idea that every dollar that you spend is a trade-off: it comes at the cost of not spending that dollar on something else. Over time, I realized that concept extended not just to money but also to time, to energy, to attention—to any limited resource that we need to allocate. It's tied closely to the theory of opportunity cost. Choosing one thing means not choosing another. Sometimes we're not aware of the fact that we are making that choice.

A lot of this is in our language choices. So many people use the "I can't" statement, and it's so disempowering. An "I can't" statement is the last thing that anyone needs, but particularly any marginalized community. The rest of the world is already systematically disempowering you enough; you don't need to further undercut yourself with the words that you use. Words matter. So, reframe "I can't" as "I don't want to" or "I choose not to"—or, if it is something that you want, we can ask curiously, "How can I?"

In values-based spending, money is a physical representation of your values. How you allocate any limited resource reflects what matters most to you. That's true across all income groups, to varying degrees. If you have an extremely low income, what matters most are the basics: food, shelter, medicine. It's still an extension of what you believe matters most. Then, as your income and your discretionary spending increase, you get to make more of those choices. In that sense, you get to express more of those values.

Your money diary is a great way to figure out what your Value Categories are. You're either already aligning your purchases with your values or *something needs to shift*.

For example, if you've settled on clothes, makeup, and coffee as your Value Categories, yet you're spending hardly any money on those three, something's off. Either you haven't identified what is truly valuable to you, or you're spending money on things you don't really like. And when I say "you don't really like," again, I'm talking about an emotional expenditure—something impulsive that provides a fleeting moment of happiness rather than something you know you will enjoy for a long time.

This is where curbing emotional spending comes in. Just like getting to the root of your emotional hang-ups regarding money, determining your Value Categories doesn't mean you're never going to find yourself making impulsive, emotional spending decisions. It's a common problem: according to an online Harris poll of two thousand Americans, almost half reported that their emotions had caused them to overspend in the last month.

To combat those emotional spending tendencies that we all have, I make it a practice to ask myself a few questions before making any spending decision.

question #1
WHAT IS MY CURRENT HEADSPACE OR EMOTIONAL STATE?

WE'VE TALKED ABOUT how substantial an impact our emotions and headspace have on our finances, and this becomes even more apparent when asking ourselves what kind of emotional state we are in before making a purchase.

Now, granted, I'm currently writing this during a global pandemic (*that hopefully is over by the time this book comes out, goddamn it*), so I am not immune to buying things to cope. At the beginning of the pandemic, I decided I needed to buy myself a Snoogle, this humongous fucking pregnancy pillow, when I was neither pregnant nor wishing to become so. At $70, it was a completely ridiculous purchase, yet *so* worth it. (A note: As I'm making final edits to my manuscript in June 2022, *I am curled up in bed with the same pillow.* What an investment.)

It's not just desperation that can cause me to overspend. I'm also susceptible when, say, I've been out on a Friday night, loving my life and my beautiful friends, and had one too many drinks. In this heightened emotional state—where, by the way, I'm feeling very, *very* good—I've moved on to the $20 cocktails, ordered some chicken tenders that I'm not even hungry for, and bought the whole group multiple rounds without thinking. Whoops.

In this way, spending can be a vice. It's really, *really* easy to try altering our mood with our purchases. We all know that certain things can bring us a lot of joy, but there are also a lot of purchases that feel good *only in that moment*.

Ask yourself this: Am I buying this thing to fill some sort of void in my life? Will this purchase give me more than a brief reprieve? Am I emotionally heightened and therefore more tempted to be careless?

It's good to ask yourself these questions to at least be aware—not to judge yourself. It happens to everyone! But I need

SPENDING **65**

you to not delude yourself into thinking that it's not happening to you. It's okay if this is a purchase you're making to deal emotionally with life, because sometimes life is fucking hard. But if you're *constantly* making purchases to cope emotionally? Yeah, that's an issue, and not just for your bank account. If every time your boss is mean you buy something, you're not fixing the fundamental issue of responding to your unhealthy work environment. The emotional spend is a temporary solution that doesn't ultimately improve your life. I don't want you relying on a Band-Aid solution that would distract you from the longer-term fix of getting real with yourself and asking, "Will this *actually* help me cope? And with what issue?"

question #2
HOW MANY TACO DOLLARS DOES IT COST?

OKAY, YOU PROBABLY READ this one and were utterly confused. Let me explain.

As few years ago, I read a blog post that changed the game for me. Lindsay Van Someren, from the money blog *Science Finance*, loved tacos—more than anything. And when she would go to buy something that wasn't tacos, she would think, *Okay, how many tacos is this worth? How much is this thing in Taco Dollars?*

For example: this jacket is $50, a taco costs $5, so this is ten Taco Dollars. I could either buy this jacket or get ten tacos.

Let's look at my personal Taco Dollars. I love to travel, so I like to think of my purchases in terms of "Where could this get me in the world?" If it's a $100 jacket, I calculate, "Okay, this could get me from Seattle to LA," or "This could get me one night in an Italian Airbnb."

You'll discover that sometimes the purchase will be worth it, and sometimes it won't. Whether it's Taco Dollars, or Airplane

Dollars, or Skin-Care Dollars, or Plant Dollars, you're viewing your purchases through the lens of what's really important to YOU. Simply by reframing your favorite thing and juxtaposing it with the item that you're about to buy, you will discover just how much worth that thing has and whether buying it is worth giving up something that you *truly* value. (We will go over how to figure out exactly what you value later on.)

question #3
AM I ACCURATELY EVALUATING THE WORTH OF THIS PURCHASE?

WHEN I SAY SOMETHING'S "WORTH," I mean it on a couple of levels: Is this thing actually worth the price tag? Is the quality of this item worth what they're asking me to pay? Will I glean a lot of value from this thing? Is this something that is worth the money, or am I just buying this thing because it's on sale?

If something's on sale, I am more likely to buy it because I feel like it's a steal. But if the original price of something was $100, and now it's 70 percent off—you'd still be spending $30. If it's something you were planning on buying before, you just got a deal! But if you're buying something that's on sale just because it's on sale, *you still lost money.*

I also like considering the cost of use of an item before I purchase it, to effectively evaluate its worth to me. By dividing the cost of an item by the number of times you anticipate using it, you can get a pretty good idea of whether the purchase is a good buy. For instance, if you've recently fallen in love with smoothies and want to make them at home during weekdays to save money, you can divide a $60 NutriBullet by 261 (the number of weekdays in the year) and realize that your cost per use is $0.23. That sounds like a good purchase to me!

I often do this with clothes, especially ones that are significant investments. If I'm buying a nice coat that costs $500—but I know I will wear it constantly, and it's good quality—that coat will last me years of wear. The cost per use is low, and I feel more comfortable making that purchase.

question #4
IS THIS A HABIT OR A ROUTINE?

I'VE HAD SO MANY CLIENTS who like coffee but use it as an excuse to take a break from work. They were having a coffee at three o'clock every single day, just to get out of the office. They didn't feel comfortable taking a break without an excuse (thanks, capitalism), so that $5 coffee was their justification. *They weren't even tasting that coffee anymore.* It wasn't something that they were looking forward to or something that brought them joy. It was a habit that wasn't serving their wallet (or their overcaffeinated bodies).

This also might look like being subscribed to a streaming service you never use anymore, staying in an expensive apartment you're not attached to even though you can afford to move, or buying yet another notebook at the start of the year when you damn well know that you have twelve empty notebooks at home (me).

Ask yourself this: Do I actually like and enjoy this thing? Is it something I really look forward to, or is this something that I'm just doing because this is the way I've always done it? Is this something that I am purchasing just because I always have purchased it, or do I feel like it's necessary to purchase?

question #5

IS THIS WORTH X AMOUNT
OF HOURS WORKED?

WE ALL HAVE an hourly rate, even if you're a salaried employee or if you're an entrepreneur. (If you don't know your hourly rate off the top of your head, take your monthly income and divide it by how many hours you work.) This hourly rate can be a good way to reflect on your output of work versus your spending.

I'll give you an example. If you make $25 per hour and you're about to buy something that costs $100, think, *Is this worth an entire Monday afternoon of work?* When I was working corporate, I'd ask myself, *Is this purchase worth the four hours I just spent being mansplained to in a meeting?*

For me, that question really put things in perspective. It was a direct line between the time I spent working and what I then spent the money on. Even if you don't absolutely hate your job, when you spend money on things you don't need or even want, it means you're not able to save that money—or spend it on something more valuable to you. For me, it kept me yet another step away from quitting and being able to work for myself.

question #6

AM I VOTING WITH MY DOLLARS?

IF WE'RE GOING TO USE our financial education to fight the patriarchy, that includes making thoughtful spending decisions. Where and how you spend money is one of your most powerful tools to change the world; after all, women control more than 70 percent of consumer spending. Now, sometimes I need shit off of Amazon, and that's okay. But before I make a purchase, I look to see if I could order the same product from, say, a mom-and-pop store, or a business owned by a woman or a person of color. We'll talk more about voting with our dollars and using money to exert positive change in our final chapter.

THE TL;DR

I'LL REMIND YOU AGAIN: You don't have to stop spending money. You just have to stop spending money on shit you don't care about.

I am not here to tell you to stop spending money, but if you do so out of habit, those things are your emotional vices. If they are not things that you truly love, it's time to let them go.

At herfirst100k.com/book-resources, we have an image you can download with these questions. Use it as a phone background to do a check-in with yourself before you make a purchase.

HOMEWORK

1. UNPACK SPENDING NARRATIVES

At the beginning of the chapter, we talk a lot about how men and women are taught different things when it comes to money. Women are fed the message to stop spending and save, while men are educated on how to invest and build wealth.

What is the narrative around money that you hear in your own circle? Do you feel pressured to save and to stop spending "frivolously"?

_____
_____
_____
_____
_____
_____
_____
_____
_____
_____
_____
_____
_____
_____
_____
_____
_____
_____
_____
_____
_____
_____

Before reading this chapter, did you consider yourself a "saver" or a "spender"? How did the idea that *we are all spenders* shift your perspective on this? Does it help you think of money as a tool instead of something evil or taboo?

_____

_____

_____

_____

_____

_____

_____

_____

_____

_____

_____

Now that you've read the interview with Ramit Sethi, what does your Rich Life look like? Visualize it below, shame and guilt excluded! How can viewing money as a tool help you build the life you want?

_____

_____

_____

_____

_____

_____

_____

_____

_____

_____

_____

2. MONEY DIARY

Now let's get into the good stuff—aka the key to spending mindfully and making purchases that bring you joy—*your money diary.*

Before completing your money diary, take a stab at what you *think* your Three Value Categories are:

1. _____
2. _____
3. _____

For the next four weeks, you're going to log all your purchases, why you made them, and how they made you *feel.* You can do this in the Notes app on your phone, in a spreadsheet, or in a notebook—your choice!

WHAT/HOW MUCH: Madewell, $70 jeans

WHY: Current jeans don't fit, so new pair!

FEELINGS: ☺

A reminder: *Do this practice without judgment.*

After two weeks, review your purchases and answer the following questions:

What went well during the last two weeks?

_____
_____
_____
_____
_____
_____
_____
_____
_____

What could be improved regarding your spending habits?

_____

_____

_____

_____

_____

_____

_____

_____

Name three worthwhile purchases.

_____

_____

_____

_____

_____

_____

_____

Name three things you bought that no longer feel necessary.

_____

_____

_____

_____

_____

_____

Which purchases from the last two weeks brought you joy?

_____

_____

_____

_____

_____

_____

_____

When you've tracked your spending for the entire month, answer the following questions:

What surprised you most about this exercise?

_____

_____

_____

_____

_____

_____

_____

_____

What was your favorite purchase from this month, and why? Your least favorite?

_____

_____

_____

_____

_____

_____

_____

_____

Under what circumstances did you spend emotionally, either positively or negatively? What triggered the purchase(s)?

_____

_____

_____

_____

_____

_____

_____

_____

_____

_____

How can you further refine your spending to align with your money goals and what brings you joy?

_____

_____

_____

_____

_____

_____

_____

_____

_____

_____

_____

Compliment yourself on three things that went "right" this month.

_____

_____

_____

_____

_____

_____

_____

_____

_____

_____

_____

_____

How can you use your findings from this practice to positively impact your money?

_____

_____

_____

_____

_____

_____

_____

_____

_____

_____

_____

_____

_____

CHAPTER 3

THE
FINANCIAL
GAME PLAN

WITHOUT FURTHER ADO, SOME RANDOM FACTS ABOUT OSTRICHES.

D id you know that ostriches have three stomachs? (I also have three stomachs, all filled with fried chicken.) Did you know that ostriches can run faster than any other two-legged animal? And unlike all other birds—wait for it—ostriches have separate holes for peeing and pooping.

Why are we talking about ostriches and their pee holes? Great question.

There's a cognitive bias that causes people to avoid situations where they might encounter information that they perceive as negative. Personal finance experts call this the Ostrich Effect.

The Ostrich Effect is burying your head in the sand and pretending that your problems don't exist. It is a *huge* reason so many of us aren't able to get our financial shit together.

Remember that scene from *New Girl* where Jess discovers that her roommate-turned-boyfriend Nick tosses his unopened bills into a box in his closet? Or the scene in *Parks and Recreation* where Ben discovers all of April and Andy's bills stashed in the freezer? Or on *The Office*, when Oscar helps Michael finally acknowledge that he's spending too much money on magic kits and workout gear he doesn't use and professional bass fishing equipment? (This is a common sitcom trope, apparently.)

The Ostrich Effect can infiltrate every aspect of our financial lives. Not checking our bank account balances. Not reviewing credit card statements. Not educating ourselves about what a 401(k) is because it's easier to just live in blissful ignorance and say, *"I'm so broke, lolz."* You can imagine just how much this practice is hurting us, right? Not only because we're ignoring the bad parts, allowing our financial problems to spiral out of control, but also because when we don't check in, we have no idea how much *progress* we're making! We can't see just how badass we are—slaying debt, building savings, and growing investments—*if we don't look at our money.*

By not looking at our shit, there's literally no way we can even develop a plan, let alone achieve it. And you know what is causing this Ostrich Effect, right? Shame. Assessing our personal finances makes us uncomfortable. Logging in to our 401(k) dashboards and realizing we know none of the jargon makes us feel stupid. So, our brains convince us that in order to protect ourselves from this fear and discomfort, it's better to just not pay attention. We just shouldn't look because that's better, right?!?!?! Better to live our lives in financial upheaval than be faced with the reality that *no one fucking taught us this.*

Of course, what happens when we "temporarily" avoid discomfort repeatedly? Things compound to the point where the thought of even looking at your bank account can cause severe anxiety.

That feeling is valid and incredibly common. And while it makes sense to feel that way, it's only going to persist if we don't take steps to address it. We want to control our money rather than let it control us.

We can't make a budget or build our savings if we don't actually know what's going on with our money; we can't refine and tweak and optimize and do better if we don't know the lay of the land. It'd be like saying you're going to bake a cake, but you're blindfolded and missing the recipe, and all the ingredients have labels written in hieroglyphics.

The other thing that keeps us from getting honest about our money? We don't know what our financial goals even are. When I work with clients for the first time, I often hear, "I know I should be saving, but I'm so scared to look at my credit card statements. And even if I were to start saving, I don't even know what I should be saving for."

We're told that progressing in our financial lives is important, but we're not given a reason. We have goals imposed on us that aren't personal, relevant, or specific. (How many times have you resolved, "Okay, but THIS year is the year I finally get my shit together!") We're just told to save money because it's "important," and that's it.

Or maybe you're encouraged to save for something that isn't compatible with your lifestyle. When I graduated college, I was advised that I should buy a house as soon as possible. Because Seattle wasn't affordable, my well-intentioned parents convinced me to check out open houses an hour outside the city, in the town where I grew up. But the truth was I didn't want to own a home. I didn't want the maintenance, the responsibility, the thirty-year mortgage commitment. And as someone in my early twenties, I definitely didn't want to live where my friends weren't and instead hang out with my parents every weekend. (Love you, Mom and Dad, but this was a recipe for disaster.) So, instead of focusing on buying a house in my early twenties, I concentrated on saving my money to travel when and where I wanted. And what happened? I became so much more motivated to put away my money because this was a goal I actually wanted to achieve.

It's impossible to bake a cake without a recipe or ingredients, and it's impossible to *want* to make the cake unless you know why you're baking it in the first place. Friend's birthday? Graduation? "Happy divorce! (We never liked him anyway!)"? No wonder you're avoiding money—you have no good reason to *not* avoid it. You have no motivation to get your financial shit together because you haven't linked it to something you care about. That's not your fault, that's literal psychology. You need to get your brain on board with *why* this is important for your life.

Why has this been so hard to figure out in the past? Well (shocker), because historically women weren't encouraged to take ownership of our financial decisions. We are told we're bad at math; we're assigned roles as dependents, not providers; we're reminded that money isn't "for women." We're not even allowed to want the coffee that gives us life in the morning. The financial ownership positions occupied by women predominantly involve managing household spending and day-to-day finances, especially in heteronormative relationships: women handle the grocery shopping, the budgeting, the general household expenses, while long-term financial decisions—the ones that actually build wealth, such as investing—are left up to the men. No wonder this concept of having a financial plan, especially a long-term strategy for building wealth, feels so foreign to us.

The key to figuring out our finances is to truly feel ownership over them—and to understand that the other side of that responsibility is freedom.

Ramit Sethi

AUTHOR AND FOUNDER OF I WILL TEACH YOU TO BE RICH

Often, as a result of our upbringings, we have what I like to call "invisible scripts": beliefs so deeply held that we don't even realize they are the scripts that guide our lives. One of the most common scripts in America is "I should buy a house." Your house is the American Dream! It's a bullshit dream propagated by the National Association of Realtors, which is an organization that you'll find in hell. The idea that "if you don't own a home, you're not a true American" has led many people, including many young people, to feel that they aren't enough. Let me be the first to tell people: I'm a millionaire, and I rent by choice. [Tori note: Me too!] When you tell people, "I could go buy tomorrow, and yet I choose to rent," they look at you like you're crazy. That is an excellent example of an invisible script.

An invisible script is something that when someone takes a different perspective, most people go, "What? How can you think that?" My belief about owning versus renting, just so we're clear, is to run the numbers. For some people, it makes sense, but for some people, it doesn't. There are also nonfinancial reasons to buy or to rent.

"You must go to college" is another invisible script. Conversely, people on Twitter have now gone the other direction to say that college is a complete waste of money. The idea that college is either absolutely required or a total waste of money is a very interesting invisible script depending on who you are and your demographic.

Another invisible script with regard to money is "I can't earn more." This is the classic puritanical, frugal-oriented American ethic, which says, "I have what I have, there's no way to get more, and therefore I'm going to fight anyone who tries to take it away."

You'll typically find people in this camp who are extremely angry and resistant to any sort of taxation. Why? That is one of the most scarcity-minded beliefs you can possibly have! "Oh, every dollar you take away in taxes is one less dollar I will have." A more abundant approach would be "I'm part of a community, I'm happy to pay my taxes, and I could just earn more money," which is exactly what I do.

Remember chapter 1? In the journal prompts, I asked you to picture what your life would look like if you were to change your relationship with money. *This* is your Why. Maybe you want to save money to afford to travel internationally every year. Maybe you want to pay off your credit card debt to improve your mental health. Maybe you want to find room in your budget to donate every month because you care deeply about a particular issue.

We're a lot more likely to achieve our goals if we put a Why behind them—not just "I want to save money" but "I want to save two thousand dollars to go to Paris"—so let's put some intention behind our goals.

Goal setting is one of the best things you can do for yourself. Big or small, your goals help you become the person you want to be and live the life you want. It isn't guaranteed that every one of your goals will happen exactly as you planned, and it's also likely that your goals will change as you start working toward them—but you're so much better off for having set them and then changed them when life demanded it, rather than having never set them at all.

So, do yourself a favor and grab a paper and pen, open the Notes app on your phone, or start a Google doc on your computer.

First up, I want you to write at the top of the page a mantra I follow and remind myself of often: "A goal without a plan is just a wish."

Sure, you can set goals and have all the intention in the world of making them come to fruition—but if you don't have a plan for your goals, it won't matter one bit how much you want them. It's not enough just to write down a goal; we need to create a step-by-step plan in order to make it happen.

Got it? Great! Next up, directly underneath that, write: "It won't get better unless I do something about it."

When it comes to money, we've been told our whole lives that we should just *know* how to handle it. We should know what to do with it when we get it, and if we don't, we're somehow less than or unworthy of it. Unfortunately, there is no money fairy who can come handle our finances for us (if only). There's no magic button to fix our financial problems. And many financial issues are not because of personal choices—each of us faces different struggles systematically when it comes to finance—so we can control only what we can actually control.

Regardless of where you're starting or what you're up against, the statement above is true. It can't get better unless you do something about it. This can be a scary realization, that you are ultimately responsible for your money. The fear of doing something wrong, the hesitancy to trust yourself and your decisions, comparing yourself with others . . . The recognition that you're on your own financially—responsible for paying your own bills, saving money, negotiating your salary, investing—can be absolutely debilitating. It can also be *liberating*.

I remember realizing that, of the stuff I *could* control, my financial life was entirely up to me. I got to choose how I wanted to spend my money, what big-life things I wanted to save for, which charities I donated to, where I wanted to invest in myself. It's the financial version of one of my favorite quotes, by the late poet Charles Bukowski: "When nobody wakes you up in the morning, and when nobody waits for you at night, and when you can do whatever you want, what do you call it, freedom or loneliness?" When it's only you responsible for your financial situation, what do you call it, freedom or paralysis? Learning to see it as freedom was one of the most powerful, exciting transformations of my entire life. It was an opportunity, rather than a set of handcuffs (and, no, not the fun fluffy kind).

So, with that sense of freedom and personalization in mind, let's set some actual goals. Right off the bat, while I want y'all to have a bunch of money and be stable as fuck, if you know that you're not going to be able to save $1 million, don't set that as your goal. Be realistic with yourself. On the flip side, like many women, I used to have the tendency to underestimate myself and play too safe, and so I would end up hitting my target too easily and with little effort. By definition, a goal is not a given but something we aspire toward and push ourselves to achieve. So, to truly challenge myself, I set goals slightly beyond my reach. Personally, what's worked in my own life is setting goals that are sticky—meaning they're not ridiculously unobtainable but also not easy. A good goal should feel a little intimidating. (My $100K goal is the perfect example of this: it was something I *might* have been able to achieve, and it propelled me forward.) That way, if (when!) I hit my goal, I feel even more accomplished; and if I don't, I still made progress that I can be proud of.

One of the ways you may be hampering your progress with your goals is by not getting incredibly specific about what you want. When you're setting intentions for your money, it's easy to be too general. "I want to get better with money" is something I hear all the time. That might be one of the core reasons you picked up this book. And you know what? That doesn't mean anything. Even if you said, "I want to get better at saving," that means little. Setting financial goals in this way is setting yourself up for failure. If you don't define "saving money," it's easy to convince yourself arbitrarily that you accomplished it; after all, saving $1 would technically count.

You should know, without a doubt, whether you hit your goal:

no grey area, no hemming and hawing. You can do this by making sure your financial goals are:

1. **Specific: a dollar amount, one source of debt, and so on.**

2. **Timely: What time frame are you going to do this in? In how many months/years? By what age?**

3. **Mission driven: Why are you setting this goal? What's your motivation? Why is it important to you?**

Let's look at the intention "I want to save money" and turn it into a goal. To make it specific, we could say, "I want to save five hundred dollars," or "I want to have three months of living expenses saved." That's step one.

To make it timely, we'll add, "I want to save five hundred dollars per month," or "I will have three months of living expenses saved by the end of this year." With goals that are further out than one month, we need to break them down in order to track them easily. We can do that on a phone calculator in less than thirty seconds: if three months of living expenses comes to $6,000, and we want to save that within the year, we take $6,000 and divide it by 12. Voilà! And so $500 is the amount of money we need to save per month.

Finally, the most important part: let's give ourselves a reason to care. "I want to save $500 per month for my wedding next year," or "I want to have three months of living expenses saved by the end of this year for my emergency fund."

This is so much more precise. You'll know immediately if you're on track, and you'll know concretely when you've achieved it. Even if you fall a bit short of your goal—in terms of the amount you saved, or the deadline you set, or both—you've still made significant progress.

To inspire you, here's a list of goals that are specific, timely, and Why driven:

* I want to save $10,000 by the end of this year to cover me in case of an emergency.

* I want to save $2,000 in ten months to go to Italy and try authentic pasta.

* I'm going to pay off all my credit card debt this year so that I'll no longer have the weight of debt hanging over me.

* I'm going to save $100 a month this year for a down payment on my dream house.

And here's my favorite hack for goals, intentions, or manifestations: write them in the past tense, like they've already happened. When we were about to launch our podcast, *Financial Feminist*, my journal entries and the Post-it note on my bathroom mirror read as follows: "I have a top 20 business podcast listened to by over 100,000 people." In fact, it ended up being a number one business podcast listened to by millions of people *because manifestation fucking works*. It's the confidence that I can do it, that I'm capable of it, and that it's already happened, like in my favorite lyric from Anderson .Paak: "'Cause if I know I can get it, then I've already had it." So let's use this trick on the example goals:

* I saved $10,000 this year that covered me during an emergency.

* I saved $2,000 in twelve months to go to Italy, and authentic pasta tasted *so good*.

* I paid off all my credit card debt this year, and now I don't have the weight of debt hanging over me.

* I saved $100 a month this year for a down payment on my dream house.

The key to managing your money is working to control it, rather than having it control you. Getting comfortable being uncomfortable is the first step: acknowledging that you want to change your relationship with money (like we talked about in chapter 1) and then creating a plan to actually make it happen.

In this chapter, we're taking a big-picture overview of what should happen—and when—with your finances, and we'll cover exactly *how* to make these things happen in upcoming chapters.

And please, if you've skipped ahead to this chapter because you're like, "I need to get my shit together *right now*, and this chapter had the word *plan* in it, so here I am!" go back and read/implement chapters 1 and 2. We can't make a plan to get better with our money without first identifying and then understanding hang-ups about money. It can be tempting to dive right in, especially if you feel like you're drowning financially, but I need you to do some emotional processing first.

THE FINANCIAL PRIORITY LIST

WE'RE STARTING the Financial Game Plan with a way to organize those goals you have for your money. Introducing: the Financial Priority List.

The number one question I get asked at this stage?

"Okay, so I have debt, but also I need an emergency fund; but *also* I wanna buy a house, and also retirement and vacations and student loans, and—

"What do I do first?"

Now, I need to get on my soapbox for a second to deliver some tough love. Please know, though, that I say it with the utmost understanding, empathy, and compassion. Often, when I bring up the Financial Priority List with a client, here's the response:

"Well, I have this unique situation, so this won't work for me."

Yes, personal finance is personal. However, in this one instance, I need you to follow the Priority List. It doesn't matter how much debt you've incurred, or how old you are, or how much you earn, or your financial goals; the Priority List has got to be followed to a tee because it works. And I know it works, because I've talked to and seen the written testimonies of the thousands of people it's worked for.

The Priority List is also something that you will use for the rest of your life. It's a step-by-step road map for your entire financial future and is something you will return to time and time again when you crave some direction. Dog-ear the page, grab a highlighter, write notes somewhere you'll see them—and come on back when you need it.

Before we get to Priority Number One, your Priority Zero is that you're covering your necessary expenses. We can't start to progress in our financial lives until we're taking care of our present selves, and you should *not* be forgoing your bills in order to build a nest egg.

financial priority #1
AN EMERGENCY FUND

YOUR GOAL IS to have three to six months' living expenses saved, hanging out in a high-yield savings account (HYSA). A high-yield savings account is just like a normal savings account, except that it offers a higher interest rate. (As of this writing, the average national bank account's interest rate is 0.03 percent; an HYSA is 2 percent on average and likely to increase in the future.) Switching to or opening an HYSA is one of the easiest things you can do to immediately make more money. I've got the HYSA I recommend linked on my website's book resources page: https://herfirst100k.com/book-resources.

Do not pass Go, do not collect $200, and do not move on to the next step until you have your emergency fund set aside.

Again, even if you're hundreds of thousands of dollars in debt, DO NOT MOVE ON TO THE NEXT STEP UNTIL YOU HAVE YOUR EMERGENCY FUND.

Why do we start with an emergency fund? Three reasons:

The first is that we don't want you taking on more debt while trying to pay for an emergency. Other financial strategies (ahem, D*ve R*msey's Baby Steps) prioritize debt payoff, leaving the individual with only a $1,000 emergency fund to start. Please don't get me wrong: saving your first $1K is a huge accomplishment and much better than having nothing in savings. But one hard-and-fast number like $1,000 doesn't account for all the circumstances that might arise. In some parts of the country, that could pay for three months of rent. But for me and many others, that wouldn't cover even one month, let alone my groceries, electric bill, or any kind of insurance. Three months of living expenses as a start is typically enough to keep you afloat until the storm passes.

The second reason is that I've found clients are in a better mental space when they've squirreled away money. However small, having savings can mean financial security. You're not wondering how you would pay for an unexpected expense. You're not losing sleep at night, feeling financially naked without any money in savings. Again, we can't underestimate the importance of the mental aspect of personal finance: that peace of mind can help you stay on track to meeting your financial goals.

The third and most important reason is that security allows you to give the middle finger to toxic situations. Let me give you an example from my own life.

As you might remember from the introduction, in 2017 I decided to leave my job for what looked like a better situation. In my new position, I had negotiated $20,000 more in pay and was promised more responsibilities than at my previous company. Plus, I'd be working under a woman I hoped could become my mentor. Something in my gut had told me this was the wrong career move, but I didn't listen to my instincts.

The reason I was able to resign? My emergency fund. I still remember the feeling of walking out of the office on my last day. It was the first time in months that I felt like I could breathe—really breathe. It afforded me time in which to process that ordeal and figure out my next steps. Yes, I was now unemployed, which came with its own worries and stresses. But I was fucking *free*. I was taken care of. Past Tori had made sure Future Tori could say "Fuck off" and find something better for herself; I could assert my value and not put up with poor treatment if I didn't have to. Escaping that poisonous workplace was one of the best decisions I've ever made.

My emergency fund also allowed me the flexibility to make sure the next position was the right one for me and not have to desperately job hunt. I could find a company that shared my values and would further my career development, rather than take the first job offered to me.

During a crisis, protecting your health is your top priority, not making money. The last thing you want to concern yourself with is your bank account balance and wondering whether you can afford to take care of yourself. So, whether that toxic situation is a job, a partner, a roommate, or something else, having an emergency fund means you get to peace out and do what's best for you.

financial priority #2
PAY OFF HIGH-INTEREST DEBT (CREDIT CARDS, PAYDAY LOANS, ETC.)

THE MAGICAL NUMBER to determine whether you've got high- or low-interest debt? **7 percent.** This is your most expensive debt, which is why it's best to eliminate it before paying off lower-interest debt.

If your interest rate is higher than 7 percent, it is considered high-interest debt. Credit cards usually start at 15 percent interest, which is why credit card debt can be so difficult to get rid of.

If your interest rate is lower than 7 percent, it's low-interest debt (which we'll discuss in a minute).

Why is 7 percent the magic number? Because it is the average percentage return from the stock market, so if we're *losing* more money than we could be earning by investing, then we want to pay it off first. (We'll talk more about how to pay off debt in chapter 4.)

financial priority #3
INVEST FOR RETIREMENT, *WHILE ALSO* PAYING OFF LOWER-INTEREST DEBT

BECAUSE WE CAN EXPECT a higher return in the stock market— 7 percent—than we're spending by reducing lower-interest debt, we prioritize retirement first, *then* paying off the debt. It's kind of a Big-Mac-with-a-side-of-fries situation, a two-parter.

We'll talk more in a later chapter about why investing for retirement is so important, but retirement is the biggest expense of your life (yes, really). Experts say you should work up to contributing 20 percent of your gross pay to retirement (which is, yep, a *lot* of fucking money). As you know, I don't play by the one-percentage-fits-all rules, so work to increase your retirement contributions whenever you can. We want to give Future You the best, most kick-ass time of her life sans work—and we get there by contributing as early and as often as possible. We also receive tax breaks when we invest for our retirement, so we want to take advantage of those.

Unlike Priority Numbers One and Two, this one often doesn't have an end that's in sight. Increasing your retirement investments or paying off your student loan debt is something you work toward slowly, consistently, and over a long period of time. This is normal and exactly what you *should* be doing. Know that this one might not give you the same serotonin rush as filling up an emergency fund or freeing yourself from credit card debt, because the "finished!" date is probably not in sight. And because Priority Three is ongoing . . .

financial priority #4
BIG LIFE STUFF

THESE ARE YOUR EXCITING life events that require savings, such as making a down payment on a car or house, having kids, getting married, taking a dream vacation, or starting a business. This goal happens while you're investing for retirement and paying down your lower-interest debt.

If you're aiming to achieve your goal in seven to ten years or less, it's recommended that you keep the money you're saving for this goal in a high-yield savings account or a certificate of deposit (CD) *instead* of investing that money. (A CD is like an HYSA on steroids, often offering a higher interest rate in exchange for your money being locked up for a period of time.) This is because you could put the money you're saving for a down payment into the stock market—and lose a good chunk of it the next day. A decade, however, is a reasonable amount of time for the market to potentially crash and then bounce back. (For most of us, retirement is more than ten years away, which is why we will be investing our retirement money!)

The only exception to the order of priorities on this list? If your employer offers you a match on your 401(k) or 403(b) retirement accounts. In chapter 5 on investing, we'll talk in more detail about what this means, but, put simply, your employer is doubling your contribution to your retirement fund. For instance, let's say that your company offers a 3 percent match. If you allocate 3 percent of your salary to your retirement account, your employer will deposit that same amount. So, a total of 6 percent of your salary goes toward your retirement, with you doing only half the work.

We want to contribute enough to these accounts to at least hit the employer match *before* we start paying off our debt, because that is *free* money, and we should do everything we can to take advantage of it, even if it means trumping this list a bit.

So, we do a *Lion King 1½* situation and slot this in right after emergency savings. I know the li'l D*ve R*msey is sitting on your shoulder kicking and screaming, but this is the smartest, most financially sound choice.

If you're getting an employer match on your retirement account, you still need to earmark as much money as you can for retirement (step 3). However, this extra money is a huge boost to your investing contributions.

So, to recap:

THE FINANCIAL PRIORITY LIST

1.   **Starter emergency fund (three months of living expenses in a high-yield savings account).**

    1.5. *If your employer matches your contributions to a 401(k) or 403(b) retirement savings account,* **pay in as much as you can.**

2.   **Pay down high-interest debt (anything with interest over 7 percent).**

3.   **Invest for retirement** *while also* **paying off lower-cost debt (again, any debt racking up less than 7 percent in interest, such as most student and car loans, mortgages, and so forth).**

4.   **Save for the Big Life Stuff.**

Now, when it comes to the Priority List, I know that it's less exciting to save for an emergency fund or to pay off your debt than, say, for a trip to Rome. So, I'd like to introduce you to the Pity Salad, a term my best friend, Kristine, and I coined for the vegetables we order as the precursor to the food we really want. (It's really just an apology to ourselves.) I eat the salad first because I know it's good for me, and because ultimately, when I'm less constipated than I would be without the leafy greens, I will thank myself for being responsible. The Financial Game Plan is the financial Pity Salad. Some parts of the Financial Game Plan—such as saving for an emergency fund, paying off your debt, investing for retirement—will often feel like the Pity Salad you eat so that you can then have pizza in Rome. It's the thing you're doing to take care of yourself, to protect yourself from financial harm and build a foundation, so you can have fun. And because I don't believe in deprivation, putting some financial goals ahead of others doesn't mean you're not living your life from day to day—we'll get to how in a second.

Remember earlier in the chapter where we discussed how to set (and achieve!) our goals? Now that we have our goals and our financial priorities, it's time to get to part two of the Financial Game Plan, which involves your favorite thing: *making a budget!* [*Cue rap air horn.*]

BUDGETING

THE WORD *BUDGET* is often associated with restriction. When old-school money experts said, "You need a budget," it was always in response to you mentioning spending money on *anything* that was deemed frivolous. And like we said in the last chapter, *frivolous* is nothing but a misogynistic word used to shame you.

Budgeting does not mean deprivation. It doesn't mean hating your life. Instead, it's actually *freeing.* Yes, really! Instead of feeling guilt for spending money, it allows you to focus your spending on things you love, without explanation or justification. It's a permission slip.

A budget is like the gas gauge in your car. You wouldn't drive a car without knowing how much gas it had, so you don't want to spend money without knowing how much is in your accounts. You want to be able to enjoy the drive, knowing that you can easily get back home. You want to be able to enjoy spending, knowing that you're not going to run out of money or go into debt. It's freeing, and it makes spending more fun by reducing the stress and anxiety that come with uncertainty. It also helps you avoid the guilt of not taking care of yourself financially: no more of that sinking feeling at the end of the month when you look at your bank account and realize you have nothing left to set aside for saving. It makes sure that you're factoring in your financial well-being *and* the things that make you happy.

If the thought of creating a budget makes you nauseated, remember that:

1. **I don't believe in deprivation in any sense of the word, and**

2. **There's a reason I created *my own* budgeting system, because none of the rest of them worked very well.**

Let me explain *why* I had to come up with my own system: budgeting apps. They overcategorize and demand that you track every penny. I won't go to the movies for three months, then I'll go see three movies the next month. And they will *yell at me* and tell me I've *gone over my limit in this category,* and I'm just like, *Jesus, let me live my goddamn life!*

I didn't want to meticulously track every penny I spent. I have better things to do (like watching Nick Kroll on *Hot Ones* for the twelfth time). And I definitely didn't like having to rely on an app or, *ew,* a spreadsheet to budget (but power to you if you do—again, personal finance is personal).

So, I created the nonbudget budget. It's called the 3 Bucket Budget. (Hydration game: take a sip of water every time I say *budget.* You can also turn this into a drinking game, but you will probably be passed out by the time you finish this page, so 0/10 would recommend.) The goal of the 3BB, as it will henceforth be known, is to take care of yourself financially *first,* while allowing you to spend money guilt free. It's flexible, completely adaptable, and requires just *one* task for everything else to fall into place (more on that in a bit).

bucket #1

THE BARE NECESSITIES

BUCKET #1 IS your *necessary expenses.*

This is everything you need to eat, sleep, breathe, move, and live.

Bucket #1 takes care of Present You's current monthly needs and includes everything that is absolutely necessary to your life that you *could not cut* in case of a job loss, like your rent/mortgage, insurance, groceries, loan payments, utility bills, and so on. And, yeah, cut off my left hand before you cancel my Spotify subscription—*but* because it is not *absolutely essential to my life*, it does not go in Bucket #1.

In chapter 2, we talked about the grey area between "wants" and "needs," so at this point, I'm trusting that what you put in here is something you're confidently and comfortably deeming necessary to your life. I like to think of Bucket #1 bills as "If I didn't pay this, I would get charged a fee and/or I'd be in trouble." Bucket #1 includes debt payments such as your monthly car payment, your student loan payment, your rent or mortgage, and so forth. If you have a credit card, Bucket #1 includes paying it off in full; if that isn't possible, and you're paying off previous debt, then paying at least your minimum payments (but, really, as much of the total balance as you can afford). Bucket #1 money generally lives in and gets taken out of your checking account.

In the Financial Priority List, making these payments is Financial Priority Zero. Paying your bills and keeping yourself alive should always take precedence. You cannot begin to save money or pay off debt if you're not first putting money toward sustaining yourself.

bucket #2
GOALS

BUCKET #2 IS your *financial goals.*

This includes the money you're directing toward the goals on the Financial Game Plan: filling up your emergency savings, paying off debt more aggressively than just your regular payments, investing for retirement, and saving for Big Life Stuff.

Bucket #2 money lives in savings, investment, and/or debt accounts, depending on what stage of the Financial Game Plan you're on.

In addition to your monthly debt payments in Bucket #1, money in Bucket #2 can go toward paying off your debt faster. (We talk more about how to pay off debt and how exactly to make the most of this extra money in chapter 4.)

Bucket #2 is where you take care of Past You and Future You. Past You, who took on debt for cool things in life, and Future You, who is saving for cool things to come in life. It's your financial self-care bucket.

bucket #3
TREAT YOURSELF

EVERYTHING ELSE goes into Bucket #3.

This is the fun category: eating out, vacations, new clothes, Spotify subscriptions, plant rescuing (my obsession), coffee, and anything else that isn't necessary to your life but makes it worth living.

Remember back in the last chapter, where we discussed Value Categories? The three areas of your life that bring you the most joy and where you'd like the majority of your fun money to go? Bucket #3 should largely be made up of your three Value Categories. Again, we want to be spending mindfully; therefore, the majority of our Bucket #3 money should align with our values and what's important to us.

So, while my three Value Categories are travel, restaurants, and nesting—and my Bucket #3 money will be spent primarily on these three things—I also will use that money occasionally to buy concert tickets, a new pair of shoes, or a nice bottle of bubbly because it was a hard Tuesday.

While D*ve R*msey makes you put literal money into literal envelopes for his "envelope system," please do not put a bunch of quarters in a neon-orange Home Depot utility bucket. But if you're asking, "Tori! If I can't put my money in an actual bucket, *what am I supposed to do?!*"—don't fret. There's a twenty-first-century answer to this question—and it's *magical*.

Wouldn't it be nice if your money just took care of itself? That seems like a fantasy world, doesn't it? One in which I eat Popeyes fried chicken whenever I want *and* I'm also happily married to Timothée Chalamet. (If you're reading this book, oh, five years after it was published, let's hope to God you're now saying, "But, Tori, I'm confused, because this *is* your actual life!")

But it is possible.

If, for some reason, your eyes have glazed over (maybe it was all the talk of *budgeting*), I need you to come back to me, because this is really, really important! It is the *one task*, as promised earlier, that helps everything else fall into place.

Here's the secret to organizing your money into buckets: automate, automate, automate.

Automating my savings was the first step I took to having my $100K saved at age twenty-five. I never had to think about moving money manually. Once the money was in savings, it meant the money wasn't going anywhere—and it was growing, because I kept it in a high-yield savings account.

Instead of trying to pay your bills manually or waiting until the end of the month to save—and your bank account is completely empty, with no money for savings—we're going to do it first. This is what makes this shit so transformational: we're getting the hard part out of the way, creating our financial foundation so we can then go spend our fun money and live our lives. It saves you so much time—no more tracking every penny in a spreadsheet (unless that's your thing); no more feeling guilty, wondering if you've saved enough; no more stress about when your payments are due. Making sure you are always working toward those long-term goals is way easier to track when you don't have to worry about remembering to transfer the exact amount of money each week or once a month, whatever the case may be.

And when it comes to our bills, it's hella faster than logging on to make your payments each month, *and* you minimize the risk of not paying your bills on time. Sounds like a win-win to me.

Generally, there are two ways you can set up automation: through your service provider or through your bank. Your service provider's website or customer service can help you automate those payments, whether it's through providing a voided check and an authorization form or through giving it your bank account and routing numbers. Of course, every bank and service provider is different, so look at their website or reach out to customer service with any questions.

Start by automating your Bucket #1 expenses. As a reminder, Bucket #1 includes your necessary and more or less predictable monthly expenses. This could include your rent, utility bills, phone bill, and so on. Route these through your checking account where your paycheck gets deposited. For most people, that's the easy part: billers and service providers are more than happy to help you pay them.

The slightly trickier part comes with Bucket #2.

Have you managed to find twelve-ish dollars nearly every single month since 2013 in order to afford your automated Netflix transfer? (For me, it's Netflixhuluhbomaxappletvplusdisneyplusdiscoveryplusparamountplus, because I need not only Ted Lasso but also Guy Fieri but also Jeff Probst.) And what about your rent? Have you *typically* come up with that money in time for the automated withdrawal (or the hopelessly outdated handwritten check) that your landlord demands?

If you can get used to those bills as an automated process for which you find money, you can do the same for your financial goals. Just think of Future You as another bill, except this one isn't from Sallie motherfucking Mae, *it's for you, baby*! You're giving yourself a little gift to build the life that you want. And that's the fucking best. It doesn't have to be a thousand million trillion dollars a month. You can get started with just $20 a month—every little bit counts. But don't pay Netflix more money than you pay yourself.

Create a list of all the Bucket #2 expenses you can automate. This can include your savings for different goals and your retirement accounts. For the automation part, one option is to set up an automatic transfer through your bank. Most banks have a recurring-payments option you can access to transfer money to other places, whether to a high-yield savings account or your investment account. Another option is to automate that money right at the source: if you're a nine-to-fiver, you can typically arrange for portions of your paycheck to be direct-deposited into different accounts. Confused about how to do this? No worries: call your bank and ask, or check with the human resources/benefits rep at your place of employment.

When we look back at the Financial Priority List, we know our first goal should be our emergency fund. So, when we set up that automated transfer of X percent per paycheck or $XXX every month, we want to direct it to our HYSA set up for emergencies.

A note: One thing you need to keep in mind when automating is that you need a buffer in the checking account you're using to pay these bills, because I don't want you overdrafting. This looks like, ideally, $500 to $1,000 of cushion. If this isn't possible for you at the moment, you can either use a smaller buffer with more diligent reminders to check your account balance, or, at the very least, just automate your bills and necessary expenses until you're financially able to contribute to Bucket #2 (your goal bucket!).

Set up reminders on your phone right before the automatic payment is scheduled in order to make sure your checking account has enough money available.

So, how much should actually go into your buckets? Great question. I frequently get asked, "How much should I be saving each month?" You're going to hate me, but there is no one-size-fits-all answer. Personal finance is personal. I don't know your life or your goals, so there isn't a set amount or percentage. Typically, 50/20/30 is a good start:

50 PERCENT IN BUCKET #1: expenses

20 PERCENT IN BUCKET #2: goals

30 PERCENT IN BUCKET #3: fun stuff

But play around with these percentages. I say the sweet spot is where you're able to afford most of the fun items and experiences you want—but also showing some restraint. For me, this looks like: "I ate out twice this week already, so I'll stay in tonight and cook." It should feel a li'l sticky: you can't purchase everything your heart might desire, but you don't hate your life either.

Let's see what this might look like with Jessica, a ~~made-up example~~ completely and totally real person who will help us demonstrate these concepts in reality. Your reality, of course, will look different.

After taxes, Jessica takes home $4,000 per month. Her essential monthly expenses, which include her rent, student loan payment, groceries, credit card payments, and health insurance, amount to $2,500.

Following the Financial Game Plan, Jessica's first step is to build up her emergency savings. She sets a goal to do so within a year. Since her necessary expenses are $2,500 a month, a *bare-minimum* three-month emergency fund needs $7,500 in it. (If that seems like a lot, I get it—take it slow and build over time. Some money in savings is better than nothing in savings! Your HYSA interest rate will also help you save—you'll be earning interest on every penny you put in.)

For most people, I recommend a bit of a cushion in addition to this, because I want you to be able to go out to eat or have something nice once in a while, even if it's an emergency! So, following this, Jessica decides to create a $200 cushion for each month, raising her emergency fund target to $8,100.

For goals beyond the month (like "by the end of the year"), you can break them down on your phone calculator by dividing the total cost by the number of months, like we did with saving living expenses back on page 87.

Again, you can base your goals around life events. If you want to go to Japan in eight months, and it will cost $4,000 to do so, you'll set aside $500 a month. Next thing you know, you're dining in Tokyo!

In order to meet that goal within the year, Jessica has to save $625 a month. So, this is what her monthly budget looks like:

✳ **She makes sure to have $2,500 to cover her necessary monthly expenses (Bucket #1).**

✳ **She sets up an automated payment of $625 a month to her HYSA (Bucket #2).**

✳ **That leaves $875 for fun things such as weekly flowers, an at-home kombucha brewing kit, and Weird Al concert tickets (Bucket #3).**

There is no magic, perfect percentage. This will take some trial and error. Jessica might decide it's worth it to move some Bucket #3 money over to Bucket #2 in order to fill up her emergency fund faster.

You will need some time to figure out how much you can put toward your goals, while also not depriving yourself too much. It took me seven months to figure out my precise percentages; every month, I would increase Bucket #2's amount by 1 to 2 percent. When I was still a nine-to-five employee, my sweet spot was 43 percent in Bucket #1, 27 percent in Bucket #2, and 30 percent in Bucket #3. Again, everyone's percentages will be different. Put everything you spend money on in its corresponding bucket and then figure out a good starter percentage for each one. Tweak as you go, and don't be afraid to play around a little bit!

Start with 5 percent automated toward your savings, and then increase it from there. A good *general* goal to work toward is 20 percent in Bucket #2, with that 20 percent being broken down for various financial goals. Now, what if your income isn't consistent? If you're a freelancer or a part-time worker, for instance, you might not be able to rely on automation, since not knowing how much money is coming in every month leaves you vulnerable to overdrafting. You're likely going to have to be more diligent and set specific and strict limits for each bucket, and, in addition, track more individual expenses, as opposed to just a general number for each bucket.

A good starting point for an inconsistent earner's budget is the bare minimum you can expect to earn. Look at your income history. How much did you make in the month you earned the least? And what's the average monthly amount you've earned over the past year (or however long ago you started freelancing)?

If your average monthly income and lowest income are close, you might want to automate conservatively: just Bucket #1 and a smaller percentage into Bucket #2. If there is a large gap between your average income and your lowest month, you might feel more comfortable automating more into Bucket #2, since you'll likely have more of a buffer carrying over, and low-earning months are more of an anomaly.

Whether you're salaried, a part-time worker, or a freelancer, you know the fluctuations of your income best. The key to budgeting is to always be mindful of the dollar amount you've automated, the money you have coming in, and how much is sitting in your checking account.

HOMEWORK

1. ## GET YOUR HEAD OUT OF THE SAND

   At the beginning of the chapter, we talked about the Ostrich Effect. What might you be avoiding when it comes to your finances? Journal about the Ostrich Effect and how it's affecting (see what I did there?!) your money and your life.

   What are some money goals you're "supposed" to set, and what do you *actually* want to achieve?

   EXAMPLE: *"I should buy a house."* → *"I could go buy, and yet I choose to rent because I like the flexibility."*

   _____

   _____

   _____

   _____

   _____

   _____

   _____

   _____

   _____

   _____

   _____

   _____

   _____

   _____

   _____

2. GOAL SETTING

Take a look at your accounts and consider some of the financial goals you want to accomplish: Do you wish you had emergency savings? Do you have debt you're trying to eradicate? What are some other life goals you wish you had money for?

In this homework assignment, you're going to turn your wishes into goals by getting specific and setting timelines, determining your Why, making plans, automating, and manifesting a visual of what that goal is.

Set goals that are specific, timely, and mission driven. Write them in the past tense, as if they've already happened, and then sketch out a plan to achieve them.

3. THE FINANCIAL PRIORITY LIST

Next, we are going to order our goals using the Financial Priority List. Simply check off where you're at—*no* judgment if no boxes are checked yet.

☐ **BUILD** an emergency fund (three months of living expenses in a high-yield savings account).

Only if applicable: Contribute as much as is needed to your 401(k) or 403(b) retirement savings account if your employer matches that contribution.

☐ **PAY** down high-interest debt (anything with interest over 7 percent).

☐ **INVEST** for retirement while simultaneously paying down low-interest debt (anything with less than 7 percent interest).

☐ **SAVE** for the Big Life Stuff.

Organize your goals according to the Financial Priority List.

_____
_____
_____
_____
_____
_____
_____
_____
_____
_____
_____
_____
_____
_____
_____

_____
_____
_____
_____
_____
_____
_____
_____
_____
_____
_____

4. BUILD YOUR BUDGET

Now comes the exciting part, building your no-budget budget.
Go through my 3 Bucket Budget and build it out. What costs/
expenses/goals are in each bucket?

STEP 1: Calculate how much you earn per month. If you're a
freelancer, use the minimum monthly amount you've made
over the past year as a starting point.

_____
_____
_____
_____
_____
_____
_____
_____
_____
_____

STEP 2: Add up all your necessary expenses to figure out the dollar amount that should be in Bucket #1.

STEP 3: Subtract your Bucket #1 expenses from your monthly income. What's left over will give you a starting point for determining how much should go in Bucket #2.

_____

_____

_____

_____

_____

_____

_____

_____

Now list all the Bucket #2 items you can automate, while making sure you maintain a buffer in your checking account.

_____

_____

_____

_____

_____

_____

_____

_____

_____

_____

_____

_____

_____

_____

STEP 4: After subtracting your Bucket #1 and Bucket #2 expenses from your monthly income, the amount of money that's left over is your discretionary spending, or Bucket #3. Remember your three Value Categories? Jot them down: a majority of your Bucket #3 should be spent on those three things.

1. _____

2. _____

3. _____

Final Steps: **AUTOMATE AND BUILD VISUALS**

Automating your buckets is a *game changer*. There's a reason they say "Set it and forget it"—because you truly will forget all about it! Beat the anxiety monster at its game. Take thirty minutes: set up auto-pay on your bills, an automated transfer from your checking to your savings account, and (if applicable) automatic contributions to your workplace retirement account.

Finally, to stay on track with your budget and goals, set visual reminders! I like to write on Post-it notes and vision boards. Give yourself a visual representation of your Why, or write down/type a few favorite affirmations for when you're feeling like you can't make it.

CHAPTER 4

DEBT

I WAS A SOPHOMORE IN COLLEGE, SITTING ON THE FLOOR OF MY FRIENDS' DORM ROOM NEXT DOOR.

We often congregated in our neighbors' room, because Gina and Alex were not only fun, but also they had a heater that was *definitely* against dorm rules. I don't even remember how the conversation started, but we were complaining about the high price of college. Although 99 percent of my university's students qualified for some kind of aid (no one paid the sticker price), a year's tuition with room and board was at least $50,000.

That's when Alex said something I'll never forget. Studying business and considering going on to get an MBA, she mentioned casually that by the time she earned just her undergraduate degree, she would be more than $100,000 in debt.

Her bachelor's degree alone was going to put her six figures in the hole. She said this with an air of exasperation yet also blissful ignorance—we were nineteen and didn't fully understand what being $100,000 in debt actually meant. We knew it was a lot of money but had no real understanding of how this debt would impact her life, her decisions, her future. It was a concept, a number written on a piece of paper, not yet a three-dimensional, real-world problem that would eventually keep her up at night.

Alex wasn't alone. Since the dawn of society, we've grappled with debt in various forms. The first recorded debt systems date all the way back to 3500 B.C.E., and some scholars claim that debt existed before bartering or even (get this) money itself. President Thomas Jefferson was in debt for almost his entire life, buying fancy shit to impress other people. (As my research assistant, Ariel, puts it, he was "a hot mess.") In 2010, real-life national treasure Nicolas Cage found himself $6.3 million in debt to the IRS and proceeded to take almost every film role offered to him—some Cage-worthy; others not so much—in order to pay it off.

In twenty-first-century America, debt is an integral part of our economy. If you have a credit card, if you had to take out student loans, if you have a mortgage, congrats! You're in the majority. The average American has more than $90,000 in debt, while the total U.S. consumer debt is currently at $14,600,000,000,000. (That's $14.6 trillion. Too many fucking zeros.)

While some debt seems "reasonable" (I put *reasonable* in quotes, because we could debate the question "Is debt inherently predatory?" for *hours*), some debt is downright bloodthirsty and should be illegal. (For example, the average payday loan interest rate is nearly 400 percent. Un-fucking-conscionable.)

Tricia Cleppe

COMMUNITY ORGANIZER

I grew up the daughter of a Filipina immigrant single mother in the American South, in an extremely white and deeply evangelical community.

One of my mother's first jobs in the United States was at a check-cashing store. The man who eventually became my godfather owned a chain of check-cashing stores, and I grew up going with her to that office every single day. I even learned how to count there, because we would count the cash on the floor.

Check-cashing and bail-bond stores are inherently predatory. It's sometimes background checks, and credit checks too. Many banks require you to have a minimum amount in your account. Check-cashing stores allow you to get cash, except they do it in the most predatory way possible: they charge you anywhere between 7 and 14 percent of the amount of your check.

If you became a member of the store, it was kind of like having a bank account with the check-cashing store—but not really. You also had to pay an up-front fee of something like $50, and then you could cash your checks for 7 percent of the overall total instead of 14 percent.

In addition to check cashing, the store also provided cash-bail services. The cash-bail program in America works like this: if you get arrested, you can be held in jail until your court date. Studies show that judges place higher bail amounts on people of color, which means the whole system relies on racism— from the arrests and the policing of minority communities to the economic state of the communities most affected. These communities don't have as much discretionary income to pay $10,000, $12,000, or $20,000 in cash up front for bailing a loved one out of jail.

But I watched people walk in and out all day to do just that.

The alternative is sitting in jail awaiting trial for months or sometimes years. There's a massive amount of people incarcerated right now in America who have never been convicted of a crime. They're just waiting for their court date, and they don't have the money to get out in the meantime.

This is an experience that I am still processing. My favorite childhood memory was going to Disney World, driving to Florida in a minivan put up for collateral by a Black grandmother to get her grandson out of jail for a drug charge. It was hard to come to terms with my family's place and complicity in these horrible, predatory systems.

White supremacy is this massive thing with tentacles woven into the systems that uphold it—but all of these systems require participation. My mother was just an Asian woman trying to provide for her family as a single mother. I don't begrudge her for that because she didn't know what she didn't know—but it doesn't make it right. I think about all that cash I took from people; I literally took it from their hands. None of it is beyond me. None of it is lost on me. It was a really uncanny master class in how these systems work together.

These predatory systems were my introduction to money.

My childhood experience speaks to this kind of grand bargain with white supremacy that many minorities fall into in America—this proximity to whiteness. You think that if you get close enough to it, you can assimilate, go through the same education systems and come out the same way. But it's just a farce. This idea just protects white supremacy.

These experiences, and the introduction I had to money as a child, made me avoid figuring out my own money issues, which created a self-fulfilling prophecy. I believed that money was evil and wanted nothing to do with it. I'd seen what money and power do to people, and I didn't want any part of it. In return, I avoided money topics and financial health. If I avoided participation, I thought I would keep myself from becoming evil and corrupt. Yet, there I was, another woman of color who couldn't seem to get a leg up on the whole financial thing, despite being fully employed and having the brains to do it.

When I first met Tori, I was in survival mode. I had a bad relationship with money and was terrified of it. I had to fight this morality around capitalism—the rugged individualism that this country requires of its people. But I've come a long way, and I've gotten to a point where I set up an emergency fund and a nonjudgmental budget, and I am able to support my mother, but those old feelings are still there. To have that confidence, and the ability to support my family, especially after everything we've been through, means everything to me.

The patriarchy isn't absent when it comes to debt (because of course it isn't). In 2019, women were more likely to have not paid their credit card balances in full in any of the last six months. Men, on the other hand, were more likely to have paid their bills in full every single month. Women hold more than two-thirds of the student debt in America—because although men start with more student debt, on average, they are able to pay it off faster. (Another factor: parents contribute more to their sons' college funds than to their daughters'.) Until 1974, a woman couldn't even open a credit card without her husband's approval. The seventies were, like, *yesterday*.

And for people of color, these statistics are (unfortunately, not shockingly) worse. Black and white college graduates leave with a $7,000 difference in debt, and it increases to $25,000 in the four years following graduation, because white graduates earn more money. There is sustainable evidence that minorities have less access to credit, and the credit they do have access to is more expensive for almost every type of loan: mortgages, auto loans, small business loans, credit cards. And being deeper in debt not only affects our current financial situation but also keeps us from saving and investing more, *and* it prevents us from improving our financial prospects because our credit scores take a hit.

Speaking of credit scores, which were created in 1974 to eliminate bias in assessing creditworthiness (it totally worked, and now racism and sexism are dead, and everything is fine!!!!!!), women, on average, have lower credit scores and lower credit card limits compared with men. Even in technology as advanced as machine learning, we see massive gender discrepancies. In 2019, when the investment firm Goldman Sachs launched the Apple Card, it relied on a gender-blind credit card approval process. Good in theory, but in practice, gender can easily be discovered from other variables, such as a lower net worth. So, because women historically have been given less credit, the algorithm continued that pattern. People of color too received lower credit lines.

So, yeah, debt sucks. But unless you're made of enough money to pay for a house or college with stacks of cash, you're going to interact with the debt economy at some point in your life. And we all want to achieve life milestones, so although debt can suck, it's also the only way we can level up. This chapter will teach you how debt works (and snowballs), give you insight into the predatory nature of some loans and how debt helps the patriarchy profit, and coach you on how to use your new knowledge to conquer that debt. Let's get some common misconceptions out of the way first.

misconception #1
I'M A BAD PERSON IF I HAVE DEBT

BOTH SOCIETY and traditional money experts are so good at telling you that incurring debt means you're a piece of shit. Having debt is somehow equated to having a personal defect: that you can't manage your life, you're not worthy of nice things while having outstanding loans, and you should be deeply, deeply ashamed. (D*ve R*msey said that taking on debt for college was "participating in stupidity.")

As I've said a million times and will say again a million times, your self-worth has nothing to do with your net worth. Being in debt doesn't mean you should live with constant sacrifice, punishment, or misery. Most people take on debt because they need to, and it's no one's place to shame you for it.

Many people go into debt because they were simply never taught how debt works. "Not understanding how a loan works" is the top reason women cited for having more debt than men. And that lack of understanding seems awfully convenient when you consider how much money creditors make off interest.

If you went to college, you might remember a sunny day on your campus quad, where credit card companies set up booths to lure you into signing up before you fully understood what having a credit card entailed. This was enough of an issue that in 2009, the U.S. Congress passed the Credit Card Accountability Responsibility and Disclosure Act, which limited how companies could advertise to young people. Offering free Frisbees, T-shirts, and the like as incentives became against the law, although many colleges still signed million-dollar deals with credit card companies allowing them to aggressively target their students. Cool.

For yet another perfect example of the patriarchal bullshit of debt, look at Victoria's Secret. No, not Victoria Dunlap's secret. (*That* secret is that, as a high school freshman, I had a massive crush on my stage husband, a very popular, very handsome senior in our production of *The Crucible*. Bet you didn't expect this kind of shout-out, did you, Rodman?)

Victoria's Secret's secret is that the company offers its customers a store-branded credit card backed by Comenity Bank, which is now the subject of a series of arbitration demands by a class-action law firm for not disclosing the card's true interest rates up front. Many retail stores brand their credit cards as a benefit. "Open up a rewards card with us and get money back on your purchases!" Sounds like a great deal, right? But the lenders that back the cards often avoid disclosing to customers what signing up for a card means, *and* they charge interest rates higher than the national average, taking advantage of a vulnerable, often financially uneducated group—women—and using their inexperience against them.

A word from
Bethany B.
HER FIRST $100K COMMUNITY MEMBER

I worked as a sales associate at Victoria's Secret in college, from 2005 to 2009. I was looking to make some extra cash to buy food, pay sorority dues, and get discounted/free stuff. It was a fun place to work because some of my sorority sisters already worked there, so I already knew a lot of my coworkers when I started.

I definitely have mixed feelings looking back on what it was like to work at the lingerie store. I'm not saying it was miserable, but there were some sketchy times . . .

Our onboarding process was very short. After a few days of shadowing other associates, we were trained at the registers on the point-of-sale system and then got about fifteen minutes of training on the Angel Card, the store credit card.

The biggest thing that didn't sit right with me was being instructed to push the Angel Card to every customer. Our manager was relentless about getting people to sign up for credit cards. She had a leaderboard posted next to our schedules in the stockroom, where she kept track of how many customers each associate was able to convert to an Angel Card holder. Top associates would be praised, celebrated on the headset/comm system that was in everyone's ear, and at times were able to pick from the bucket of items that were returned without tags.

The phrase "Are you shopping with your Angel Card today?" haunts my dreams. We had to ask *everyone* that question, and if they said that they didn't have the card, we would ask them if they would like to open one that day. I just hated pushing the cards and did so only when my manager was in earshot. I didn't even really understand credit cards myself, so I definitely should not have been the one pushing them on others.

There were different approaches we were told to take.

We could make it seem like they were getting personally invited into a really cool club, using statements such as "I'd like to invite you . . ." and "This is such an amazing offer right now; I'd love for you to be a part of this."

If that didn't resonate, we went the route of discounts, since a lot of the time there was an instant dollar amount off (sometimes $15 or higher) as a sign-up bonus. That felt like the most manipulative part, because we would say, "You could get fifteen dollars off today if you sign up for the Angel Card," and I don't think it clicked with people that they were actually signing up for a credit card. (For one thing, we were instructed to refer to it as an "Angel card," not an "Angel credit card.") We were to advertise it more like a rewards account, like what you have at the grocery store, than a credit card. Some of my coworkers would hold up an item from the customer's merchandise and ask, "Do you want this for free?" or "Can I give this to you for free today?" or "How about I don't charge you for this one?"—to which a customer would obviously respond, "Oh, hell yes!" and the associate would say something like, "I can do that when you open an Angel Card." It was a high-pressure and intimidating tactic.

One of the worst examples that I remember is when our manager pushed a woman to sign up for the credit card, and there was a very significant language barrier between both of them. I think our manager said something that made it seem like the woman needed to open a credit card in order to buy her stuff, almost forcing her to open the account. When one of my coworkers and I asked our manager about it, she said something like, "Well, she can call the number and press two to speak to someone who can actually explain it."

I have a lot of guilt when I think about how many people I coerced into opening a credit card. Sometimes young women would use their Angel Card at the register, and the card would be declined. I never really put it together until now, but I bet they never paid their card statements. They probably didn't even know how to. Shit.

And to think: I did it all to chase the possibility of getting a free bra each month. I actually did win once, and you know what? Since I'm a 34DDD, they had only *beige* in stock. So I did it all for a friggin' beige bra.

Anyone who makes you feel bad about yourself for being in debt is both ignoring economic realities and justifying the predatory behavior of multinational corporations. Whatever your reasons for going into debt, shame and guilt will not get you out of it. Give yourself some grace, and let's figure this out together.

ALL DEBT IS "BAD" FOR YOUR FINANCIAL HEALTH AND SHOULD BE AVOIDED AT ALL COSTS

RIGHT ON THE HEELS of "I'm a bad person if I have debt," we have the narrative that all debt is bad. If you were "stupid enough to get yourself into it," then you should do everything you can to immediately eradicate it.

When you're drowning in debt, it's easy to feel like it's all the same burden. But not all debt is created equal. Student loans are different from mortgages are different from medical bills are different from credit cards. Some debt is worse than others in terms of its financial cost, which depends on the interest rate, how that interest accrues, and the length of your loan. We'll talk about how this all works in a moment.

Most people go into debt because they have to. It's a privilege to maintain a debt-free lifestyle. Taking on student loans—the trillion-dollar elephant in the room—was what many of us were "supposed" to do, regardless of the cost. We were told that a college degree ensured a good job with good benefits and that we should just suck it up: "If I had to pay a whopping twelve dollars for college, you should be able to pay for it too; not sure why you're complaining."

But here's a thing that will blow your mind: debt isn't called *debt* when it's held by rich people—it's called *leverage*. It's fucking labeled differently depending on your financial status, and while one is "bad," the other is smart and financially savvy. Leverage can be as simple as getting a mortgage on a property even if you can afford to put down cash (because you can often earn more in the stock market than what the average mortgage costs you in interest). For richer people, taking on debt is often a smart business decision—and they're rewarded for it.

Avoiding debt at all costs is just not realistic. Nor is it necessarily good for you. Just like leveraging can benefit finances, assuming debt is often how you move up in this world. Maybe you're buying your first home, building your business, or getting a bachelor's degree. These are net positives, which, yes, I wish were more accessible to all of us without having to take out a loan. But since we currently live in a world where we can't avoid debt, we have to beat it at its own game.

misconception #3
I CAN NEVER BECOME DEBT FREE

I KNOW. You log in to your student loan provider's website, and that huge number feels like a slap in the face. Every time you pull out a credit card, your gut drops. At night, your medical debt haunts you like Björk's swan dress at the 2001 Oscars.

You're staring at the Mount Everest of Debt, wondering how the fuck you're going to climb this thing.

But just like that quote about eating an elephant, you eat it a bite at a time. You *can* pay off your debt. Not only is becoming debt free a massive personal accomplishment, but also it's yet another way we fight patriarchal, bullshit systems.

Now, let me be clear: *being* debt free is an act of rebellion, but the act of paying off debt isn't. Paying the (unfortunately necessary) interest, sending in your hard-earned money every month to a massive corporation or the government, is soul sucking and icky. If you're a woman, a person of color, LGBTQ+, disabled, and so on, being debt free is a "fuck you" to a system that wants to keep you under its thumb. Being debt free, just like every other financial milestone, is bigger than you.

I'm not going to sugarcoat it: It will be hard work. It will take patience and consistency. It will be a challenge. But when have you ever been afraid of a challenge?

A QUICK OVERVIEW OF HOW
A LOAN WORKS

THE GENERAL IDEA of debt is simple: you borrow money, and you have to pay it back. (This works the same for all kinds of debt, from student loans, to mortgages, to car loans.) The original sum of money you borrow is called the principal. Depending on the terms of your agreement with the lender, you have to pay a certain amount within a certain period of time—often called a monthly payment. This payment not only includes part of the principal balance but also interest.

What is interest? Well, financial institutions are not lending you money for free, so in exchange for the money, they charge you more money, which you'll usually see presented as a percentage per year. For example, you might have $350 due on the fifteenth of every month to your student loan provider (principal + interest). If you do not pay the full amount on time, you could be hit with late fees. With certain kinds of debt, like credit cards, you have the option of paying a "minimum payment" without incurring a late fee, but because you didn't pay the full amount, you'll have to pay back both the original sum AND the interest charged.

If you borrow $1,000 with a 25 percent annual *simple* interest rate, you'll owe 25 percent of $1,000 (that's $250) in interest every year. This is the preferred type of interest for when we're borrowing money, but because it's not as lucrative for the debt provider, it's the less common option.

Continuing with our example above, now let's say the interest *compounds* instead. Compounding means that the interest isn't just on the principal—it's also on any interest accumulated during the compounding period. At the end of year two, you don't owe 25 percent of $1,000, but 25 percent of $1,250 (the principal plus the interest from the year before). Compounding is great when we're the ones collecting the money—say, through an HYSA or investing—but not when we're in debt.

One more thing. The *frequency* of compounding also makes a difference regarding how much is owed. So far, we've seen what happens when interest compounds annually, but what happens if it's compounded *daily*, like most credit card debt is? If your annual interest rate is 25 percent, you would divide 25 by 365 to calculate the daily interest, which would be 0.0684 percent. So, if you borrowed $1,000, the following day, you're now in charge of paying $1,000.68. And the next day, you're in charge of paying 0.0684 percent *again*, but this time the interest is calculated on the previous day's total of $1,000.68, not the original $1,000. And so on and so on.

This might not seem like a lot in the first few days, but at the end of the year? That's $1,283.92—more than the $1,250 you'd expect if the interest compounded only annually.

You can see why compounding debt is a slippery fucking slope. When you send in your monthly minimum payment, you are slowly chipping away at your balance, *but you're not making much progress because the interest is still accruing*. This is why you see all those stories about how someone put $5,000 on a credit card, has been paying the minimum payment for two years, and now owes, like, $8,000. I get tagged in someone's TikTok video about this at least once a week. (Maybe it's *your* story.) Creditors intentionally make the required minimum payment low, so that you'll continue to owe them way more than you ever bargained for.

And, of course, we're assuming you're not adding to this balance. If, say, you continue to put additional money on your credit card without paying the full balance—if you spend $2,000 per month but pay only $1,000—that debt is adding to the original $1,000 *plus* the mounting interest. This is why it feels like you're drowning trying to pay off debt: you're sending in money but seeing little to no progress. Because remember: Interest. Never. Stops. Compounding.

PRINCIPAL AND INTEREST	HOW MUCH YOU OWE AT THE END OF YEAR 1	HOW MUCH YOU OWE AT THE END OF YEAR 2	HOW MUCH YOU OWE AT THE END OF YEAR 3
$1,000, 25% simple interest	$1,250	$1,500	$1,750
$1,000, 25% interest compounded annually	$1,250	$1,562.5	$1,953.13
$1,000, 25% interest compounded daily	$1,283.92	$1,648.44	$2,116.46

And the interest rate isn't the only thing you have to think about. Every kind of loan has different terms. For example, some don't charge interest for a certain time period, and some loans have higher monthly payments but are less lengthy, so you're done quicker. For example, I opted to pay $100 more per month for my car, saving two years of payments and interest.

Being in debt means you're constantly one step behind. It's no surprise that being in debt can make you feel powerless, like you're at the lenders' mercy. Of course it feels miserable. Someone (typically a huge corporation) is literally profiting off your financial instability, without batting an eye.

HOW TO PAY OFF DEBT

THE HOW to paying down debt is actually shockingly simple. It starts with the difference between the principal and interest. Recall that the principal is the amount of money you originally borrowed, with the interest accruing on top—either simple interest or, more frequently, compound interest.

As you'll remember from when you made your Financial Game Plan, there are two different groups of debt: high interest and low interest. I consider high-interest debt to be anything over 7 percent interest, while low-interest debt has an interest rate under 7 percent. Payday loans and credit cards are always high-interest debt, while most student loans, mortgages, and car loans charge low-interest debt.

The reason we prioritize high-interest debt is because it's costing us more money than we could be making in the stock market. If we're losing more money being in debt than we could be gaining by investing, we should aim to eliminate that debt first before investing.

Now, let's say you send in extra money with your regular monthly payments to start paying down your debt. (Good for you, you badass!) You send off $300 instead of $250. The potential catch: next month's bill will just be $200. You paid $50 off next month's bill. Which is cool but really didn't get you anywhere. It was applied to your principal *and* your interest, not just the principal. You just saved Future You $50 that you would have paid, instead of chipping away at the total balance.

A quick anecdote explaining what I mean: my car loan was through Toyota, and my monthly payment was $500. When I first started paying it down in 2016, I had an extra $50 one month, so I sent in my normal $500 plus an extra $50, expecting it to go to the principal.

But when I opened my bill for the month after, it was $450. Lower than normal, but again, it didn't actually pay off the car any faster. The extra $50 I sent in just went toward next month's balance. Past Me was just saving Next Month Me $50, but Future Me still had just as much debt.

So when I called and asked the loan division how I could put money toward the principal, they said, "Oh! Well, you have to send the extra money you want to go to the principal *to this random PO box in Iowa* that you didn't know the address of until you called and asked very specifically." That's some bullshit.

Lenders are sneaky. Sometimes they make it inconvenient for you to whittle down the principal because the longer you remain mired in debt, the more money they make off you. Paying toward the principal shortens the lifespan of your loan, thus saving you money in interest—but, of course, they won't tell you that either, because they'll make more money if you're in the dark.

To pay down debt faster, we need to put extra money toward the *principal* balance of the loan. In addition to your normal monthly payments, you're going to funnel any additional money toward the principal balance of the loan that's weighing you down with the highest interest rate. The way to do this depends both on the type of loan and the lender. Call your loan provider and ask, "How do I start paying down the principal of this loan?" (Highlight that previous sentence, it's incredibly valuable and you're going to need it.)

Some lenders are easier to work with, but all are required legally to tell you the exact steps you'll need to take to apply more money to the principal. Take notes on everything they say.

And while you're on the phone, another fun thing to try: sometimes your loan provider will be open to lowering your interest rate. This will be most advantageous if you're currently paying off your debt. (A lower interest rate means, of course, less money charged in interest!) Just ask the company's customer service. (You might recognize this script, since it's basically the same as the one for lowering your bills. Work smarter, not harder.)

Here's your script:

> "Hello, [name], how are you? I'm doing great—thank you for asking. I'm having an issue, and I would love for you to help me. I saw that [a competing company] is offering a significantly lower interest rate and better card benefits." [Or] "I'm currently going through a tough financial period due to [reason—job loss, COVID, or other medical issue]. I'd love to discuss your lowering my interest rate. As an [elite card holder, five-year Capital One customer, reliable lendee, and so on], I'd really love to continue being a loyal, valued customer. What can you do for me?"
>
> If they say it is not possible to lower your interest rate at this time, ask again: "I want to have a great customer experience today with [company name]. What can you do for me?"

When you're in debt up to your eyeballs and you're fucking *stressed*, you'll do almost anything to make it go away. So, when you hear about strategies or tools that sound almost as if they can make your debt magically disappear, you're completely on board. I get how tempting it is to use these as Easy buttons to get out of debt, but I need you to be cautious. Folks often end up using these tools as life preservers during a time of stress and panic about their debt (completely reasonable) without really considering the consequences or making a debt payoff plan. They don't work for every person or every situation (personal finance is, you guessed it, personal), and they *especially* do not work if you don't have a plan.

First, student loan forgiveness—a topic I am asked about almost daily. Politicians often talk about student loan relief and/or forgiveness; it's become such a political buzzword that it feels almost inevitable. And we already have some student debt forgiveness programs in place, such as Public Service Loan Forgiveness (PSLF) and Pay as You Earn (PAYE) (do your own research to see if you qualify!)—and many companies are starting to offer debt repayment as part of their benefits packages. We also have income-based repayment plans, which definitely don't offer forgiveness but can offer some relief. However, you may end up paying more in interest over time. (And as this book was in production, President Biden announced loan forgiveness for individuals making less than $125,000—$10,000 for most individuals or $20,000 for Pell Grant recipients—which we hope actually materializes. So, yay! Let's applaud progress while also demanding more.)

I want broad student loan forgiveness more than I want to marry Timothée Chalamet (which should tell you how much I fucking support it). However, I don't recommend anyone banking on it happening. Too many people I talk to are like, "My student loans are awful, so I'm just not going to worry about them because forgiveness maybe?" But here's the deal: I don't trust the campaign promises of politicians, who then won't or can't get shit done when they're battling against other politicians yelling about how they could afford a house in 1765, so the rest of us should just suck it up. Do we honestly think that our lawmakers will come to an agreement? I wish they would, but I'm not holding my breath. So, while we vote for and support student loan forgiveness, it's not a guarantee. We continue to work toward paying off our debt and making our payments.

Let's talk about the Holy Trinity of Debt Quick Fixes: balance transfers, zero percent interest, and debt consolidation. All of these are a potentially slippery slope. They work *only* if (1) the math checks out, and (2) you have a debt payoff plan. I'm providing you a bit of information about each of these, with the expectation that you'll do more research as it pertains to your own situation.

A balance transfer is moving your debt from one place to another offering a lower interest rate: for example, moving $10,000 in debt from a credit card charging 25 percent interest to one with 18 percent interest, to slow down the accumulation of debt. Another strategy is to transfer money from one card to a new card that entices customers with zero percent interest for the first X months. This could be a great Pause button on your debt, but, again, only if you have a plan. Delaying the inevitable with no strategy to pay off your debt by the time the interest kicks in—or using zero percent interest as an excuse to purchase something you can't afford—is not a smart decision. You can use this tool to buy you some time, come up with a plan to pay off your debt, and stick to it. (More about this later in the chapter.)

Finally, there's debt consolidation. Exactly what it sounds like, it involves taking multiple debts and putting them all together with only one interest rate (often a lower rate than you were paying before). Yet again, this works only if you have an actual plan to pay off your debt and if the math checks out. Let's say you had three debts, each with an average interest rate of 15 percent, and then you consolidated them all under a 12 percent interest rate. This might sound like a better deal, but like I mentioned before, interest rate is only part of the equation. What if your loan length increases? What if it was a two-year loan and is now a five-year loan? While you might be temporarily paying less in interest with a lower rate, you could pay more over the long run if the term length increases.

With all that in mind, let's make a plan.

STEP 1

The first step to paying off debt is *knowing what your interest rates actually are.*

This is one of those money steps that many people avoid, either because they don't understand exactly what interest is, or because they are ostriches who bury their heads in the sand and don't want to look at it. (Both reactions are understandable and totally normal.) But we cannot proceed unless we understand what we're working with!

The easiest way to check your interest rate is by looking at your monthly statements or logging on to the company's online platform and finding it there. You can also call customer service and ask.

I recommend doing this even if you think you know what your interest rates are, because often, when you first sign up for a credit card, you're enticed with a more favorable interest rate than you actually have to pay down the line.

STEP 2

This money step is a little like ripping off a Band-Aid. Grab yourself a bottle of wine and *check your debt balances. All of them.* You can log this in a spreadsheet, a notebook, or an app if you have one you like.

Now you're going to organize your debt in two ways: first by interest rate, then by the current balance:

CHASE FREEDOM CARD: **22 percent interest; balance, $6,275.92**

BANK OF AMERICA CARD: **16 percent interest; balance, $4,679.00**

STUDENT LOAN: **4.5 percent interest; balance, $45,670.00**

Got it? Now that we know the lay of the land, let's proceed.

While we will be aggressively paying down our debt, it's *extremely* important to not go into more debt, especially more *credit card debt*. In other words: emergency funds are for emergencies, and credit cards are not. This is why we set aside an emergency fund first, to cover our asses should something happen. It's super hard to dig yourself out of a hole while at the same time shoveling sand back in it. (Stanley Yelnats knew that better than anyone.) You should be doing everything you can to not put something on your credit card that you cannot pay for. You're now president of the On Time/In Full Club.

Once we have that list, we'll start by paying down our high-interest debt (anything with more than 7 percent interest). In the example above, that's the Chase Freedom card and the Bank of America card.

Wait, Tori, what do we do if we have multiple debt balances over 7 percent interest?

Good question.

Look at the hypothetical example. You've got one card with more than $6,000 on it, at 22 percent interest, and another with 16 percent interest and a balance of more than $4,000. Which should you pay off first? Pure math would tell you to start paying down the one with the highest interest rate: the Chase Freedom card.

However, if you know you need to see progress in order to stay motivated and keep going, grab the lower-hanging fruit: the Bank of America card with the lower balance. Personal finance is, yep, *personal*, so choose what's right for you.

Although you need to pick one to focus your energy on, *please dear God*, make sure that you pay at least your minimum payments on all credit card debt you have. Do not try to aggressively pay down both at the same time and do not spread your money between both of them! This could overwhelm you and make paying off your cards a more tedious process.

STEP 3

Following last chapter's Financial Priority List, now that your emergency HYSA is fully funded with three months of living expenses, you're now going to take the money you were allocating there and reroute it toward your high-interest debt. As with filling your emergency savings, it doesn't have to be $1 million a month—every little bit counts.

In order to figure out how long it will take to pay off your debt, you can use a debt payoff calculator. Simply plug in your interest rate, your balance, and how much you plan to contribute every month. It's easy to play around with numbers and see if you can lower your time in debt by increasing your contribution. Google "debt payoff calculator" to find one.

Remember Jessica from last chapter, whose take-home pay (after taxes) was $4,000 a month and whose budget looked like this?

* **BUCKET #1: $2,500 for necessary expenses**

* **BUCKET #2: $625 toward an emergency fund in an HYSA**

* **BUCKET #3: $825 for all the fun stuff**

After a year, Jessica's HYSA has the $8,100 she needs for her emergency fund, so it's time to tackle her debt. She has a balance of $6,275.92 on one credit card with a 22 percent interest rate and $4,679 on another one with a 16 percent interest rate.

What does she do now? Using a debt payoff calculator, Jessica figures out she can pay off the $6,275.92 credit card in about nine months if she ups her Bucket #2 contributions by $100 a month, which she decides is worth it. So, for the next nine months, she plans her budget as follows:

- ✳ **BUCKET #1: $2,500**

- ✳ **BUCKET #2: $775 toward paying off credit card debt**

- ✳ **BUCKET #3: $725**

Once that first card is paid off, Jessica uses her debt calculator to plan how to eventually eliminate the $4,679 on the card with 16 percent interest. She could keep that $775 payment steady and pay it off faster, but after all her hard work, she decides that she deserves a little more fun money. She calculates that if she adds an extra $100 a month back into Bucket #3, she'll be in debt for just a bit longer, which feels okay to her. So, she decides to ease off the pedal:

- ✳ **BUCKET #1: $2,500**

- ✳ **BUCKET #2: $675**

- ✳ **BUCKET #3: $825**

And that's how you pay off debt. Once that first debt is gone, you move on to the next account. And the next. Until you're done.

Again, the How isn't complicated (putting money toward the principal). Where you can and will get tripped up is in staying consistent, which is why it's important to find what works for you and adjust if necessary.

There is no magic wand to wave and make all your debt disappear. It's hard fucking work. That's why we put our extra contributions on automatic, so even when we're like, "Ugh, God, seriously? *Again?!*" it happens anyway.

Paying off debt can feel isolating. Know that you're not alone, and that I'm here to support you and cheer you on.

HOW TO TAKE ON DEBT RESPONSIBLY

GOING THROUGH LIFE in our economy without ever taking on debt is almost impossible—again, because of lack of access to capital, lack of education, and (the ever-present reason) systemic oppression. We've just gone over how loans work, but to make this super easy, I'm going to give you the top three questions to ask when deciding to take on debt:

1. What is the interest rate and loan term?

Is the interest rate around the average? What's the length of the loan compared to the amount of interest?

2. What is the creditor's ethics, credibility, and customer service like?

Avoiding predatory companies is hard. It requires you, the consumer, to be knowledgeable about a company's business practices and make informed choices about what kinds of companies you'll do business with. Let's be honest: in this capitalist hellscape of a world, it'd be a full-time job for you to make sure that every single purchase and every single financial institution you involve your money in is an upstanding organization that doesn't kick puppies or contribute to climate change. (Trying to avoid these companies also tends to be super fucking expensive for us, the consumer, and is a privilege in and of itself.)

In addition to learning how debt and loans work, one of the best pieces of advice I can offer to avoid predatory companies is to aggressively research them. You want to make sure that this company is credible, transparent, and trustworthy. In 2010, while the country was still reeling from the aftershocks of the Great Recession triggered by the collapse of the U.S. housing market and predatory lending practices, Congress passed and President Barack Obama signed into law the Dodd-Frank Wall Street Reform and Consumer Protection Act. In addition to imposing regulations intended to prevent a repeat of the worst financial crisis since the Great Depression, Dodd-Frank established the Consumer Financial Protection Bureau (CFPB), an independent government watchdog agency charged with helping to ensure that consumers are not misled or taken advantage of by banks, lenders, and financial companies. The bureau's website has an amazing database to get you started, where you can type in a company and view complaint information.

Above all, trust your gut. It may sound simplistic, but if something doesn't feel right, it probably isn't. Many of the folks I talked to about their experiences shopping at Victoria's Secret mention a turning point in their conversations with the sales associates: namely, when the application asked for their Social Security number. Something didn't feel right, so they turned down the credit card offer.

3. How could this improve my personal or financial life?

As I've mentioned before, loans have the incredible power to change your life for the better. It can be an opportunity to accelerate your goals. For many people, student loans are their only option for attending college. Likewise, a mortgage is typically the key to homeownership.

But be wary of the kind of debt that does more harm than good—credit card debt being the likely culprit. But credit card debt is different from a credit card itself. D*ve R*msey will tell you that credit cards are terrible. (He once compared them to cigarettes, saying, "Cigarettes don't kill everyone that smokes them. But they are good for no one that smokes them"—again, a real thing he said.) That's bullshit. You're an adult, and I'm going to treat you like one: you can handle a credit card. Let me repeat that: You. Can. Handle. A. Credit. Card. Credit cards are a tool. I like to tell my community that they're like a knife: yeah, they can cut you, but if used properly, you've got yourself a yummy veggie stir-fry!

When you're done with the struggle of paying off your debt, especially credit cards, it might be tempting to never use them again. But you know what's the ultimate "fuck you" to credit card companies? Using them responsibly.

If you use a credit card responsibly, there's nothing better. Credit card companies make their money from charging you interest. So, when you pay your balance on time and in full every month, they don't make a profit off you.

When choosing a card, think about your lifestyle. For instance, if you don't fly Southwest Airlines, a Southwest credit card—with its bonus points that can add up to miles in the sky—isn't going to help you much. A good everyday card is one that gets you cash back on everything, no rotating categories. You'll find recommendations linked in my book resource page at her first100k.com/book-resources.

It bears repeating: credit cards are dope, but only if you pay your monthly bill on time and in full.

Knowledge is power. A predatory relationship means one party has control and power over another. We've seen how creditors have a long history of exerting power over vulnerable populations for their own gain, and how it took interventions by the federal government to curb the worst of that predatory behavior. When we take out a loan without knowing how it works or what it means, the lender has power over our money. When we know and understand, we can make better decisions to protect ourselves and those around us. By using a credit card knowledgeably and responsibly, you are claiming back some of that power.

HOW TO IMPROVE YOUR CREDIT SCORE

IT SUCKS THAT this is the case, but managing your debt and ability to assume credit opens up so many more doors in your financial life. I'm talking about your credit score, or, as I like to call it, your report card from corporate America. And although credit scores are kinda bullshit, doing what you can to boost your score is one of the best tools you have for bettering your financial future. If you have a less-than-great credit score, lenders will interpret that as irresponsibility with money, so they might increase your interest rate to compensate. On the other hand, if you have a good score, you're more likely to get lower interest rates on loans, because lenders trust that you're more likely to pay them back. Basically, if you want to have anything adult in life—a car, an apartment, a house, a credit card—you're going to need a credit score.

The three major credit reporting agencies are TransUnion, Experian, and Equifax. A perfect credit score is 850, but that is pretty much impossible to attain, so anything over 750 is considered a "good" credit score. And yes, I once asked a guy on our second date what his credit score was, and I stand by that decision 100 percent. (*It came up naturally, okay?!*)

Let's talk about how to increase it. I'm going to uncomplicate this shit for you: there are three basic things that make up your credit score: your credit history, whether you pay your bills on time, and credit utilization.

Your credit history is simply the age of your oldest line of credit. The longer your credit history, the higher your score. I opened my first credit card when I was eighteen, so my credit history is a decade old. Unfortunately, your credit history is probably the least in your control, because you either started building credit at a certain age or you didn't. If you don't have credit yet, that's your first step: get a line of credit, typically by opening a credit card account. For my recommendations, go to herfirst100k.com/book-resources.

Another factor impacting your credit score is whether you pay your bills on time. One of the biggest myths I see is that carrying a balance on your credit card from month to month boosts your credit score. This is completely false. It does not increase your score; it just puts you in debt. Do not, unless you absolutely have to, keep a balance on your credit card, allowing it to roll over to next month's payment.

What does this look like in action? Let's say you charged $100 to your credit card. A month later, you receive your statement. Your minimum payment due? Just $25. Woo-hoo, right? Nah. Boo-hoo. Because as we've learned by paying the minimum, you'll be charged interest. Now that $100 purchase has ballooned into a more expensive purchase. Always pay the full amount if you can and be sure to not miss any payments. This is one of the biggest building blocks for developing a solid credit score.

The third aspect of your credit score is your credit utilization. This is one that you probably can exert a good deal of control over. Say you have a credit card with a credit line of $10,000. Your credit utilization rate is simply the percentage of that $10,000 you are using. So, if you put $5,000 on that credit card, your credit utilization is 50 percent. If you're maxing out your credit cards, this means your credit utilization is 100 percent. Not only is that potentially dangerous financially—are you spending more than you make?—it can decrease your score significantly. The best way to boost your score is to keep your credit utilization as low as you possibly can. Experts recommend under 30 percent, but to boost your credit score quickly, you really want to be under 10 percent.

One of the best ways to lower your credit utilization rate is to increase your credit line *and then not use it*. So, in that hypothetical example of the $10,000 credit line: if we request an increased credit line of $15,000, and if we continue to spend $5,000, suddenly our credit utilization rate is so much better (33 percent instead of 50 percent). Often, credit card companies will happily give you a credit line increase, because for most people, it means that they'll spend more money. So go ahead and call your credit card companies—all of them—and request credit line increases. *Then don't use them.* I recommend doing this about every six months. However, if a lender tells you it will need to conduct a hard credit inquiry in order to increase your credit line, decline. A hard credit inquiry entails a creditor or financial institution pulling your credit score, and you could see an unnecessary drop in your score, which we obviously don't want.

Something I hear often is "I just paid off my student loans, and my credit score *fell!*" or "I just paid off one of my credit cards, and my score decreased ten points! Why?" Unfortunately, credit bureaus don't exactly give you clear reasons. However, since your credit score is a measure of how much you can take on debt and pay it off, your credit score might dip once you no longer have debt to demonstrate you can pay it off. But please, *please* note that this does not mean you should seek out debt in order to boost your credit score. This decrease in your credit score is temporary and totally normal, and usually your credit score goes right back up in a couple of months.

A myth I hear all the time about credit scores is that checking your score decreases it. That is not true. Checking your credit score is one of the best ways to stay on top of your personal finances—and it's free, through places such as Credit Karma and your credit card provider. This myth exists because people confuse checking their credit scores with the aforementioned hard credit inquiry. Creditors or financial institutions typically do this when you're seeking a new line of credit, like a new credit card, a mortgage, a car loan, or even a rental apartment—but you want to avoid these pulls for unnecessary things.

If you're getting ready for a big moment in your life, such as buying a car or a house, a high credit score is going to be so essential to making that a positive experience. When you're prepping for one of these big life events, take steps to boost your score, because most likely, it'll give you a lower interest rate on this huge purchase.

Ultimately, just like everything in personal finance, your credit score should not define you. Your credit score is not a measure of your success. It's not a measure of how much you deserve nice things. Unfortunately, as cumbersome and frustratingly opaque as credit scores can often be, they are one of the best tools you have for building the life that you want. Like I say all the time about personal finance, it gives you options. Gaining control over your credit score is one of the best ways to increase your financial mobility, not just for you but also potentially for generations to come.

So, establish credit as soon as you can, pay your bills on time and in full, and, last but not least, decrease your credit utilization rate by increasing your credit lines. Go get 'em!

HOMEWORK

1. **DEBT MISCONCEPTIONS**

   Go back to the beginning of the chapter and reflect on the misconceptions about debt. Which ones have you been believing? Have you been considering debt evil or inherently part of your self-identity? What sorts of mind-set shifts do you need to have a better relationship with debt?

   _____

   _____

   _____

   _____

   _____

   _____

   _____

   _____

   _____

   _____

   _____

   _____

2. **NEGOTIATE YOUR RATE**

   Make sure you're getting the most favorable interest rates possible for you.

   Call your credit card company and try negotiating your interest rate. Write about the experience in your notebook or a Google doc and what you learned or might want to try next time.

_____

_____

_____

_____

_____

_____

_____

_____

_____

_____

_____

_____

3. CREATE A PAYOFF PLAN

STEP 1: Figure out your debt interest rates. Log in to your account(s) or call customer service to ask.

STEP 2: Organize your debt by interest rate, then balance owed.

STEP 3: Decide which high-interest debt you are going to conquer first. Do you need to focus on the loan with the smallest amount to keep yourself motivated, or are you ready to knock down the one that is costing you the most?

STEP 4: Once you're at three months of living expenses in your emergency fund, use the money you were putting toward your emergency fund as *extra* money toward the principal of the debt you've decided to tackle. (If you're not sure how to do this, call your creditor to find out.) Set it up on an automatic transfer, if possible.

STEP 5: Rinse and repeat, until all your debt is taken care of.

CHAPTER 5

INVESTING

IT'S THE FIRST WEEK OF MARCH 2020, IN THE "BEFORE TIMES."

'm on a solo trip to New York City after splurging on the ultimate gift to myself: front-row mezzanine tickets to *Moulin Rouge!* on Broadway. I have a free afternoon, so I'm walking around the financial district down by the water, when I realize: I'm a finance expert and I haven't seen the Wall Street bull since I was a child.

For those unfamiliar, *Charging Bull* is a brutish, broad bronze sculpture that has been guarding the New York Stock Exchange since 1989. The thing is massive—eleven feet tall and weighing more than seven thousand pounds—and on a winter afternoon, I was one of thousands who visited it. As I walked up, I saw the normal line of tourists, but they were doing something strange.

They were touching the bull's balls.

I had forgotten about this little piece of Wall Street lore: that if you rub the sculpture's testicles, you will receive good fortune and financial prosperity. Folks were squatting with their phones between its cheeks to get a photo of its burly bulge. The bull's balls are even a noticeably lighter color than the rest of its body, from all the oil on people's hands.

The symbol for financial progress, in the country's (really, the world's) epicenter for wealth, is a massive masculine symbol that offers security in exchange for a scrotum stroke. So no wonder we as women don't feel investing is for us.

If I had a nickel for every time I've had someone comment on one of my Instagram posts, "I want to start investing, but I'm intimidated," I'd have dozens of $100Ks.

We talk about the pay gap a lot (as we should), but what we don't talk about as much is the investing gap. Women either wait longer than men to invest or do not invest at all, and that's a HUGE problem, because the investing gap leads to a wealth gap, costing us not only millions over the course of our lifetimes but also limiting our options and lifestyle choices, including the ability to stop working someday. In 2019, the median wealth for single women was $36,000, while the median wealth for single men was $43,800. For women of color, these statistics are so much worse: for example, the median wealth for Black women was a shockingly low $1,700, and for Hispanic women, $1,000. And largely because of the investing and wealth gaps, women over sixty-five are more likely to be living in poverty than men.

One of the reasons women aren't investing as much goes back to the wage gap: because women don't earn as much as men do, they have less money to put into the stock market. When we're starting out from an unequal place, it's harder to advance, even if we're doing everything right. An analysis by Fidelity Investments showed that, on average, women saved higher percentages of their paychecks than men did, but in *dollar amounts*, they were saving less—because men made significantly more money. Men don't need to invest as much of their salary as a percentage to be on par with how much women invest.

Not having as comfortable a financial starting point is one thing, but even when women are financially able to invest, there's still an overall pattern of women avoiding investing. According to a recent survey, only 28 percent of women report feeling confident investing. I've seen it over and over again in my experience as a financial expert: women try to grow their wealth and advance their financial lives by putting away their money in a savings account and calling it a day. Every single woman I've advised to start investing told me the reason she hadn't before was *fear*. In my online investing workshops (more about these later), I have a slide in my presentation deck that asks participants to comment in the chat if fear is the reason they haven't started investing. And every single time, the chat blows up with "Yes, that's me!" The fears are numerous: fear of doing it incorrectly, fear of losing money, fear of making a mistake, fear of even getting started. I feel like a broken record, but again, this fear isn't our fault. It's ingrained in us because we're taught that investing isn't for us. Financial advice—but especially investing advice—is gatekept by straight white dudes.

It has been that way for ages. In the 1860s, Victoria Woodhull, a leader of the women's suffrage movement, and her sister Tennessee Claflin became the first two women stockbrokers on Wall Street. At the age of thirty-one, Woodhull was a millionaire. She made history again in 1872 as the first woman candidate for president of the United States. Victoria decided to run for the White House, she explained, because "woman's ability to earn money is better protection against the tyranny and brutality of men than her ability to vote." A decade later, long before she could even vote, a stockbroker named Mary Gage started a women-only stock market after being shut out of the all-male New York Stock Exchange. However, when she accused a male banker of impeding "her social progress and that of her daughter," she was arrested and faced "lunacy proceedings." Women like Gage and Woodhull were considered jokes in their time, labeled either "sirens" or "hags" by the public in an attempt to discredit and silence them.

Today only 15 percent of Wall Street traders and only 23 percent of financial advisors are women. The so-called GameStop boom of 2021—where Redditors drove up the share price of companies like GameStop by buying their stock and quickly selling, causing severe financial consequences—was often heralded in the news as "the democratization of wealth," yet women, people of color, and other marginalized groups were left out of the conversation.

Within the realm of investing, women are treated like they can't or shouldn't be involved; one study even found that young women investors received inferior advice compared with young male investors. Financial advisors would ask men more questions to better tailor their investing strategy and were less likely to advise women to invest in stocks or bonds (the very backbone of investing; we'll define them in a bit). And the craziest part? Advisors were more likely to have women transfer money into an investing account before giving them any advice. Women were pressured to work with an advisor before even knowing if the advice was good or not.

Given this patriarchal state of affairs, it's no surprise there are so many misconceptions holding us back from feeling confident as investors. Let's talk about some of them so that you're able to start taking action and grow your wealth.

investing misconception #1
I DON'T NEED TO INVEST—SAVING MY MONEY IS ENOUGH!

DO ME A FAVOR and look up the highest interest rate a savings account is offering at the moment. Probably around 2 percent, right? This is better than the national average of around 0.06 percent but not nearly enough to beat inflation (you know, the fun thing where the price of milk was, like, two pennies in the 1950s but is now multiple dollars). Savings accounts are meant for short-term goals, where you need to access the money easily (à la an emergency fund), *not* for long-term wealth building.

Meanwhile, the average annual rate of return when investing in the stock market is 7 percent (or 8 to 10 percent, according to some less conservative experts). We've seen the S&P 500 (five hundred of the largest companies on the U.S. stock exchange) soar more than 30 percent annually. Other years, as in 2008, when the wheels were coming off the U.S. economy during the peak of the Great Recession, we've seen it dip into the negative, then start to increase again the following year.

Let's say that five years ago, you were deciding what to do with $1,000. You could have put it in either the stock market or in an HYSA with an interest rate of 0.5 percent.

I love high-yield savings accounts as much as the next financial expert, but there's simply no competition between investing and saving in an HYSA, especially when we consider inflation,

	YEAR 1	YEAR 5
HYSA with 0.5% interest	$1,000	$1,025.25
S&P 500	$1,000	$1,402.55

which reached a record high 6.8 percent in 2021 (and, as I'm editing this in 2022, is even higher). Shit is getting more expensive every passing year, and a checking account, mattress cash, or even a high-yield savings account is no match for inflation. But investing is.

If you're in debt—especially if it's credit card debt—the amount you owe is compounding right now at a higher rate than your HYSA can keep up with. You are more in debt now than you were when you began reading this book. Does that piss you off? It should! This is why you cannot afford to wait to start investing. You need these powerful investment returns working for you.

Please note that this doesn't mean you should immediately dump your emergency fund into the stock market. Unlike an HYSA, with its generally consistent *positive* rate of return, investing in the stock market is like a roller coaster: sometimes it goes up, sometimes it goes down. The last thing you want is for it to go down when you have an emergency. Don't put your backup money in something that brings with it inherent risk.

This brings me to . . .

investing misconception #2
INVESTING IS GAMBLING—WHAT IF I LOSE ALL MY MONEY?

THIS MISCONCEPTION IS NUANCED, so allow me to explain my cardinal rule of investing: it shouldn't be sexy. Investing should not be sexy! I know when you think of investing, you're visualizing Leonardo DiCaprio shouting into a phone *Wolf of Wall Street*-style, but that's really not it. A lot of the flashy stuff (Crypto! Day trading! Hot stocks!) is, at best, speculative, and, at worst, gambling. Investing does carry risk, but smart investing is consistent, stable, and sustained over a long period of time. It successfully mitigates that risk. This is a long game we're playing here, like

Leo finally winning that Oscar (not for *The Wolf of Wall Street*, ironically).

I want you to read this paragraph really closely: highlight it, circle it, install a neon sign next to it. If you put your money in the stock market for only one day, historical odds of making money in the stock market are 50 percent. This means that if you were to invest in the market and then sell your shares the very next day, you're just as likely to make money as you are to lose money. But if you hold your shares for a one-year period, your odds of making money increase to 68 percent. Over a ten-year period, your likelihood of profiting is 88 percent. Investing for the long term—twenty or more years—raises your prospects of seeing a return on your investment to 100 percent. This is based on trends observed throughout the more than one hundred years of the American stock market's existence. If you invest and ride it out for two decades, you will not lose money. In fact, during every single twenty-year period (yes, even during the Great Recession), investors *made* money. Long-term investing—steady, patient, consistent—does not lose. It never has.

After all, the very definition of the word *invest* is to put time/effort/energy into something with the expectation of a worthwhile result. It's not immediate gratification but patience and consistency. There will be stock market highs and stock market lows, but the key is to ride the wave and trust that time will take care of you. Again, we've seen from the data that it always has.

The flashy, "sexy" investing you see discussed most on Reddit forums and in TikTok comments—the kind that feels too good to be true? It is. It is too good to be true. *That* is gambling. Anyone you see getting rich off short-term investing either (1) got extremely lucky (and there *is* luck involved) or (2) is lying to you. Again, I wish all personal finance was money trees and Easy buttons from Staples. It's not. Beware of these get-rich-quick schemes, especially when it comes to investing.

So, if you're afraid of losing money, the answer is to not panic when the market dips. Remember, it's a roller coaster (I'll take Thunder Mountain at Disneyland, please), except that you'll be strapped in your seat for twenty or more years, with the knowledge that it will trend up.

investing misconception #3
I CAN WAIT TO INVEST

NOW THAT YOU KNOW investing demands playing the long game, it's easy to have your next thought be, *Okay, then, I'll just wait to invest until I'm older and have more money.* And that's completely valid reasoning, especially when you consider emergency funds and student loans and credit card debt and, oh yeah, just that whole staying-alive thing. But here's the deal: you cannot afford to wait.

Dwight Schrute voice "Question: Would you rather have a million dollars now? Or a penny that doubles every day for a month?"

I know you already looked at the picture, you sneaky sneak.

Watch what happens to this penny over thirty days:

Yes, look at it: $5.3 million. Not too shabby. And if we went with a month that has thirty-one days, we'd have more than $10.7 million. *tosses hair over shoulder*

This is the power of time.

So many folks think, *I can't start investing because I don't have thousands of dollars.* But really, with investing, *time* is more important than the amount of money, which is why we have to get you investing *now*. Not in a week, not in a few years, not "when I'm making more money." Even if you have only a little to invest, start now.

If you're still in the early stages of the Financial Game Plan—saving an emergency fund, paying off higher-interest

DAY 1	$0.01	DAY 16	$327.68
DAY 2	$0.02	DAY 17	$655.36
DAY 3	$0.04	DAY 18	$1,310.72
DAY 4	$0.08	DAY 19	$2,621.44
DAY 5	$0.16	DAY 20	$5,242.88
DAY 6	$0.32	DAY 21	$10,485.76
DAY 7	$0.64	DAY 22	$20,971.52
DAY 8	$1.28	DAY 23	$41,943.04
DAY 9	$2.56	DAY 24	$83,886.08
DAY 10	$5.12	DAY 25	$167,772.16
DAY 11	$10.24	DAY 26	$335,544.32
DAY 12	$20.48	DAY 27	$671,088.64
DAY 13	$40.96	DAY 28	$1,342,177.28
DAY 14	$81.92	DAY 29	$2,684,354.56
DAY 15	$163.84	DAY 30	$5,368,709.12

debt—that's totally cool. These are the necessary steps you're taking to be able to invest soon. You're making progress in your financial life and setting the stage for you being able to start investing.

Investing is the thing that makes you rich. You can just get started with a few hundred dollars—every little bit counts. Time matters more than the amount of money. If you invested only $100 a month for thirty years—$36,000 without interest—Future You would have more than five times more, about $185,000. It's all about how much time you have for it to grow.

investing misconception #4
INVESTING IS COMPLICATED AND DIFFICULT

I HAVE ANOTHER not-so-conspiracy conspiracy theory. The finance bros who have dominated investing and Wall Street for decades—and created the jargon used to describe the stock market—*love* to deliberately use those cryptic terms with laypeople: Short selling! Blue chip! Dividends! I believe they've done this for two reasons: one, to make themselves feel smart. They're deluding themselves that what they do is really, really hard. They're justifying their price. So, it's not just about keeping people out, it's about keeping their egos intact. Classic straight white men shit. And two, *to make you feel like you can't do it.* It feels intimidating, like a different language, and so it's just easier to go, "Nah, that's not for me." Of course, when a finance bro mansplains it to you, you don't feel safe or comfortable saying, "I don't understand that," or "What does that mean?" If they tell you investing is complicated—and use lofty language to gatekeep wealth building—then of course they can keep their club to themselves or charge hefty fees to do it for you.

The truth is that investing is ridiculously easy. Truly, it is. My favorite part of the workshops I lead is when a new investor walks in slightly scared and, forty-five minutes in, goes, "Wait, that's *it*? That was so much easier than I thought!" (I like to think this is partly because it is indeed that easy and also because the way I explain it makes it easier.) When it comes down to it, investing is simply putting money into financial products (we'll define them all in a bit) with the expectation that they'll make us more money.

The hard part is learning *how* to start doing that and staying consistent. Learning how to invest is like climbing stairs—maybe the first step seems twenty feet high, but after that, all you have to do is put one foot in front of the other. Reading this book gets you on an escalator.

I can't stress enough how important it is for women to invest, and not only to close the wealth gap, build wealth, and gain financial power, which are all reasons enough! But women also need to invest because, dear God, we would really like to retire and stop working someday! I want sixty-five-year-old me to be drinking a sauvignon blanc with lunch, adopting dogs left and right, living in a beautiful Tuscan mansion, and flirting with Luca the hot Pilates instructor.

"But, Tori, *wwwwhhhyyyyy* would I start investing for retirement? That's so *far away!*"

This is going to sound harsh, but you literally cannot afford not investing. I'm going to say that again: you literally cannot afford to not invest. Retirement is the costliest expense of your life. It's more expensive than a house, college, or paying for your kids' college. And because women live seven years longer than men on average, we need even more money than the bros who earn more than us and have more invested. (Absolute bullshit, Lord, don't I know it.) The average person will not be able to afford to retire if they don't invest, and I want you to be able to stop fucking working someday.

Let's break this down. From roughly age twenty to sixty-five, you'll probably be working (about forty-five years). You'll work to make money, then save and invest that money in order to eventually not work anymore. The average life expectancy for women in the United States is currently eighty-one years, but we are steadily increasing our time on Earth.

So, let's say you live to be ninety-five. (I hope we all do!) That means for thirty years, you'll need to sustain yourself financially without working. You're working five-plus days a week, forty-plus hours a week, for forty years straight—in order to support yourself without working a day for another thirty years. And, with increased medical and living costs, this is likely to be the most expensive period of your life. Whew.

Investing your money in a tax-advantaged retirement account such as a 401(k) or an IRA is the only way the average woman will be able to stop working someday. The *only* way. Let's learn from the mistakes of others: not saving early enough for retirement is the number one financial regret of U.S. Baby Boomers (surprisingly, their first regret isn't shoulder pads), and women over sixty-five are twice as likely to be in poverty compared with men.

So, investing—building wealth—for our futures is absolutely imperative.

Now, if you're thinking, *I'm not in my twenties; is it too late for me?* the answer is no. Investing works if you're eighteen, thirty-eight, or eighty-eight. You're never too young and never too old to start investing. The key, again, is that you actually start.

A quick pause before we go further: this is the most finance-heavy chapter, and it might be tougher to get through and to grasp fully the first time. Please know that you can take breaks and reread to your heart's content. We also have a guide at the end where we'll break down your exact investing steps and where to go if you're still confused. (I helped develop a whole investing education platform because this initial shit is *that* confusing!)

So, let's do an introduction to investing: how to do it, what your options are, and who to do it with.

YOU CAN EITHER INVEST FOR A GENERAL GOAL OR INVEST FOR RETIREMENT SPECIFICALLY

AN INVESTING ACCOUNT used for a general goal is called a "brokerage account." It's the default way to start investing. The flexibility is a huge plus: you can put in as much money as you want and pull it out at any time. On the flip side, brokerages don't provide tax advantages (a fancy way of saying that the government incentivizes you to save by giving you tax benefits, such as lowering your taxable income). All your earnings are taxed, and if you hold your investments for less than a year, you're subject to *higher* taxes.

Retirement accounts are obviously specifically for retirement, and they are tax advantaged. The government gives us (ordinary people, not billionaires) very, very little in terms of financial benefits, so take advantage of these sweet, sweet tax breaks to the fullest extent by doing everything you can to contribute up to the full limit for these accounts! With these tax benefits comes one big drawback: you will usually incur some sort of financial penalty if you withdraw money from your retirement account early—because it is for retirement, after all. This isn't supposed to scare you but instead remind you that you should definitely not be putting vacation money in these accounts.

I personally use a brokerage account for investing after I've maxed out my retirement accounts, or for goals that are seven to ten years out (as opposed to traditional retirement, which is thirty-plus years away for me). A reminder again that the more time your money spends in the market, the odds of profiting go up, so while you could invest money for a shorter-term goal (buying a house in two years, for example), your risk of losing money before you need it for your goal is significantly higher. The stock market may dip and not be able to recover to meet your timeline.

TRADITIONAL 401(K) OR 403(B) ACCOUNT

Typically offered by your employer, a 401(k) account allows you to invest a percentage of your wages for retirement. A 403(b) is the public sector's equivalent to a 401(k).

* Investing through a 401(k) or 403(b) is one of the most advantageous ways to invest, since the government is giving you tax breaks.

* Your employer will sometimes match what you contribute, up to a certain percent. (FreE mONaY!) Remember from our Financial Game Plan that this is the trump card: if you have an employer match, take advantage of it.

* Maximum yearly contribution: $20,500, which means you can contribute any amount up to that limit. This does *not* include any employer match, so go crazy. (This and all other retirement account maximums are current for the 2022 tax year.)

INDIVIDUAL RETIREMENT ACCOUNT (IRA)

This is an individual retirement account, meaning it's not tied to your employer. You have to open it up on your own, and it's yours forever.

* Good news: you can have both a 401(k) *and* an IRA!

* Maximum yearly contribution: $6,000.

* You technically have fifteen and a half months to contribute that $6,000. The government lets you put money in your IRA during the twelve months of that year, plus the first months of the following year leading up to the tax filing deadline. A little confusing, but stay with me: if you want to contribute to your IRA in 2023, you will have from January to December 2023, *plus* January to April 15, 2024, to hit that $6,000 max. So, let's say that you're rounding out the year of contributions at $4,500. That means you have another three-ish months to get the full $6,000! More time, yay!

* If we're already in the new year, and you want the money to specifically go to the previous year's IRA, you simply need to specify that when you contribute. It's usually as easy as checking a "previous year" box.

Let's talk about the most common retirement accounts.

In addition to the differences above, 401(k) and IRA accounts come in two flavors: traditional and Roth. The main difference between these accounts is in how they're taxed.

In traditional accounts, you won't pay any taxes on this money until you withdraw it at retirement. You get the tax benefits *now*.

Roth accounts require tax payments now, so you don't have to pay them later. You get the tax benefits *later*.

In some cases, you can make both traditional *and* Roth contributions into the same account.

I personally like the Roth flavor for a few reasons. The first: it's like giving sixty-five-year-old me a little gift: "Here's this lump sum of money that I already paid taxes on; go take Hot Luca on a trip to Costa Rica." I also have no idea what the fuck tax rates are going to be when I retire. I'd rather pay them now than leave it up to chance. Also, most people's salaries grow throughout their careers; I expect (hope!) that you'll be making more in twenty years than you do today, so you could contribute and pay less in taxes now, when you're in a lower tax bracket.

In addition to a Roth IRA or a traditional IRA—which are available to both W-2 and self-employed folks—here are some additional retirement account options (contribution limits and other rules around retirement accounts are subject to IRS changes from year to year, so make sure to keep up to date):

SEP-IRA (SELF-EMPLOYMENT IRA)

Another kind of IRA. As with a traditional IRA, you pay the taxes you owe when you withdraw money—for instance, at retirement age.

* Made for solopreneurs or companies with a few employees.

* If you side hustle, you can have a SEP *in addition to* a trad/Roth IRA *and* a 401(k), even if you do not work full-time for yourself. This is one of the biggest reasons I was able to hit my $100K goal. Take those tax-advantaged accounts and contribute as much as you can.

* Maximum yearly contribution: 25 percent of your income, up to $61,000.

SOLO 401(K)

Similar to the employer-sponsored 401(k) plan, except that you're your own sponsor! You can have a Roth and/or traditional IRA in addition to a solo 401(k).

* This is an option only if you're self-employed full-time, and you cannot have both a SEP-IRA and a solo 401(k).

* Maximum yearly contribution: $20,500.

INVESTING IS A TWO-STEP PROCESS

THIS IS the number one investing mistake I see people make, so highlight the hell out of this section.

Let's say you have $1,000. If you were to save that money, that involves only one step. You deposit the money into your savings account, and you're done. However, with investing, you take your $1K, deposit the money into your investing account (or "fund" it), and then you need to decide what to buy—or invest in—with that $1K. You are not investing until you take the second step of choosing investments. It's like putting money on a gift card. You still have to *spend* the gift card! You loaded up a TJ Maxx gift certificate, and now you've got to go buy your plants and candles and throw pillows.

A few years back, I was sitting on a panel at a women's self-development event, and one of the other panelists, a financial advisor, told one of the most tragic stories I've ever heard. (I'm literally close to tears as I type this, but you need to hear it too.)

A client of hers—a cute seventy-year-old woman we'll call Rose—was ready to retire. Rose had been prepping diligently for her retirement for more than thirty years, putting as many hard-earned pennies of her teacher's salary as she could in her 401(k). Except one problem: Rose had never actually *invested* that money.

Rose had never done step 2. She deposited her money into her account, but never chose her investments. She had, using our metaphor, put money on a gift card but had never bought anything. Her money was in financial purgatory, sitting there for thirty years earning no interest and never growing one bit. Rose could no longer afford to retire, because even with her pension and monthly Social Security checks, she did not have enough money to sustain herself.

(After I wrote this, I started crying, then had to rewatch that episode of *Kroll Show* where Liz gets bangs, just to cheer myself up.)

Please, *please*: do not just put your investing money into the account, but go choose your investments. I need you to make sure that you and everyone you love do not end up like Rose. If you are already an investor, perhaps through your employer's 401(k) or something else, please make a note to confirm that you're actually invested!

This brings us to choosing our investments.

THERE ARE TWO BASIC PRODUCTS YOU CAN BUY: STOCKS AND BONDS

ONE OF THE REASONS investing seems intimidating? "There's so many things to invest in!" But in reality, there are only two (yes, two!) basic investment purchases.

STOCKS are tiny little slivers of companies, so owning a share of stock in, say, Amazon, makes you a part owner of the company. Granted, it's like owning a grain of sand on Bezos's beach, but you still own a slice!

You can invest only in companies that have gone public, meaning that they have chosen to make shares of stock available for trading on the stock exchange. (Typically, this is for larger, more established companies.) If you've ever heard about a private company "going public," it means the business has held an initial public offering, or IPO, and is now allowing the general public (folks outside of its investors and employees) to buy and sell its shares. A few examples of publicly traded companies are Google, Microsoft, Meta, Johnson & Johnson, and PepsiCo.

When you consider the process of investing, you might visualize the rapidly scrolling list of stocks on CNBC. This is called a stock ticker, and the reason it's not boring as hell to watch is because stock values fluctuate from second to second when the markets are open. The price of a stock can go up or down depending on numerous factors, including the company's performance, global events (such as a war), and the state of the economy. These individual stocks are volatile but also more profitable.

BONDS are a company's or government's debt. When you buy a bond, you are giving a company/government a loan and earning profits on the interest. Bonds typically generate less money than stocks do but are also less volatile.

Now, financial guidance generally advises investing in stocks when you're younger (usually under ages forty to forty-five, assuming you'll retire at around ages sixty-five to seventy) because you can afford to be more aggressive. You've got more time for the stock market to recover should it dip, and you've got longer until you need the money. As you age, you can modify your collection of investments, or portfolio, to become more conservative and bond heavy.

Because stocks can be unpredictable, picking a company and buying its stock—perhaps twenty-five shares of Amazon, or Tesla, or Bumble, or Stitch Fix—is actually one of the riskiest things you can do, especially if this is the only investing you're doing. One of the cardinal rules of investing is to *never* put all your eggs in one basket. What if you decided to invest in only one company— Delta Air Lines, for instance—and something completely unforeseen happens, like, oh, I don't know, *a global pandemic of epic proportions that basically shuts down airline travel?* Well, you can see how that might not have been the best idea. This is also why it's dangerous to put all your money in a single industry, even if you divide it among different companies. Even if you invested in Delta *and* Spirit *and* American *and* JetBlue, they're all affected by the same global forces and trends, causing them to potentially tank at the same time.

A better way to invest is to do it through groups of stocks. Not only is it less likely that they'll all lose value at once, but also this option tends to be cheaper. Funds made up of groups of stocks diversify your portfolio for you, so you don't have to worry. You've probably heard of a few of these—exchange-traded funds, index funds, mutual funds—which I profile below.

TYPES OF FUNDS

MUTUAL FUNDS. A group of stocks tracking a particular part of the stock market that can be traded only when the stock market is open. They are actively managed, meaning that you'll pay an extra fee for an "expert" to pick stocks for you.

EXCHANGE-TRADED FUNDS (ETFs). A group of stocks tracking a particular part of the stock market that can be traded at any time, even when the stock market is closed. Typically, ETFs are cheaper than a mutual fund, because they are passively managed (no manager to pay).

INDEX FUNDS. One of the most popular choices in the personal finance community, an index fund is a mutual fund or an ETF that's designed to track a particular part of the stock market, such as the S&P 500. I'm index funds' biggest fan: they are diversified, extremely low in fees, and more stable than individual stocks.

TARGET-DATE FUNDS. A popular fund used for retirement investments, this one is actively managed (meaning more in fees), with managers picking investments that become more conservative every year as you approach your retirement "target date." So, let's say it's 2023, and you're looking to retire in thirty years; you'd choose something like a 2053 fund, which, honestly, doesn't feel like a real year.

So, instead of buying individual stocks, you can buy something like VTI (Vanguard Total Stock Market Index fund, if ya nasty). It's an index fund that has Tesla, plus a bunch of other companies. When I'm thinking about my own personal investment strategy, it's a no-brainer. Why would I buy into one company when I can buy parts of the whole stock market? It costs less, *and* it makes me a less risky investor! That's the magic of funds: you get a bunch of different options, not just one or two. The diversification work is done for you.

I'll give you a metaphor: picking individual stocks is like making your own fried chicken. Sure, you can buy chicken thighs, and paprika and cayenne and cumin and salt and pepper, and oil, and panko, and also a fryer. And it's all a lot of work. Or you can just swing by Popeyes and buy a bucket of chicken, where they've done the work for you, and it's deliciously Louisiana Fast. (Popeyes, please don't change your slogan before this book comes out.) Although typically I'm all for a home-cooked meal, when it comes to investing, the simpler the better. Again: We Want You to Just Get Started with the Least Amount of Overwhelm Possible! (Is this a Panic! at the Disco song?)

The other thing about trying to cherry-pick individual stocks in order to get the highest return? You very rarely do. Even professional stock pickers who oversee investment vehicles such as mutual funds and target-date funds (again, called "actively managed"), and whose full-time job is to choose what they believe will be the highest-performing stocks, *aren't that good at it!* (*And* they charge you extra money for their services!!!!) A report from the ratings and research agency Morningstar found that only 47 percent of hedge funds, which get paid millions of dollars to study the market, outperformed the average index fund in 2020 and 2021. "It was what you would expect from a coin flip," said Ben Johnson, the report's author and director of global ETF research. When you look at a ten-year period, it's even worse: only a quarter of the stocks managed by pickers perform better than index funds.

It turns out that when you pit professional pickers against a kitten, the cat chooses stocks with higher returns. As reported in *Forbes* magazine, in 2012 a British house cat named Orlando did a better job at picking stocks than the professionals. While the managers used their years of investment knowledge and traditional stock-picking methods, Orlando chose his stocks by *tossing his favorite mouse toy on a grid of numbers assigned to various companies.* At the end of the year, the professionals had £5,176, while Orlando amassed £5,542. (Side note: When I did the research for this section, every article just had a stock image of a cat. I was committed to finding out exactly what Orlando looked like. So, in case this is also you, let me give you the specs: the four-legged master of stock selection is orange with white stripes, a cute li'l pink nose, and very scratchable ears.)

GET STARTED INVESTING: DIY OR ROBO-ADVISORS

DIY, FOR DO-IT-YOURSELF, means that you're the one choosing the stocks and bonds you're buying. You can go through companies such as Fidelity, Vanguard, and Charles Schwab and pick exactly what you want to invest in. This means you have complete control over your investments but also implies that you should really know what you're doing. I personally DIY my own investments because it saves me money, *and* I feel confident in choosing what's right for me.

Your other option is to rely on a robo-advisor: a digital platform that automates your investing. You'll be asked a series of questions, such as: What are your goals? When do you want to retire? What is your risk tolerance? Then, based on your answers, the algorithm (with a little human supervision) will make your investment decisions for you. Some examples of robo-advisors includes Acorns, Betterment, Ellevest, Wealthfront, and Wealth-simple. Robo-advisors take a fee (usually 0.25 to 0.5 percent) *on top of* any fund-specific fees, so you could easily be paying 0.5 percent or more—which, as a reminder, adds up quickly! ·

Through my work, I realized that neither of these options was ideal for beginners. Total DIY was too stressful: trying to learn how to choose your own investments with no help is *scary*. And although robo-advisors are great for getting investment newbies started, the process is too passive; they don't really teach you *how* to invest or show you what they're doing, so you don't know what you're invested in, why those investments were chosen for you, etc. They're fishing for you, rather than teaching you how to fish.

What if you could Hannah Montana your investments and have—wait for it—the best of both worlds? I found that Her First $100K community members needed to be guided through how to start investing, but in a nonjudgmental place where they could be supported and ask questions. So, I built my own option: a platform called Treasury that provides investing education and community. Not only do I teach you how to invest step by step, but Treasury actually gets you started by helping you to make your first investment. It's an amazing place to have conversations about wealth building, while also doing the damn thing in a jargon-free, finance-bro-free environment. More about Treasury and how to sign up at herfirst100k.com/book-resources.

So, how do I actually choose my investments?

Do me a favor. Grab your phone and google "VTI." Click on the first of the more than thirty million search results. Are you immediately overwhelmed? Because I sure would be. Even though we've just gone over what VTI is, how funds work, and the basics of investing, everything seems *so fucking stressful*. There are graphs and charts and terms that may as well be in Klingon. You might really want to go the DIY route, but this is the stage where it's tempting to bail immediately.

It's important to make solid, educated decisions you feel confident about, but, honestly, most platforms drown you in information *you don't need to start investing.*

In order to make this super easy, I'm going to give you the top three things I personally consider when I'm researching a potential fund to invest in. There's always more you can look into (people like my dad treat the stock market like a hobby), but as we just talked about, you don't need to do that to make money. Let's avoid brain overload or analysis paralysis and just get fucking started. (Shameless plug, but this is another reason Treasury is so awesome: we give you these exact three things in an easy-to-read format, so that you don't have to scroll through Yahoo! Finance, all confused and crying. We also explain this in 3D-level detail in our Treasury workshops, so if you leave this section still a li'l confused, we'll see you there.)

1. PERFORMANCE

The first thing to look at is simply the investment's performance over the past few years or even the past few decades. Overall, does the stock or fund chart trend up (with some explainable dips, such as March 2008 [Great Recession] and March 2020 [pandemic])? Or does it seem to be losing value all the time? When assessing performance, we want to look for a fund that seems to be on an upward trend in the long term—we don't care about the day-to-day (long-term investing, remember?). I personally look for the longest time period I can, typically since the fund's inception, but anything beyond five years is typically a valid measurement.

2. FEES

The second thing to look for is the fees associated with buying into the fund, particularly one called an "expense ratio." Back in the olden days, you had to diversify your portfolio yourself and basically create your own fund. You had to cook your own fried chicken. But now, index funds and ETFs exist, so in exchange for that work being done for you, you'll pay a fee. This fee is baked into the price per share and charged annually, so no reason to stress about getting a bill.

Now, here's where you can get bit in the ass. Many funds charge a fee of around 1 percent. That doesn't sound like a lot, but 1 percent of $1 million is $10,000—a good chunk of change! Actively managed funds, such as target-date funds commonly used for retirement investments, tend to have higher fees; for example, the average target-date fund is going to charge you more than 0.5 percent in fees. Let's compare that with the average index fund fee, which is 0.2 percent—with some as low as 0.02 percent. (My personal favorite, VTI, is 0.03 percent.) That's a *helluva* lot better than giving a huge amount of your hard-earned money to some random investment manager.

You also might pay fees every time you buy or sell investments, although many investing platforms are starting to waive these fees.

3. HOLDINGS/COMPANIES

The third thing to look at is the fund's holdings, otherwise known as the companies that particular fund invests in. Remember that a fund is just a group of stocks, so when we're researching, we're interested in checking out the individual companies that make up the fund. For example, my personal favorite, bad bitch VTI, holds Apple, Microsoft, Amazon, and Tesla, among others. It actually holds every company on the U.S. stock market (hence, "total index"). You need to make sure your portfolio is well diversified, meaning, again, that you haven't invested in just one company or just one industry, such as tech, health care, or agriculture.

If a fund's holdings are predominantly in one industry, that's not necessarily a reason to stay away from it, as it might have good long-term performance and low expense ratios. Don't forget those other two factors! This is because when we're investing, we don't have to choose just one fund and call it a day. We can choose multiple diversified funds across the stock market. Therefore, if you want to buy a tech fund, you can make sure that the other funds in your portfolio are not also all tech funds.

Going back to our fried chicken metaphor, *because it's so fucking delicious:* let's say you want to order twenty-four chicken tenders, half spicy and half mild. You could do one box of a dozen spicy and another box of a dozen mild. But maybe you're ordering these twenty-four tenders to eat with someone else, and you'd rather not keep passing the box around and tracking how many of each flavor you've eaten. So, if you both want an equal number of mild and spicy tenders, you might want to order two boxes, each with six spicy and six mild. You're still going to end up with twelve spicy and twelve mild wings—you've just diversified a little differently.

The bottom line: I choose my investments based on whether they

1. **have a graph that charts up;**

2. **have low fees, typically under 0.1 percent; and**

3. **are well diversified, whether within an individual fund or throughout my portfolio.**

The best education I can give you? Make an informed decision quickly and start investing (or increase your contribution). Every day that passes without your money in the market is another day that you're missing out. Don't be afraid to ask questions. (Again, shameless plug, but this is why I built Treasury!)

And above all else, remember that the investing game is a long one. Even if the stock market is down, you have not lost money *unless you sell your investments*. I want to repeat that: you have not lost (or gained!) money until you cash out. What happens to the stock market on a random Tuesday doesn't matter in the scheme of thirty years. Stay the course.

To see how this works in the larger strategy of the Financial Game Plan, let's check in on Jessica, who was paying off her second credit card through the following budget:

* **BUCKET #1: $2,500 for necessary expenses**

* **BUCKET #2: $675 toward paying off credit card debt**

* **BUCKET #3: $825 for all the fun stuff**

She has successfully finished paying off all her credit card debt, but she still has student debt at 5 percent interest. What should she do next? Because her student debt is less than 7 percent—the average stock market return—she should focus on contributing as much as she can to her 401(k) or IRA. (If she maxes out one, she should start contributing to the other!)

Of course, the question now is how much more should she allot for retirement?

There's a common misconception that everyone can retire once they're a millionaire, but that's far from accurate. Your retirement number is unique to you. Experts recommend that you total up your yearly expenses and multiply that amount by 25, the assumption being that you'll withdraw 4 percent of your money per year. So, if you spend $30,000 a year, you'd need $750,000 before submitting your notice, throwing water on your least favorite coworker, and riding a mothafuckin' chariot out of your cubicle and into the sunshine. This "expenses/year x 25" rule assumes that you only take out what you need to live for the year, leaving the rest of the money to continue making gains. It also assumes an annual inflation rate of around 4 percent (and unfortunately, it's continuing to rise) and that your yearly expenses won't change.

A reminder: investments increase in value, so you don't have to contribute that full amount in cash yourself; you'll hit your retirement number through your returns—hence why my $100K at twenty-five will be worth over $1.6M at retirement, even if I never contribute another penny.

In order to understand what that number—25 × your annual expenses—means for you today, you can use a "retirement calculator." You can find this with a simple Google search, but your brokerage or retirement account provider probably offers one too. This will show you what percentage of your salary you need to invest every month in order to retire comfortably. You'd be shocked at how much working time gets shaved off if you increase your contributions. For example, sometimes adding as little as $50 more per month is enough to enable you to retire a year or two earlier.

So, before Jessica starts paying down her student debt more aggressively, a good goal might be to max out her IRA before funneling additional money to her loans. Since the annual IRA limit is $6,000, Jessica would have to contribute $500 a month.

As a reminder, the Financial Priority List says she should pay off her low-interest debt alongside investing for retirement. So, when she wraps up paying off her last credit card and with her retirement contributions set, she decides to put her Bucket #2 money toward paying off her student loan debt faster. Now her bucket distribution looks like this:

* **BUCKET #1: $2,500 for necessary expenses**

* **BUCKET #2: $500 toward her Roth IRA and $175 extra toward paying off student loans**

* **BUCKET #3: $825 for all the fun stuff**

For the time being, this works for Jessica: she's on track to meeting her financial goals without depriving herself too much.

Of course, as you've heard me say a million times, personal finance is personal. Maybe for you, reaching your retirement number quickly is more important than having a bigger Bucket #3. There's actually a whole community of people working to retire early by increasing their investments and living off that income. It is called the FIRE movement, which stands for Financial Independence, Retire Early. I personally am more interested in the financial independence half of that equation, because I love my company and its impact, and don't plan on stopping work anytime soon. However, my job is now optional, meaning that, at twenty-seven years old, I never have to work another day if I don't want to. Which . . . hell fucking yeah!

A word from
Kiersten Saunders
COCREATOR OF RICH & REGULAR AND COAUTHOR OF
Cashing Out: Win the Wealth Game by Walking Away

I first discovered FIRE back in 2015-ish. At first, it was a hard "no" for me, because many of the people who were the leading voices were very in the "sustainability" corner, so their ways of saving money were very bunker style: things like switching to reusable toilet paper, eating big bags of rice, big bags of beans, keeping all meals under $1.50, etcetera. I understood the Why, but it just didn't work for me.

I thought the FIRE movement struggled with inclusivity, especially with women. One specific instance is its view of childcare. Day care is expensive, especially if you live in a major city, and the idea that it's somehow not going to be expensive is bullshit. Also, the idea of a bare-bones budget that doesn't include grooming, hair products, makeup—have you tried interviewing as a Black woman without your hair done? You can't do that. In general, I thought they excluded the work experience of Black people. I just don't know that you can talk about what to do with income without talking about what you have to go through at work.

There was also a disconnect between how much money you'll need to make at a job to both afford necessities while still working toward FI. The presumption is sometimes that if your income is low, your expenses are low. That's a big leap to make.

At the time, I was doing well at work, and I felt like I could have a long career for as long as I needed to, so I didn't have any real motivation to get into FIRE. My partner, Julien, discovered FIRE through real estate forums and content creators, and when he brought it to me, I said, "Absolutely not." We had already done the debt-payoff R*msey shit, and this felt even more extreme than that.

Julien and I got married on Labor Day weekend, and we didn't go on our honeymoon until October. We had to go back to work for about four weeks and then took two weeks off in Africa. During this time, we started to reassess what was important to us. There was enough time to unplug from work and remember who we were. That was when we asked, "How can we do this more often?"

To us, the FI (financially independent) part is more important than the RE (retiring early). We tend to talk about retirement as this onetime event, and that's such a weird way to talk about a word that means as much as *retirement* can—we recognize that it's a spectrum we can move in and out of. Even if you hit this "magic" number you've set, that could change tomorrow. Many people don't think about wealth or FI in a nonlinear way. You can work seasonal jobs—you can be a seasonal contractor or freelancer or work part-time at Target if you want to—and then not work the rest of the year after March! Think of your income differently instead of spreading it out into fifty-two weeks of the year.

A lot of these income-generating opportunities didn't exist prior to five years ago, when we didn't have these marketplaces on the internet where you can sell a skill. I think people are waking up to the idea that they can earn money outside of traditional ways.

One of the big wins that led to us achieving FI was paying off our mortgage in 2017; we stayed mortgage free for about a year and a half before moving in 2018. That time of not having that big bill was awesome. Another big win was being able to quit our jobs. At the time, Julien was in a capital-*T* toxic situation, and while my situation was nothing like his, it wasn't great. Being able to quit on my terms was something I'd never been able to do before, and I feel like that's something everyone should be able to experience. I quit just because I fucking could, and it felt amazing.

Being a Black woman who's achieved FI means that I can tell the truth. What the world needs now are more truth tellers. I can afford to be honest about how fucked up things are and what people need to do. When I was dependent on an institution, I couldn't be honest, and I couldn't just leave if something wasn't working for me. Now I get to be the speaker who walks into these same companies and says, "It's pretty fucked up that you don't have any Black leadership."

If you want to achieve FI, start with what you care about. Hold those things close to you and let them be your motivation for figuring out what the rest of your lifestyle can cost. Then build the life that you want around it. Don't assume that everything is fixed: that means not assuming that whatever income you start with is the income you're going to end with. Create a baseline plan that allows you to get what you want without sacrificing your soul at a job you hate.

Let's wrap up by touching on an investing topic that is commonly inquired about: socially responsible investing, often used interchangeably with impact investing or ESG (environmental, social, and corporate governance) investing. This strategy aims to generate both financial gains and social change through avoiding harmful companies and/or investing in impact companies. These funds also generally bring higher returns, as they include many tech companies and shun oil, which hasn't performed well in decades.

Defining what is socially responsible gets a little precarious, of course. As an individual, you might have a different idea from Wall Street's of what this is, based on your own values. There are, however, general rules for socially responsible funds, such as no firearm companies, no oil companies, and no private prisons. However, you can take this a step further and venture into enterprises that are more in line with your values, perhaps companies founded or led by women, or B Corporations, companies that meet verified metrics for environmental and social performance.

Socially responsible investing is a great way to practice financial feminism. However, as our next expert interview expands upon, it shouldn't be the be-all and end-all, and it isn't perfect.

A word from
Tim Nash
CERTIFIED FINANCIAL PLANNER AND FOUNDER OF GOOD INVESTING

The language around socially responsible investing gets tricky. There are a lot of different terms for it: responsible investing, socially responsible investing, sustainable investing. Those are all broad umbrella terms that kind of mean the same thing: investing not only with a financial lens but also with ethical, religious, progressive, or sustainable considerations.

For so long, the economic system has viewed social and environmental issues as externalities, but with socially responsible investing, the idea is to bring in those social and environmental criteria into the investment decision-making process. The genesis of socially responsible investing was within religious communities in the last ten years: the Mennonites in Canada, plus a few other religious communities in the United States, felt strongly against investing in "sin stocks," such as alcohol, gambling, and tobacco. Now socially responsible investing has taken on the form of this language around ESG, where some people will screen their investments for what they want to exclude from their investment portfolios. Those original "sin stocks" might be excluded, but there's also a focus on excluding things like for-profit prisons and fossil fuel companies.

We're now starting to analyze companies not only on financial metrics but also on these sorts of ESG metrics. I'll be honest: we don't have consensus on what this means. To some degree, it has been hijacked by Wall Street, such that we now have sort of Wall Street's perspective of sustainability and ESG, which is not usually in line with most people's expectations. I would say if you're on the more sort of radical, feminist, progressive side of the equation, you might have a hard time with some of Wall Street's definitions.

I personally get really excited about impact investing, which is a little bit more niche, so it often gets overlooked. Impact investing is when we eschew Wall Street entirely and invest directly in things such as community bonds and microfinance. As an example, let's say a nonprofit organization in your community needs money to purchase its real estate. If you can loan the organization that money, you can have a large impact supporting a local nonprofit while also earning interest. This is something I suggest people do as *part* of their portfolio, but you want to be careful and not make it your *entire* portfolio.

The language that I use is that most of your portfolio is going to be in "doing less evil" funds. The less evil funds are broad index funds, but with exclusions. When I started in this industry ten to twelve years ago, there were so few options available, but now ESG funds have caught fire and are available through the big ETF providers like Charles Schwab, Vanguard, and Fidelity. Then we can carve out part of your portfolio for doing more good, whether this is through themed ETFs or bonds focused on renewable energy, clean tech, or water infrastructure, or through impact investing.

There are three fundamental trade-offs when it comes to responsible investing. Number one is going to be higher fees. That's not necessarily the case all the time, and sometimes it's just a matter of a few basis points, but if fees are your big concern, then there are some options for you that are sort of a small step in the right direction. What's been awesome about this is that fees have come down dramatically. It used to be like buying organic avocados, but now fees depend on how far on the spectrum you want to go.

Number two is going to be diversification. The more sustainable you are, the more things you're cutting out, so the less diversified you're going to be.

The third is this notion of risk exposure. Now, this is one that cuts both ways. At this moment in time, the two things that are doing well since Russia invaded Ukraine are weapons companies and fossil fuels. These are two things that socially responsible investing excludes, so right now we're underperforming. This is the tension between investing for value reasons and doing it for risk reasons. Some people—especially women—they just won't invest if some of these companies are in there. For me, if it's a value thing—where there is a benefit to getting rid of those things—then it's a no-brainer. Then for everyone else, it's really about managing ESG risk.

I recognize that ESG profits could be lower, especially during times of turmoil, when energy and military stocks do well. What I do know for sure is that the more sustainable you go, the more you're going to deviate from the benchmark, for better or for worse. To me, those are the trade-offs that I help clients walk through: "Okay, what is this tension between finance first and impact first? What are your ethical deal breakers?" For everyone who's trying to figure this out but understands the yucky aspects of colonial patriarchal capitalism, it feels really weird investing in it. Just how do you navigate this? It's going to be different for everyone.

I want to communicate that there is a wide range of options. To do less evil, understand what you're comfortable with in terms of participating within this capitalist system, because by refusing to invest, really what you're doing from the math standpoint is losing money to inflation. You're losing money to the system. Unless you can go totally off grid and grow your own food and be entirely independent and self-sufficient, you're participating in the global economy. But the way we participate matters.

When you choose what job you take and what kind of company you want to work for, you're making a decision about how you participate in the economy. When you decide between the big-box store and the mom-and-pop shop, or between buying something made in China and something made in your neighborhood, you're making a decision regarding your participation in the global economy. The *biggest* one is how you invest your money. Achieving financial independence and having a retirement investing strategy is the biggest decision that we make, especially for people with larger portfolios, and it's a decision we often make only once: we decide how to invest, and then that becomes the default option. It drives me nuts that I meet so many people who spend more time choosing an avocado in the grocery store than they spend choosing investments for their portfolio. Please at least go through and look at the companies that are inside the fund that you want. If you have an emotional reaction to that, I want you to know that there are other options.

You kind of have to play the game: It's important that we do participate in the economy and the market. As citizens, we have the same responsibility we have when we vote. If the economy implodes and it all goes to shit, then yes, your biggest assets are your community: how friendly you are with your neighbors and how good of a gardener you are. It doesn't matter where your money is invested in that scenario. However, if capitalism endures, then you want to be in a position in retirement where you are financially self-sufficient, where you are able to look after yourself and your family but also able to give money away and donate and volunteer. If you can retire early or cut back on your hours to give more in society and to your passions, this is what financial freedom allows you to do. For some of the most ardent anarchists, their worst-case scenario is to end up in retirement in government-assisted living, fully dependent on the system. If capitalism endures and you don't participate, that's the worst place you can be.

In my mind, I'm trying to find the balance: I acknowledge that capitalism in general is to a large degree unsustainable, exploitative, and sucks. That said, right now investing is the best way for us to be able to earn money and save for retirement. What I want to do is to be intentional about that, to dance within that balance. This is the best option that I've come up with. It's not perfect, but in my mind, it's like the best out of bad.

I'm not here to say sustainable investing is the be-all and end-all, but this is another arrow in our quiver in terms of impact, systems change, and advocacy. I would argue that in the world today, our markets and publicly traded companies are more powerful than our governments.

If you're voting and lobbying and participating in democracy but are investing blindly in the stock market, then, to me, there's a disconnect there. I believe most people would be comfortable paying slightly higher fees, having slightly less diversification, and having a little bit more deviation from that benchmark in order to align their investments more directly with everything they're doing in the rest of their lives and with their vision of the world that they want to retire in.

More than any other financial to-do, investing is our most powerful form of building wealth. It's easy to spend hours picking the "perfect" investing platform or worrying for weeks about whether a Traditional or Roth IRA is better. However, your time is better spent picking an investing account and actually getting started, even if it's just a small amount of money. Don't let analysis paralysis keep you from being able to retire someday!

THE TL;DR

LET'S BREAK DOWN your exact steps to start investing. If you need extra help with any of these steps—or this chapter felt extra confusing to you—no worries. This is exactly why my team and I started Treasury, to walk you through step-by-step. (See you over at herfirst100k.com/book-resources!)

1. Decide on your investing goal (probably retirement).

2. Decide if you want to DIY, work with a robo-advisor, or let us walk you through it on Treasury. Open an investing account, such as a 401(k) offered through your employer or an IRA.

3. Put money in the account (as little as $100).

4. Buy your investments. (Index funds are a popular option.)

5. Rinse and repeat steps 3 and 4 as often as you can.

HOMEWORK

1. NANA YOU

A fun assignment today! You're going to write about sixty-five-year-old you, fantasizing about how dope you'll be as a retiree and how you can support Future You right now. (This is in no way supposed to be a set-in-stone kind of scenario; don't let this exercise panic you. *It should be fun, all you type A personalities!*)

Who are you? What is a standard day like for you? What's your favorite article of clothing, hobby, place to travel? What are your hopes and dreams?

Then, in six months, or two years, or ten—when you're wondering, *Why am I putting away all this money?* and considering ripping apart this book—pull out your journal and imagine Old You.

I'll give you mine in brief. (Please wax poetic when you do it, though.)

> I own property in Seattle and in the Italian countryside. I also own a cabin in the mountains where I do puzzles and read books. I travel constantly. (Luca can come if he wants.) I eat incredible food—nothing subpar passes my lined lips—and I take my girlfriends on a dope trip every year à la Sara Blakely, the founder of Spanx. I run a foundation that uplifts women and girls. And I'm somehow, miraculously, almost unbelievably, more badass than I am right now.

2. START INVESTING TODAY

STEP 1: Decide on an investing goal—retirement (tax advantaged) or something else that is long term (non-tax advantaged). If you don't know where to start, a retirement account is your best bet.

STEP 2: Choose an institution to get started investing, much like you'd decide on a bank. You can go DIY or robo-advisor, or I'll see you over on Treasury for the step-by-step walk-through! If your work offers a 401(k) plan, it has already chosen the institution.

STEP 3: Open the account of your choosing and put money into it; an e-transfer from your bank account to your new investing account is the easiest way.

STEP 4: Once the money is in your account, choose your investments to purchase. I'll remind you that index funds are the most popular option, as they're low fee, low risk, and well diversified.

STEP 5: Boom! You're an investor!

CHAPTER 6

EARNING

MEET TWENTY-ONE-YEAR-OLD TORI.

Bright-eyed and bushy-tailed, I had just graduated college with dual degrees in organizational communication (like a marketing degree with less math) and theater. (Yep, I'm now a financial expert. I'm wondering how that happened too.) When I dreamed of my career, I imagined a high-profile marketing job in the city, where I wore a pantsuit and heels (that's how you know it was a fantasy because, WOW, heels are *awful*) and commuted in to work with a coffee in hand (also a fantasy, because caffeine makes me absolutely crazy). I dreamed of being a VP of marketing by age thirty, working my way up the corporate ladder, gaining more and more experience until I fucking conquered the world.

Within two weeks at my first corporate job, that Technicolor dream started to fade. Although it was a fantastic position in terms of experience to put on my résumé—I was the youngest manager at a global Fortune 500 company, my coworkers were fun, the office was in an amazing location—I was getting to see how the sausage was made. And it was not pretty.

Many folks can go months or years before realizing that the company they work for is run by awful people, but I had the gift of seeing that within a month. I had a front-row seat to a toxicity master class. My direct boss was a top executive in a company dominated by men; the culture was a mess of alcohol abuse and sexual misconduct, and a manipulative but disingenuous "we're not coworkers, we're family" mind-set. (Always be wary of a company that says seemingly well-meaning shit like this. We share a cubicle, not a fucking bloodline.) It was an incredibly unhealthy environment, and I hated it.

I hated helping to make someone I didn't respect rich. I hated contributing to a company that didn't share my values. But, then, I hated the whole nine-to-five life: having to stay for eight hours with my butt in a chair just to prove I was working and having to ask for permission to take a vacation.

Even when I left for less toxic environments (and there are plenty of less toxic environments out there), I wasn't thriving, no matter which marketing job I took in which industry. Throughout my life, I had dabbled in various things trying to figure out what to do: I worked at a music store in high school. (My parents joke that they went to more high school football games my senior year than I did.) In college, I played piano for Mass and other events (can you tell I went to a Catholic university?), worked in the admissions department as a campus tour guide, led the yearbook staff as the editor in chief, and would then come home on breaks to work as a cashier at the local hardware store. All of these experiences taught me that I just wasn't a person who could work for someone else.

In retrospect, it was inevitable that I would make multiple attempts at entrepreneurship. I started my first business at nine years old: owning gumball-type vending machines, with the profits going toward my college fund. (Ask me fucking *anything* about peanut M&M's.) I didn't invent anything, I didn't go on *Shark Tank*, and I didn't make that much money—but I learned how to pitch myself, how to manage business finances, and how to deal with rejection. When I started working nine to five after college, I was always thinking about what I could pursue on the side—in part for the extra money but also mostly because I wanted to be an entrepreneur. First, it was freelance writing, then it was social media management for clients, then it was a blog for twentysomething women. (Hello, HFK origin story!) I thought that full-time entrepreneurship wouldn't be possible for me before I turned thirty. Turns out, it happened five years earlier than that. What I was building was my life's mission.

My career looked very different from what I was told it "should" look like. And yours can too. Everyone's dream job and career trajectory are unique, and I can't necessarily tell you what yours can or should look like. But the pitfalls and struggles along the way are largely the same: being underpaid, fearing to ask for more, withstanding toxic environments just to get a paycheck, trying to get ahead in an environment not built with you in mind— the list goes on.

Every piece of the Financial Game Plan starts with you earning money. You can't begin to build your savings, pay off debt, or invest unless you're making money. This is largely the reason women and people of color are financially disadvantaged.

One of the most infamous and familiar stats in discussions of gender and money concerns the gender wage gap: on average in the United States, women make 82 cents to a man's dollar, while for Black women, it's 77 cents; Latina women, 75 cents; and Indigenous women, 70 cents. Asian women are the closest to closing the gap, at 95 cents. Disturbingly, this disparity in compensation only widens for women as we progress up the corporate ladder. For instance, Pacific Islander women at the executive level earn 60 cents to a white man's dollar. And while there has been improvement since 2015, this is likely a result of lower-income women dropping out of the labor force altogether.

Honestly, it's crazy that I have to spend any more time writing about such a well-established fact at this point, but if you look at my TikTok comments, there are still people who believe this whole "wage gap" thing is a complete myth. A common retort is that "it's illegal to pay someone differently based on their gender identity," so therefore the wage gap isn't real. But we know better.

The reasons for the wage gap are numerous: women not negotiating at the same rate that men do or being denied their requests at a higher rate than men and labeled "ungrateful"; women making up the bulk of lower-paid workers, especially in professions such as teaching and health care, whose societal value is not reflected in their economic compensation; and the big elephant in the room: terrible family-leave policies that penalize women for having children. Meanwhile, their male partners—who are also parents!—actually experience what researchers call the "fatherhood premium": a bump in compensation due to the perception of them as more committed, stable, and deserving.

Many a book and think piece have been written about the pressure placed on women to not only work but also maintain a household and take care of children or ailing family members—in addition to the unpaid emotional labor that is expected of us; for instance, the responsibility of managing others' feelings at work, like being told to "put on a smile" for clients and customers. I'm not the first to talk about this, and I probably won't be the last. Despite dozens of books, thousands of articles, and global conversation about the stress women feel to "have it all"—and about how "having it all" often means doing uncompensated labor—these inequalities persist.[*] Women made up the majority of COVID-related job losses, and women are penalized professionally and financially if they need to provide care to family members.

To make matters worse, women struggle with lower compensation and undervalued labor in a system that conflates our economic productivity with our worth as people. Capitalism can literally put a price tag on a human life. (If you're curious, it's around $7 million. One way of estimation is based on average lifetime earnings, which means women are valued less under capitalism when compared with men. Cool.) It's even in the language we use when we talk about compensation. "Earning our worth" sounds positive, but it's equating our monetary "value" with our value as humans, leading us to hustle culture: the feeling that we're never doing enough, that we need to keep grinding.

Hustle culture (read: capitalism) tells you that you are not inherently worthy, that the only measure of your worth is your work: how often you work, how tired you are, how successful you could be if you just worked harder, smarter, faster. Working yourself to the bone is a badge of honor in hustle culture. It scoffs at time off, equates rest to failing, and consistently asks for more than you can and are able to give, while calling you weak. It causes, promotes, and incentivizes burnout and exhaustion.

We've spent so long believing that if we just work harder and break more glass ceilings, our financial and personal lives will all fall into place, but that's not the reality—which makes for a chapter very challenging to write. More than any other topic in personal finance, earning is the one least within your control, affected by dozens of factors, many of which are *not* how hard you work or how deserving you are. The minimum wage in your state,

---

[*] Useful further reading about this fuckery includes *Fed Up: Emotional Labor, Women, and the Way Forward,* by Gemma Hartley; *Invisible Women: Data Bias in a World Created for Men,* by Caroline Criado Perez; and *Unfinished Business: Women Men Work Family,* by Anne Marie Slaughter.

whether you had the (often privileged) opportunity to attend college, your industry's standard salaries, whether your company's workforce has unionized and has the bargaining power to demand more from your employer—all of these can impact your earning potential and are further evidence of why financial feminism is not just about personal choices; it also must be focused on policy and systemic change.

Now, it's possible to work hard (or have a side hustle) without "hustle *culture*." It's possible to be ambitious and care about your job without falling victim to or contributing to the "grind no matter what" mentality. When you love what you do, sometimes you do find yourself hustling, like I did when I was building Her First $100K. There were some sacrifices I was willing to make, but others I wasn't. I was willing to often devote a few nights a week to work, but I wasn't willing to give up eight hours of sleep. You can work hard and care deeply about your work, while also honoring your needs, taking breaks, and doing what you love. But I also want to be clear that under our current economy, there is a large subset of people for whom a side hustle is not a passion project but the thing they have to do to survive.

Like I've said over and over again in this book, we control only what we control. Yes, it's awful that you could do the difficult, brave, and vulnerable work of evaluating your worth in capitalistic terms, build up a strong case, negotiate expertly—and still not get that promotion or raise through no fault of your own. But I need you to advocate for yourself anyway. Whatever you have to do for work, I want it to set you up for success in every possible way down the line, and that includes financial success.

A word from
Anonymous

Growing up, I thought if I worked really hard in school and got good grades, then there would be a good job for me when I graduated—which happened in 2010 during a recession when barely anybody was hiring. I eventually ended up in a job where I was working sixty to seventy hours a week. It was a really toxic environment: people constantly talked about each other behind their backs. I quit without a job lined up and ended up working with a florist. The role definitely wasn't part of my plan, but I took it out of desperation, and the florist later brought me on as a co-owner. Then she ended up moving, and we separated, resulting in me being unemployed for a year.

It was difficult trying to get a job with my florist background because a lot of companies couldn't see how that experience could be beneficial or helpful. I was penny-pinching to an unhealthy degree. I intentionally didn't wake up until maybe eleven o'clock or noon, so I wouldn't have to worry about eating breakfast.

My college's career counselor recommended I pivot to social media marketing again, so I started emailing people nonstop, asking if they'd be interested in marketing services. For a couple of months, I was an administrative assistant to an entrepreneur. Then my grandmother on my mom's side became terminally ill, and I stopped working to be with her until she passed a month later.

Around the same time, a friend who was leaving her company put my name in for a job, and I got hired for a full-time role as a billing clerk. I worked hard to stand out in the role, and within a year, I was moved up into a billing coordinator position.

The company became my life. My closest friends were my colleagues. I ended up going on an international trip with a coworker, who became one of my best friends. I even dated a person there. I finally felt like I had a purpose. The company created an environment of feeling like you didn't need to ever go home. I got a lot of great opportunities from it: amazing lifelong friends, a partner, and the ability to move to Seattle.

However, when I first arrived in Seattle, I was given a huge workload that really should have been done by two or three people. I worked about seventy to eighty hours a week without additional compensation. I didn't know what boundaries looked like at a workplace—nobody at the office did. We were all staying late and being overworked. Unfortunately, I had a boss who also didn't have great boundaries. I once even got a phone call while I was on the beach in Mexico, and I was regularly working on Thanksgiving and Christmas.

I thought that level of work was expected, because there's a belief that if you really want something, you'll work hard for it, but it was toxic because it always felt like a competition of who was working the hardest. It wasn't until my partner at that time said, "You don't really have a life outside of work," that I realized the extent of the situation. That's when I started to do comedy. Through comedy, I met so many friends outside of work. In January 2016, I told myself that I'd work for a year and then quit and pursue comedy full-time.

Then I was sexually assaulted.

On a work trip, I was sexually assaulted by two coworkers who worked at a different office. It completely derailed my plans. I had never experienced the emotions I was having. Searching for another job felt impossible when I remembered how taxing job searching was earlier in my career—job hunting, interviewing; and starting a new job often means having your worth questioned repeatedly and having to prove yourself. At that point, I couldn't do that for myself. I was barely keeping it together.

I had to rely heavily on my existing job because I needed money to live. I needed health care to go to therapy—a lot of therapy.

However, I drastically stepped away from that toxic work culture. I stopped putting in that amount of hours. I switched departments. I knew I wanted to leave at some point, but I needed to feel safe and level before I did that.

I really liked my new department and my boss, but I hated that I was staying longer than I planned. But then again, getting better took longer than I planned. I thought I'd do six months of therapy and be fine, but it took a solid three years for me to stop dissociating and depersonalizing. Anybody who's going through something like that isn't going to be the same as they once were.

Cut to COVID in March 2020. I pushed for working from home and told my employer that because of a preexisting condition, I didn't feel comfortable coming into the workplace. They made me prove the preexisting condition, and eventually we agreed that once Washington State hit phase three, I'd come back to the office. It was a job I could do remotely, which I proved by implementing a lot of new projects while working from home for a little over a year. In March 2021, Washington did go into phase three, but the vaccine rollout had only just started, so I told my boss that I still didn't feel comfortable returning. That was my boundary.

My boss agreed with me that I'd done excellent work from home, but the higher-ups didn't care. It felt like another full-circle moment of looking at my health, but this time, instead of staying at the job for my mental health, I had to leave it for my physical health. I had a boundary I wasn't willing to cross.

They gave me the option to work in LA because I was living there temporarily, but it didn't matter what office I was going into—the boundary was still and had always been that I wasn't comfortable going in. They weren't listening to my underlying issues. I gave them the month's notice they asked for, and they still told me to come into the office. I said no and used my leftover PTO—then left.

After I put in my notice, a company recruiter hit me up and asked me to list all my skills and job responsibilities. Two weeks later, I looked at the posting for my old job. It had a new title and was a manager position, paying $20,000 more than what I was making after I had been with the company for eight years.

I'm lucky I had the financial means to leave my position, and that it was enough money to take a year off. I was able to see my other grandmother more before she passed away. I was able to work on projects and go on a trip to Europe for a couple of months. When I talk to people and recruiters about my time off, they think it's great. I've been told that it's amazing how I was able to recognize I needed a break and to take it. Usually people go from one job immediately into another.

Job searching feels a lot different now because I have much more experience. When I wrote down the job responsibilities for my previous position, I realized my accomplishments. I know it'll take a while to get a job, but I feel confident discussing my job experiences. It felt like I had to make stuff up before. Now it feels authentic.

My story is a complicated one. I think it could be perceived that I stayed at the job for too long, but I did what I needed to do to keep myself safe and be healthy again. I'm learning to be kinder to myself. The metaphor I use is to imagine you're dying of thirst and someone asks you to play in a softball league. You can't. You're just trying to function. That's how dire my state was after the assault. I always thought the job was going to be a temporary thing, since my original plan was to work there for a year. Because of that, I kept thinking about what I *should* be doing. I still fight my thoughts of *should*. What I've learned is in order to make a change and get out of a situation, we have to lay the groundwork first.

Earning more money helps so many parts of the financial puzzle fit together, but please remember that we're not pursuing money for its own sake here. Earning more money doesn't mean submitting to hustle culture. Hustle porn and financial feminism do not mix. I don't want you to work so hard that you burn out or come to equate your income or productivity with your self-worth. I don't want you to embrace the mentality of earning the most money possible and fuck everything else. That's not what I'm about, and it's not what this chapter is about either.

The point of increasing your income is to fund your dream life and make it easier, not to work more. The occasional sacrifice in your career is to be expected, but if you're regularly giving up your time, your mental health, and rest, this is the opposite of what we want. We work to increase our income and get paid fairly: for our mental health, our financial goals, and our own stability, and to make society better.

This chapter is a guide to make sure that when you do find work you love—or at the very least, work that fits the kind of life you want—you're compensated fairly for it; that you're treated well by your boss, your company, and your clients; and that you do what's within your power to make a fair wage.

As in previous chapters, we'll first dive into some misconceptions that actively hold us back in our careers and our earning potential. (These narratives apply whether you work a more traditional full-time job, are a freelancer, own your own business, or are somewhere in between.)

narrative #1
IT'S NOT THE RIGHT TIME

"I CAN'T START a side hustle right now, not when so many other people are doing the same thing!"

"Quitting my job to run my business full-time right now is just so scary. What if I fail?"

"It's just not a good time to ask for a promotion; my boss isn't having a good day."

Why should someone who runs a similar business prevent you from starting your own? If you have the ability to be an entrepreneur, why should the fear of failure keep you from trying? And why should your boss's having a bad day stunt your career?

Here's the hard truth: it's never the right time. Ever. And a decision that feels brave will always mean overcoming a little bit of fear, no matter the circumstances. One of my favorite people on the planet, author Elizabeth Gilbert (*Eat Pray Love*), talks about fear in her incredible book *Big Magic: Creative Living Beyond Fear*. She has a fantastic exercise for when she's embarking on something new. (Fun fact: it's something I've had to do *many* times while writing this book.) She will literally take a chair out from her kitchen table, mentally place Fear in the seat, and talk to it. She tells Fear that she's about to head off on a road trip with Creativity, and although she knows Fear will kick and scream in protest, it is allowed to come along on the excursion. But it has no vote—it cannot pick the snacks, or the destination, or the playlist. And Fear *definitely* doesn't get to drive.

Feeling apprehensive about making a huge career change isn't some kind of character flaw. Blame your brain. It turns out that our brains don't know the difference between something as seemingly harmless as trying something new and literally dying. Whether we're asking someone out on a date or about to skydive, the part of our brains that registers fear feels the same terror. Your brain is trying to protect you from the risk. It's fight, flight, or freeze. So when we're about to do something vulnerable—something that puts us out there, that we're not an expert in, that is going to potentially bring rejection or shame—it feels like life and death. But it's not! Your asking for a raise or quitting a job or starting a side hustle is a blip on your life's radar—what a relief, right?—and might actually be the start of something incredible.

narrative #2

I WORK HARD SO THAT THEY'LL NOTICE ME

WE'VE BEEN TOLD that hard work equals promotions and raises. ("Shame's first demand is conformity," as my friend Alexis Rockley said in chapter 1.) You consistently outperform your goals, you show up on time, and you bring innovative ideas to the table. You do such good work that your boss would be *crazy* to not see it. This is a narrative meant to keep you in homeostasis: "work hard because it's the right thing to do, without the expectation of a reward."

A company, no matter how seemingly well intentioned, is almost never going to just hand out raises and promotions without your advocating for yourself. If an employer can underpay and overwork you, he's going to keep doing it—it saves him money! In fact, you're *making* him money. A carrot is being dangled in front of you, but you'll never actually get to chow down on it.

narrative #3

LOYALTY IS IMPORTANT AND WILL BE REWARDED

THIS ONE DRIVES ME CRAZY.

For decades, job hopping was frowned upon. It was a red flag that displayed a lack of commitment and direction. "Job hoppers" were flight risks. But so much of how we think about jobs and our careers has changed. That kind of narrative is outdated. In a survey of roughly 1,200 millennial employees, 91 percent said they expected to stay in a job for less than three years. Pensions aren't a thing anymore. You no longer stay at a company—or even in a particular industry—for a decade.

Starting a new job arms you with more negotiating power to increase your salary than you will ever have again at that company. Seriously. I never stayed at a job for more than two years, and, frankly, that's partly what I attribute my financial success to. It meant that my salary kept growing.

Even if you signed an Ursula blood oath and pledged undying loyalty to your company for the rest of your life, it has zero loyalty to you. Zero. That sounds harsh, but it's true. Employers will lay you off, break a contract, fire you, cut your benefits—with little to no pause. I need you to be as ruthless as they can be. If something is no longer working for you, do everything you can to leave and find better. It's out there, I promise. Which leads me to . . .

narrative #4
"THIS IS AS GOOD AS IT GETS"

WHEN WE'VE BEEN TRAINED by society to play small, we believe that our current environment is as good as we deserve. We don't believe we're worth the best, so we stick it out in situations that we shouldn't tolerate. Corporate culture's endless pressure to conform and sacrifice seeps into our psyche, convincing us that we don't deserve better. Worse, we're being told *constantly* that these companies that we're pouring our blood, sweat, and tears into are great places to work. (Cue: "We're a family!") They tell you how lucky you are to have the job you do, at the place you do, with the salary you do, with the title you do. And, slowly, you start to believe them.

When you're in the thick of it, it's extremely difficult to see the forest for the trees. When you're in the daily slog of your commute or in constant communication with a client (please give me a metaphorical hand for that alliteration), it's almost impossible to even consider that you might not have to put up with toxicity. It's like being in a bad relationship: only when you break up do you realize that your friends were right and it wasn't healthy, and also him telling you on a beach in Hawaii that you should maybe lose some weight was actually the most *insane* red flag (definitely not speaking from personal experience).

You start to believe that this job, this client, or this gig is tolerable—even when a tiny voice in your head tells you differently. Trust your gut. Trust that there's better out there, even though you've been conditioned to believe there isn't. I promise you, there is.

There are companies and organizations out there that will value you both personally and professionally, provide you opportunities for growth, and compensate you for the worth you provide. (That company or organization might just be the one you start.)

narrative #5
JUST DO IT BECAUSE YOU'RE PASSIONATE ABOUT IT, NOT FOR THE MONEY

I HEAR THIS all the time from people who work at nonprofits or in the public sector. I also see it with artists and with entrepreneurs leading a social cause: "I know I'm going to be underpaid, and that's just the reality." Like every other narrative we're debunking in this book, this one is perpetuated to keep you underpaid and overworked. Mission-led work doesn't inherently mean you should get paid poorly. It's a narrative that guilts you for asking more from "good" companies or places with tight budgets. But you deserve to be compensated fairly, regardless of where you work.

Passion and money are not mutually exclusive.

Yes, it might be harder to negotiate because of either smaller budgets or bureaucracy, but just because it's harder doesn't mean it can't happen. I've worked with dozens of teachers, government workers, and nonprofit employees who successfully prepared their material before sitting down with their boss to discuss their salary; asked for their worth, making a compelling case why they deserved a raise; and received an increase in pay and/or benefits.

Lorena Soriano

CORPORATE SUSTAINABILITY CONSULTANT AND
FOUNDER OF EVERY POINT ONE

There is a big lack of intersectionality in advice for women and in the professional workforce. For example, the housework and domestic workforces that are predominantly made up of women of color and immigrants are still paid the least. White women have been able to accomplish their professional goals because of women of color in these industries.

There's also a lack of corporate responsibility. We know for a fact that more women of color are entering the corporate world. However, because of a lack of focus on retention and building workplaces that sustain diverse talents, you end up with a higher turnover. It gets worse: we have corporations who take advantage of immigrants and women of color via implied threats to their citizenship or their family members. They leverage this "guilt" to suppress the demand for change. They end up spinning the narrative that says, "You should feel lucky that you even have a job," or threaten deportation.

Even women who have their citizenship, like my mother, experienced this firsthand. They felt so "lucky" to have the opportunity, and companies take complete advantage of that. My mother was working six days a week, and whenever I brought up that legally they can't make her do extra work, she'd fall back on how lucky she was to have a job when so many other people didn't.

Women of color especially have to care for their mental health. We need rest days—we need breaks. But then, when we take them, we fall to a societal stigma that says rest is lazy and we should be working to accomplish our goals.

> For me, changing these narratives started with getting the best job I could out of school, which gave me the ability to earn money and finally have the final say on things I wanted to do. I also sought out the mentorship of a friend who helped me learn to negotiate and advocate for myself. I also had to learn to set healthy boundaries, both with my family and with myself. It was hard but so necessary.

narrative #6
I CAN'T LAND A JOB IF I DON'T MEET EVERY REQUIREMENT

IF YOU'RE JUST GRADUATING or changing industries, you might believe that you have no shot in getting a certain job, let alone negotiating your salary. That's simply not true.

Let me tell you a story about my friend Hailey, a newer grad who wanted to get into corporate human resources and recruitment. The problem was that she didn't have any recruiting experience. Her only job following college was as maître d' at P. F. Chang's. Hailey didn't know how to interview prospective job candidates or even how to sort through résumés.

However, when interviewed for jobs, she framed her years in the hospitality industry in such a way as to make them relevant to the position she sought. She explained how she thrived in the fast-paced environment of a restaurant, where she had to be detail oriented as well as an excellent communicator with both patrons and staff. She managed expectations and worked to resolve issues with difficult customers. She was a self-starter who knew how to wear multiple hats and time manage her ass off, all to ensure that guests had wonderful experiences.

Just because you've never held a particular job title or even worked in a certain industry doesn't mean that you don't have what I like to call "bridge skills" that match the job you're applying for. While Hailey didn't have any specific experience in being a recruiter, she could take the experience and skills she did have and package them up as evidence that she was a perfect fit. Hailey tailored her résumé to include all the examples of how her talents in the restaurant industry were natural bridges to the skills needed to be a successful recruiter.

Be like Hailey. Find your bridge skills and practice highlighting them on your résumé. Use specific examples of times you've "been a team player" or shown "attention to detail."

(Also worth noting: Men will apply for jobs where they only meet 60 percent of the qualifications. However, women won't apply unless they meet 100 percent of the requirements. This ends now, y'all.)

narrative #7
I CAN'T ASK FOR MORE BECAUSE THE COMPANY IS GOING THROUGH A ROUGH TIME RIGHT NOW

IT DOESN'T MATTER how well or how terribly the company is doing—you deserve to be compensated fairly. Always. Getting paid well for your work has nothing to do with company performance (unless you're, like, the CEO). Your salary or rate is based on your quality of work, not on how well or terribly the company is doing. They're mutually exclusive, just like you wouldn't expect a raise *just* because the company is doing well. If budgets are tight, and management isn't able to increase your salary at the present time (make them tell you this after you ask—don't just assume), there are other forms of compensation you can request. More on that in a bit.

WE CAN INCREASE OUR INCOME in three basic ways: get paid more in our current situation, get paid more by finding a new situation, or get paid more by creating our own situation. We can either negotiate our current salary or contract; leave and find a better-paying salary or contract; or start a side hustle or our own business. We'll spend most of this chapter discussing how we can advocate for ourselves and get paid more no matter our situation—because whether we're salaried employees, freelancers, entrepreneurs, or some hybrid, we all deserve to be paid fairly.

NAVIGATING THE NEGOTIATION

LEARNING TO NEGOTIATE is key to increasing your income throughout your career. You can do it at any time, but most commonly when you're faced with one of three scenarios: you're starting a new job, it's performance review time, or you discover you're being underpaid.

A not-so-fun negotiating fact: women who do not negotiate their salaries miss out on more than $1 million during their lifetimes compared with women who do. Yep, $1 million lost. And if that's not powerful enough, let's frame it like negotiation expert Alexandra Dickinson does: "Are you willing to lose out on $1 million just to avoid a handful of uncomfortable conversations?" Are you willing to lose out on *$1 million* just to avoid getting some knees weak, arms are heavy (Mom's spaghetti)? It's not just the salary increase that comes from getting a new job or a raise, it's what that money can do for you over the course of your entire career: your salary at your next job will likely be higher; higher returns on your good investments because of compound interest; more flexibility for your present-day finances, as well as in your future.

Moji Igun

FOUNDER OF BLUE DAISI CONSULTING

I never negotiated my salary until I turned twenty-five. I was getting a 3 percent cost-of-living raise every year, and I was just grateful for whatever was offered to me.

As a full-time employee, my salary was $50,000, but the company wanted to switch me to a contractor role. So, I had to do the math to determine if switching from full-time to part-time would lose me money, plus factor in taxes. I previously took Tori's online negotiation course called Navigating the Negotiation, but this was the first time I'd written a script on a piece of paper and put it next to my laptop's camera. My hand was shaking, and I said, "Um, what do you think about giving me this much per hour?" I was nervous they'd think I was ungrateful and that I was taking advantage of them, then say no and fire me.

After I finally did it, they came back to me, saying, "I'm sorry, no, we can't do that." That actually gave me more courage to advocate for what I needed outside of salary. I would say no to more projects, and I was firmer with my boundaries about hours. The act of negotiating gave me more confidence to stand up for myself in the workspace and be bold.

I also learned that my coworkers were in the same situation. I wasn't the only person freaking out. I brought it up over coffee, saying, "I tried to ask for more money, and this is what happened. I'm kind of bummed about it." I kept hearing, "Oh my God, I had the same experience." We started spilling the tea instead of tiptoeing around it. Openly discussing negotiation with my coworkers and friends created a shift in me.

Then I got a call from the City of Seattle to work for them on a project. They said, "There's no budgetary limit. What does it cost to do this?" That's when I realized, "Oh, I can actually think about what I'm worth, name it to a point where I don't feel resentful, and be comfortable."

Starting a new job or project without worrying about inconveniencing anyone was also a whole new shift. I was literally shaking during my first negotiation, and now here I was, saying, "No, that's what it costs; you can change your budget if you need to," with no qualms. Then I watched *them* get a little bit nervous. They said, "This other consultant we pay doesn't charge as much as you." I responded, "I'm not that consultant. I'm Moji. It's not outlandish—it's slightly higher. You can do it." They said, "Actually, we *can* do it."

And that was it. I think that's where I felt respect—both for myself and from them—because they weren't prepared for me to stick to my guns. I think they thought I would be accommodating, like I was previously in my career.

I feel like as a Black woman, I have been conditioned to be small. If I get a really big opportunity to have a multiyear contract with an established organization, I should just be grateful to be there. Now I was willing to walk away if they weren't going to at least have a conversation about salary. That felt powerful because I don't think any of my Black women friends feel like they're able to walk away if someone's not treating them the way they need to be treated. That energy is powerful. A small skill of knowing what to say *and how to truly believe it* transformed that interaction.

Knowing how to negotiate also helped me set boundaries. If they weren't going to pay me enough, I wasn't going to work more than forty hours per week. In my contracts now, scope creep is a firm boundary. If they ask for more than what we've already agreed to, I'm like, "Actually, no, that's not part of our agreement. I can't do that for you without additional compensation." That mentality bleeds over into my personal boundaries of rest as well. I say, "This is how I can help you, and this is what I can do." I am clear about that, or else I'm burning myself at two ends, and that's not healthy.

To anyone afraid of negotiation, be honest with yourself about what happens if you don't ask. If I stayed in the same circumstances of my last job, I would have grown resentful. I would have been in the same place, and I wouldn't have given myself the opportunity to create a healthy environment. I would never have been able to accomplish my overall goal of wanting to have good well-being and space for vacations and rest.

It begins with trying, then practicing, and then we can get better at it and keep moving forward in the future. It's important to get comfortable with trying.

I want to quickly redefine what a "successful" negotiation means. A negotiation "success" is not getting what you asked for, although there's no better feeling. As we mentioned before, whether you get what you ask for is not entirely within your control. Instead, I want you to think of it like this: being a successful negotiator means that you thoughtfully prepared and organized your materials, advocated for yourself firmly but politely, and were brave enough to try. *That* is a successful negotiation, regardless of the outcome. Negotiating is something you'll do for the rest of your life—not just in the context of bargaining with an employer but also in other areas. Every time you do it, you learn more for next time. You strengthen your negotiating muscle. So, our goal here isn't solely to get what we want, everything else be damned; it is to come to the table as prepared as possible and learn to advocate for our compensation in a fair way.

Too many people approach a salary negotiation with a misguided ask. They'll think, *Well, I just need fifty thousand dollars* to cover *my bills or pay off my debt, so that's what I'll ask for.* Or: *I work really hard and deserve to make X dollars,* but *X* is a random number they've made up in their heads.

My amazing friends over at Bitches Get Riches, a personal finance blog, have the best metaphor for this. (Fun fact: cofounder Piggy from BGR is my literary agent. Hi, Pigs!):

> Choosing the right number for your salary is like guessing how many jelly beans there are in a jar without going over. Working backward from your budget is sort of like formulating your guess around how many jelly beans you personally want to eat right now. *I really only want a handful. So, I will guess twelve.* "Are there twelve?" Not a winning strategy. It's also unwise to make an uninformed guess, like blurting out some random number and hoping it will be right. "Are there two hundred and ten? Because I told the universe that I wanted the answer to be two hundred and ten, and I'm trying to manifest my will into reality." The go-with-your-gut strategy is fine for low-stakes church fundraisers, where the prize *is* actually jelly beans. But setting your salary is the highest-stakes guessing game you'll ever play. It's imperative that you use every tool and strategy you can to maximize your odds of being right.

Instead, when you're approaching a negotiation, you need to come armed with a clear understanding of your market rate. Your market rate is the range of jelly beans in the jar. You can tell there's definitely more than twenty, and there's no way two hundred fit in there, but narrowing it down is the tricky part—and the most important. The people you're asking for more money are most likely very data driven and need to see the evidence as to why they should pay you more. Rather than propose a random amount, you need to ask the right questions and do the right research to figure out your market rate.

Your market rate is based on two things: the data and your value-add.

When I say data, I'm referring to market research that tells you what you should be getting paid relative to other people in your industry with your experience level. We're looking for that market rate. You can find this through third-party platforms such as Glassdoor and PayScale, where employees of various companies anonymously list their salary information by role. However, use the data on these platforms as your jumping-off point. These salary aggregates are very two-dimensional. They typically ask only for the job's title, your location, and how many years of experience you have. They're not seeing the full 3D you, with your unique skill set, certifications, and background. They also tend to give a HUGE salary range—sometimes multiple tens of thousands. That can be a helpful start, but since it's not immediately clear what differentiates people at various points in the range, we need to dig deeper.

Another good place to look online are the dozens of Google Sheets containing anonymous salary information. The spreadsheets proliferate across the internet, for all different levels and industries. These are even more powerful because (1) they're anonymous, and therefore typically more accurate, and (2) these spreadsheets are often put together and organized by women or people of color committed to helping others earn more money. You can find these by literally googling "salary data spreadsheets."

To get the most accurate data, the kind you can bring into a negotiation, you'll want to talk to your colleagues. These should be people in your network who could share their thoughts—previous bosses, friends who work in the industry/field, recruiters, even random people you've met at networking events. Ask them, "Hey, based on this job description and the skills and experience that I have, what should I be getting paid?"

For instance, if I'm a marketer, I'm going to talk to other marketers. I might follow up with people I met at a networking event for marketers. I'll message previous bosses or previous coworkers too. I might chat with friends in recruiting who hire marketers. Whomever I eventually end up talking to, I'll show them the description of the job I'm going for (or currently doing) and ask, "Based on what you know about my experience and skill set, what would you price this role at?" This conversation is going to be a lot more specific to your unique situation than a random Glassdoor entry.

The second thing that helps you figure out your market rate is your value-add. It goes without saying that this shouldn't be taken to mean your value as a person, and, of course, you're adding value to your company regardless. Figuring out your value-add is more about creating hard metrics out of what you, uniquely you, are able to do at work. How much money did you save your company over the past year, and how? What sorts of projects did you implement? Who do you manage? What additional benefits do you bring this company by going above and beyond your job description? In what way can they really not afford to lose you? How do you contribute very distinctly to the company culture? (And when applying for a new job, reflect on these questions both in the benefit you added to previous workplaces and how you can bring that same energy to your new job.)

We can display this value very easily. If you're asking for a raise, find your original job description for the position you were hired for. (If you're negotiating for a new job, the description should be right in front of you.) Go to the bullet points—where they list the job's requirements—and prepare specific narratives or statistics that show how you not only checked that box but exceeded expectations.

An example: let's say I'm working as a social media marketer, and the first bullet point is "Manage and grow our social media accounts." I will come to the negotiation with something along these lines: "In the past year, I've grown our following more than 30 percent across all channels." Be as specific as possible, not just with numbers or statistics but also with anecdotal evidence. Stories can be just as powerful. Let's go down to the next bullet point: "Foster connection in our online communities." I could mention a story about how one community member commented favorably on another's post, and how they're now friends in real life, supporting each other.

These examples can go beyond job-specific accomplishments. Someone who's congenial to work with, on top of being good at her job, is a value-add anywhere. In 2019, the last year I worked corporate, I was preparing for my annual review, focused on getting a raise. As part of my negotiation, I emphasized the fact that I instituted a gratitude practice every Monday during team meetings: I initiated those meetings by inviting everyone to say what he or she was grateful for both personally and professionally—something that built trust and vulnerability (two of the company's core values) and allowed team members to be recognized and appreciated by their colleagues. At my annual review, I said, "Hey, not only have I contributed in all of these ways, very specifically to my job and to the outcome of the company, but I have also helped in terms of our company culture—I'm exemplifying our company values and fostering them." My boss told me later it was one of the reasons that I received a 20 percent raise.

Claire Wasserman

COFOUNDER OF LADIES GET PAID

When it comes to earning more, the thing you can't get away from is negotiating—regardless of whether you're a freelancer, asking for a raise at your current company, or applying for a new job.

Women are so hard on ourselves—it's baked into how we're socialized. We want to be perfect, and we're conditioned to see most things in life as a test. We do well in school, we get the As, we're the majority of college graduates—it's worked well for us so far. So, we go in to interviews and also see this process as some sort of test. Or worse, if we have imposter syndrome, we use the results of this "test" as a reflection of our worth. We wade into existential territory, and it becomes much bigger than just trying to get the job. This is compounded around our money fears on top of everything else.

The first thing I want to tell someone who's feeling anxious about negotiation is that every single company expects you to negotiate. If you don't negotiate, *you're subsidizing somebody else who is.* You should be very wary of underpricing yourself for two reasons:

1. We pay a price that's commensurate with what we deem to be valuable. If we don't think you're that valuable, we'll pay you less. If I feel like you're already coming into the conversation with that sort of energy, I sometimes wonder, *Why is this person charging me so little? Is something wrong?*

2. When you underprice yourself, you're bringing down wages for everybody. If we're all competing with one another to see who can price the least, we're racing to the bottom. This gives way too much power to the employer. A trick to employ if you're unsure of what to ask for: say, "Here's the amount that I normally charge; however, I know budgets are tight. I really

want to work with you. What were *you* thinking?" The key in this scenario is to make sure the first number you put out is a really big one. If you're starting with a really big number, chances are you're not underpricing yourself.

Leaving your job to find a better environment or higher paycheck can feel really scary, especially for women. (We have this fear of retribution.) Instead of convincing yourself of the reasons you should stay, maybe the question should be: "If I stay, what am I missing out on?" List them. Are those things rooted in a place of fear or growth?

The one upside to the workplace disruption that's happened in the past few years is that we've punched hustle culture right in the fucking face. Employees have more power than they ever did before. We still live in a capitalist society, so of course we still need the money, but things are shifting. At the end of the day, you are the one that matters. You, your health, your family—not your job. We have so much more power than we realize.

Now that you've done your homework, you're all set to walk in to a negotiation. When negotiating for a new job or at your annual review, there will be a natural opening in the conversation to bring up your compensation and to present your prepared materials. However, if you've discovered you're being undercompensated, you're going to send an email to your boss like this:

Hey, [name]

Hope you're having a great day. It's recently come to my attention that I'm being undercompensated for my work and the value I provide to our team. I'd love to chat with you about my compensation, as well as my expectations and goals for my position—when would be good for you next week?

MY FIVE KEYS FOR NEGOTIATION SUCCESS

key #1
NEVER GIVE A NUMBER FIRST

COMPANIES ARE LOOKING to underpay you, so they'll ask, "What are your salary expectations?" This is a classic job interview question, one that disproportionately affects women and people of color—because members of marginalized groups consistently believe they're worth less than they actually are, and they've been proven to undercut themselves time and time again.

Companies will do this almost immediately: after posting a vague job description and calling you in for a thirty-minute, first-round interview, they nail ya with the "How much money do you expect?" zinger, catching you *completely* off guard. If the company wanted to make sure that you fit comfortably within the position it was trying to fill, it would have been transparent and put the salary range on the job description. (Memo to companies: you look shady AF when you aren't transparent.)

There's no way, after a thirty-minute phone conversation, you can accurately assess what would be fair compensation for this job. Here's what you should say:

"It's hard to understand the full scope of the role at this stage in the process, so I'd love to know your budget."

Nine times out of ten, they will tell you the salary range. Then you can say if that's in line with your level of experience. And if this is a required question on an online application, put "$00,000."

If they push back—"We'd really love to see if we're aligned"—you can either give the range that came up when doing your market research or say kindly but firmly, "I'd be happy to tell you if your budget meets my expectations!" Remember that you're interviewing them as much as they're interviewing you, and if they get weird when talking about compensation, that's a red flag.

This "What is your budget?" question is also magic if you're a freelancer or entrepreneur. The hundreds of messages I receive along the lines of "Tori, we'd love to have you speak at our event!" or "Please contribute writing to our blog" all get an almost automated email response of "Budget???????" This is particularly useful for us self-employed folks for two reasons: (1) we don't want to leave money on the table, and (2) this makes a response such as "We don't want to pay you real money but instead pay you in eXpO$uRE!" look like the stupid shit it is.

If you're optimistic that your current company is likely to offer you a raise, the same rules apply. Don't be so gung-ho to negotiate that you play your cards immediately—let them tell you their anticipated increase first.

key #2
NEGOTIATIONS ARE COLLABORATIONS, NOT CONFLICTS

TOO MANY PEOPLE go into negotiations thinking they're going to have to put on their boxing gloves and fight tooth and nail in order to get what they want. But that's not a negotiation.

A negotiation should be a compromise. A collaborative process. You and your boss/potential boss are not on opposing teams. You are on the same team, working to solve the problem of you not being compensated fairly.

You're a good problem solver. It's probably one of the things that makes you a good employee. You know how to work with others to find a solution to said problem. And that's exactly what you're doing here. I know it seems terrifying, but I promise: a calm, collected attitude makes this process so much smoother.

And approaching it with the mind-set of "How can we work together to solve this?" is transformational in terms of getting what you want. Frame it as working *with* your company, as opposed to against it.

key #3

IN A SALARY NEGOTIATION, DO NOT ASK FOR THE NUMBER YOU WANT

COMPANIES EXPECT YOU to negotiate. Yes, really. They expect to have a conversation with you about compensation, so they will purposefully offer you less than what they actually prepared to pay you. This is true if you're negotiating for a new role or if you're asking for a raise. And fun fact: men are more likely to negotiate when it is ambiguous whether salaries are negotiable. However, in situations where it is clearly stated that salaries are negotiable, the gender gap disappears. If you have felt terrified in the past to ask for more, take solace in the fact that companies are fully expecting to have this conversation—and they're actually *more* shocked if you just accept the first offer. (It may even cause them to view you as less qualified than they thought you were!)

Therefore, when you give your number in a negotiation, make it higher than what you would actually accept. Let me give you an example. If a company has offered you $50K, and you know from market research that you should be getting paid $55K to $58K, do not ask for $58K. If you do, you'll end up at $55K, which is better than when you started, but not your market rate. Ask for $62K to $65K, and then you'll settle somewhere in the middle. (Collaboration, remember?)

YOU'RE INTERVIEWING THEM TOO (AND YOU HAVE JUST AS MUCH POWER AS THEY DO)

IT'S EASY TO BELIEVE that a company holds all the power in a negotiation. Especially when you're doing the scary, vulnerable thing of asking for more, it can feel like the company is the one in control. But the truth is you are interviewing this company or client as much as it is interviewing you—even if you currently work for this organization. You're gathering information about this company, its leaders, its values. And you're then deciding if this is the right place for you.

And when you negotiate, in addition to getting paid your worth, you're also conducting a little test: How will this employer respond to you advocating for yourself? Is this a healthy environment, where the company is willing to have a transparent, give-and-take conversation about your compensation? (That should be the bare minimum, y'all.) Or does it get weird, defensive, and turn the "you should just be grateful to be here" narrative on you?

If a company is not willing to entertain a healthy conversation about your value now, it will be unwilling and unable to do so during the entire time you work together. Ask yourself if this is the environment you want to work in. (Hint: it's probably not.) And although it will be uncomfortable to have a bad experience negotiating, they're doing you a favor. They're showing you what the company is about—believe them.

Both you and the organization you're negotiating with have the same three options. You can accept, counter, or walk away. These are pretty self-explanatory, but you can either accept the offer that's been given, counter the offer with one of your own, or decline. The company has the same three options: accept your counteroffer, counter again, or decline. It doesn't have any option that you don't also have. You need to constantly ask yourself,

Which option is in my best interest right now? These options are a form of agency: you get to decide what you want to do every step of the way.

key #5
A NEGOTIATION IS VERY RARELY ONE CONVERSATION

A SALARY NEGOTIATION in and of itself is a counter: they offered, and you're countering. Typically, both parties counter back and forth until an agreement is reached. I think we all have this fantasy that we can write an email where we ask for more money, the company goes, "Lemme think for two secon— Yes, done!" and it's over. (Because *we* desperately, *desperately* want this to be over). It's that feeling of asking someone out via text, then checking your phone to see if they saw the text, then checking their Instagram to see if they're active, which would mean they *had* to have seen your text, then wanting to call the whole thing off: "I wasn't serious, what a funny joke, LOLZ!" That's because being vulnerable is scary. Instead, a negotiation can take a while.

But just because it's taking a while to hear from the company doesn't mean you fucked it up; Debra from HR may be out sick, or the people in charge might be juggling other projects and also have to go through some bureaucratic shit to approve wage increases. I once worked with a client to help her ask for a raise: from the time she first brought it up to the time her increase finally got approved, *three months had crawled by*. Unfortunately, this isn't unusual, and it is something you might have to remind your boss of—politely but consistently. It will feel weird, but as my mom always says, "The squeaky wheel gets the grease." Take a deep breath: You didn't fuck up. This is normal, and it's all going to work out.

And in the spirit of "this won't be one conversation," let me remind you that you have the same power. You shouldn't feel pressure to respond right away or to accept the first (or second!) offer. Ask for the time you need in order to research, to consult with mentors, to think through your decision. A simple "I'd love to have till Monday to look this over; does that work for you?" will suffice.

What if you come across the rare occasion where they really won't budge on the salary? The good news is that you can still negotiate: PTO, flexible work schedules, health benefits, and so on.

My two favorite things to negotiate are a better job title and an education stipend. I love negotiating a more impressive title because it costs your employer nothing, while setting you up for better opportunities in the future. An education stipend (typically around a few thousand dollars a year) pays for you to take an online course, attend a conference, expand your skill set, and so on. With this stipend, you're not only bettering yourself as an employee at this current company (which benefits your employer) but also beefing up your résumé for the rest of your career.

I advise people to practice negotiating by starting with low-stakes scenarios. (I've been training you like Rocky Balboa throughout this entire book for this moment!) For example, calling your credit card provider to lower your interest rate. If you botch it, you're never going to speak to Brenda from Capital One again. If you have children, you are already a prime negotiator.

I still have to amp myself up before negotiating. I blast Beyoncé and punch the air a couple of times. It's never truly easy; it just gets easier because I know the dance now. It's like ballroom dancing: the first time you go out on the floor to dance, it's going to be terrifying. But when you keep practicing, you'll still get stage fright, but at least now you know the moves to the foxtrot! Keep in mind, it's never going to be a walk in the park, but still, you know how to walk it.

Here's a laundry list of everything you can negotiate for besides salary. Keep in mind that some of these might not be relevant to your particular job or industry.

* Health benefits (or employer-paid coverage)

* 401(k) or similar retirement program or a 401(k) match

* Relocation stipend

* Flex/work-from-home schedule

* Additional PTO days

* Transportation stipend or a public transit card

* Signing bonus

* Annual bonus

* Stock options

* Profit sharing

* Commission on sales

* Health/wellness stipend (such as a gym membership)

* New equipment (like a new laptop)

* Professional development or education stipend (à la a free or discounted bachelor's/master's degree program, or new certification)

* A better title

* Childcare stipend

* Parental leave

Now, there will be some instances where the company will just not budge. And that fucking sucks. (Please make sure you've already asked for more, and that they've actually confirmed they don't have any flexibility.) Here's what you say:

"What sort of goals or metrics do I need to hit in six months in order to be compensated at this level?"

This does a few things. One, it shows, again, that you're willing to work with the company in order to find a compromise. (You'll make these goals together with your boss or potential boss.)

THE THREE TS TO CONSIDER BEFORE STARTING A SIDE HUSTLE

TIME

Time is going to be both your greatest friend and worst enemy. It's easy to think you have more than you do, and overextending yourself could result in poor client or coworker relationships and burnout. When considering adding a source of income, you need to think about the amount of time commitment you're willing to make, as well as how much time you have available. When you're considering time, there are two factors: How much time do you *have,* and how much time do you want to *spend*? You might have ten free hours a week, but do you want to work an extra ten hours on top of your day job?

Here are some questions to consider:

* Do you want the flexibility to choose your own hours and be able to hit Pause on your hustle when life gets crazy?

* Do you want weekends free, or would you be cool working Saturday and/or Sunday?

One easy way to accurately visualize how much time you have is by writing out a typical week's schedule.

Two, it gives you a very specific to-do list to go out and *kill* it. And three, when you inevitably *do* kill it, you get to waltz back into your boss's office with receipts and say, "Money, please!!!!!"

Get this agreement in writing, even if you just send an after-meeting email that says, "Thanks for meeting with me. As a reminder for us both, here's what was outlined." Now you're on your way.

And if they go back on their word then? You know what you're willing to accept and what you're worth. Now is when you would turn to other opportunities—or maybe create your own.

Include your wake-up time, commute, work, kids, gym, social life, and anything else that you do on a weekly basis. Once you're done, it's time to ask the question:

"Where would a side hustle fit in?"

Looking at your weekly schedule, do you see openings where you'd want to work? Do you have obligations that need to be first priority before bringing in a second income?

You may discover that you have more time than you'd thought and want to fill some of it with your side hustle. However, what you (most likely) will discover is that you have way *less* time than you think you do.

If your schedule is already jam-packed, one of two things needs to happen:

1. you need to carve out room in your schedule for a side hustle, or

2. you need to pick a side hustle that fits into your current lifestyle.

Add where you'd fit your hustle in, or make a list of what you'd need to cut back on in order to make it work.

TALENT

Next, it's time to think about what skills you can use to get another source of income.

There are three different approaches to leveraging your side-hustle skills:

1. Use the experience and knowledge gained from your nine-to-five or prior education to start your side hustle.

2. Revisit an old hobby or something you used to do, gain a fresh perspective and up-to-date knowledge on the skills needed to carry it out efficiently, and turn it into a side hustle.

3. Choose a brand-new skill and start learning it from scratch. This takes a little longer, but if it's a skill that really sets your soul on fire, and you're ready to dedicate your time and energy to it, it may be the way to go.

My personal experience followed the first approach: before taking Her First $100K full-time, I was a social media marketing manager. I used the skills that I learned in my day job to do social media contract work on the side and then, later, used my marketing experience to grow Her First $100K into a global business.

However, not everyone loves her day job enough to also consider doing it part-time. Some people want to do something completely different—something that doesn't feel like work. I'm thinking of an accountant who looks at numbers all day and wants to do something more creative. This means you may be better off using skills from a hobby or learning new skills in order to foster that creativity.

Something to note: if you want to learn new skills and get paid for it, you're going to need to put in the time and will likely start at a lower rate of pay than if you were to choose a side hustle for which you already had valuable experience.

TREASURE

The third and final thing to consider when choosing your side hustle is what amount of money you want (or need) to be making. Is your side project going to be a hobby or something you monetize?

* Is the money necessary?

   People can always benefit from earning extra cash. However, if you're someone with high debt or worried about paying bills each month, chances are a side hustle is more of a necessity than a luxury. (Yay, capitalism.)

   If you're looking to start a hustle because you're interested in learning a new skill, gaining a new hobby, or growing a sustainable business, money may not be your first priority (at least not immediately).

* How much money do you bring in each month already, and do you already have a budget?

   Understanding whether a side hustle is necessary means that you already have a good understanding of your current budget. If not, head back to chapter 3.

* Do you need this money now?

   Building a business from the ground up is now more lucrative than, say, a part-time job as a barista, but it takes time. It took me more than three years to see significant profits and growth in my business. I had to be patient, persistent, and consistent. Starting a business from scratch is not the way to go if you're looking to make money immediately. Do you have time to grow something organically, or do you want to make money ASAP?

* Do you want to set your own schedule or take gigs as they are offered?

  Depending on your skill set, experience, and reputation, you can still make a decent amount of money by choosing which projects to take on rather than reflexively accepting every offer that comes your way. However, the more aggressive approach might be preferable when you're getting started, as a way to gain experience and build your portfolio.

For an example of what this might look like:

* **TIME:** Jessica looked at her weekly schedule and found about fifteen free hours that she could use to put toward working a side hustle. She enjoys having flexible hours and prefers to participate in creative activities.

* **TALENT:** Jessica likes her everyday job as a graphic designer and could do it outside of work as well.

* **TREASURE:** Remember that Jessica has credit card debt that she wants to pay off ASAP. She wants to earn extra money as soon as she can in order to focus her Bucket #2 money on other financial goals, like retirement.

Jessica has set a short timeline to pay off her credit cards. She also has a decent amount of time to dedicate to a side hustle. She likes what she currently does for work and wants a flexible schedule. Overall, it sounds like she would do well with a side hustle as a freelance graphic designer.

Alyssa Davies
FOUNDER OF MIXED UP MONEY

I started my career right out of university in marketing and communications. My entry-level position had too much responsibility and terrible pay. It wasn't enough to pay my bills and put money aside, so I lived paycheck to paycheck. I tried being a restaurant server on the side, but my day job was bleeding into my evenings.

I realized that everything I went to school for, even though I loved it, wasn't going to pay me what I needed to get ahead in life. That's a sad realization for many women, especially if they love their careers. I was working at a nonprofit, and it felt like I couldn't both give back and earn a living.

Starting my blog really changed my life. That one side hustle helped me get a new job, because I had built a portfolio that proved my value. Then I turned that side hustle into nine streams of income. Some of them come directly from my work as a writer and content manager, and others are passive, like dividends from my investing portfolio and royalties from my books. These income streams provided me with a sense of financial security I would never have had with my regular job.

One of my biggest values is security, and multiple income streams are my backup plan for my backup plan for my backup plan. That totally comes from anxiety. I grew up with the mind-set that if you're not working, you are not allowed to enjoy your life, and I saw that part of hustle culture for me was rooted in anxiety more than the actual desire to hustle. When I was doing that hustle culture thing, I didn't have any free time. I stopped contacting my friends. I stopped doing all the things I loved, because I felt like the balance wasn't achievable. I realized I needed to make a realistic plan. Otherwise, I'm staring at the wall every night, asking, "Who am I doing this for if I don't get to enjoy anything for myself?"

I had to stop saying yes to everything that came my way, and I set up a list of my values and would ask myself, "Does this new opportunity align with those values?" Because if this is going to take away from my family and my freedom, then it's not worth it. I've finally come into the space where I'm doing only the things I love and can hire people to manage all the boring things I hate.

To build a successful side hustle, you have to have a solid support system. My husband is fully committed to supporting me at home, which is the greatest thing in the world. I'm also really good at compartmentalizing my time. I have a strict schedule to keep myself sane. During the week, I go to the gym at six thirty in the morning; that's my mental health "me time." Then I work from seven to three at my full-time job. I'm completely offline from three to six, which is my family time. And then from six to ten o'clock at night is my side-hustle time. I keep my weekends free for family and friends, so that I can live the life that I want to live. Committing to this schedule is the one thing that gives me the ability to do everything I do.

I incorporated my side hustle to become a business just at the end of last year, and I told myself I was going to stop calling it a side hustle. At this point, it's a full-blown business. To call it a side hustle is doing a disservice to myself.

The biggest questions I get asked about multiple streams of income are from other people who have kids and families, because they don't think it's possible. All that I have to share is you have to start with one at a time and slowly build up your plethora of income streams. There are several types of passive income, and you can choose any mixture of them. You probably have more than you think just by preparing for the future: if you invest or have a high-yield savings account, you already have streams right there!

My best tips are to first start with a natural source. If you already have a full-time job, what's the next option? Are you investing? Do you have a side hustle? Do you have a part-time job? Next:

What is your Why? What's the connection between the financial side and something more meaningful? That's the moment it becomes much easier to control your planning. For me, it's my kids. I'd give up nights and weekends to know they can have the life I want for them. The third tip is to be patient. It's taken me six years to build nine streams of income, and that's amazing, but it took time.

If you need ideas for what kind of side hustle or income stream to start, I recommend writing down every idea you have of how you can make money. From there, ask yourself: How much time will each option take you per week? How much will you make? Then you do the math of time versus money. Does it add up? Does it align with your values?

I cannot say enough that having a side hustle should add to your life, not subtract from it. It should not be in the name of "rise and grind." If a side hustle is contributing to your burnout and is only an option (not a necessity), reevaluate. Not every person wants or needs a side hustle—and at the same time, for many, side hustles are not glamorous choices but rather necessary second or third jobs in order to survive. Passion and necessity are two different things.

As we've spent this chapter discussing, disparities in earning are plentiful and often tied to systemic issues and lack of equitable policies. But one way we can personally move the needle is talking about how much we're earning. It all begins and ends with transparency.

Currently, surveys show that 69 (ayyyeeee) percent of employees find it socially unacceptable to ask coworkers about their salaries. And even more dramatically, those who perceive themselves to be higher relative earners are less willing to reveal their salaries to peers. This is how the status quo is maintained, and unless we start becoming comfortable having these conversations, nothing will change.

Getting comfortable talking about money is the simplest way that we as individuals can make a difference. Look at Moji's story: a simple conversation with her coworkers allowed her and others to realize they were being underpaid and overworked. It gave her the green light she needed to find something better. Talking about our salaries, our freelancer rates, or our benefits allows us to feel less alone.

As an entrepreneur, I have reached out to so many women in the personal finance space and said, "I'm getting pitched by this company to come speak. I was thinking this amount of money; what do you think?" We're all transparent with one another, so, of course, one might go, "Oh, I was paid two thousand dollars more!" We talk hard numbers. We advocate for one another.

Although workplaces will often discourage you from discussing your pay, it is illegal to prohibit you from doing so. Therefore, we *must* discuss our compensation with one another. White women, we must be committed to talking to our colleagues of color. And men, you must be committed to talking to your women coworkers about how much you're making. Your salary, your benefits, your promotions.

This invitation to talk openly about money extends to opportunities too. Open the door to opportunities for your marginalized colleagues. Use your privilege to help others. At the end of press interviews—when I'm interviewed for *Forbes* or CNBC or *Entrepreneur* magazine—I often say, "Let me know if you need help with any future stories, and I can connect you to someone." I have a network of women of color, LGBTQ+ folks, and disabled individuals, and when I offer the reporter my network, I'm connecting those individuals to opportunities that could hopefully change their lives.

If you're looking to start these conversations to learn if you're being compensated fairly, I love the advice of the "over and under" rule: if the person you're talking to doesn't want to divulge her salary, you can ask, "Are you making over or under X amount a year?" So, I could ask a colleague, "Are you making over or under seventy thousand dollars?" and when she says, "Over," I can ask again: "Are you making over or under eighty thousand dollars?" If the response is "Under," I now know she's earning between $70,000 and $80,000 per year.

Lastly, this fight is bigger than you. Like Claire mentioned, we have opportunities to use our collective power to demand better of the folks compensating us. In the past few years, we've seen employment trends such as increased flexibility and remote work, the rise of entrepreneurship during the COVID-19 pandemic, teachers and health care workers going on strike to receive wage increases, and the commitment to unionizing. Just look at recent headlines about the unionization of Starbucks stores. If opportunities to better your and your colleagues' lives don't exist currently, you can create them. When I think about my corporate career—often working for people I didn't respect, making rich men even richer—I knew that I had to create my own opportunities. Now, not only do I make more money than I ever thought possible, but my mental health is better. My business changes women's lives every day. I get to create jobs and opportunities for more than a dozen people, mostly women. There's no better feeling.

HOMEWORK

1. AFFIRMATIONS, BABY

Take an index card or a piece of paper and write an affirmation for you to repeat to yourself as you prepare to negotiate.

It can be as simple as this:

"I am worthy of negotiating," or

"I will choose to advocate for what I know I'm worth."

In the week or even month leading up to negotiation, tape it to your bathroom mirror or stick it in the visor of your car, and repeat the affirmation to yourself every time you see it.

_____

_____

_____

_____

_____

_____

_____

_____

_____

_____

_____

_____

_____

_____

_____

2. **GET YOUR DATA**

Research two sources of salary data. Print them out, highlight the data, and staple them together. (You can also save the data digitally.)

Start a conversation about salary with two different colleagues on LinkedIn or over email. Others you can ask might include previous bosses or coworkers, recruiters, folks you met at networking or industry events, etc.

3. INTERVIEW PREP

Check if the "What is your current salary?" question is illegal in your state. If it's not, start planning how you'll respond if it comes up in the interview, as well as how you'll respond to being asked your desired salary. As a reminder, you don't want to give a number first.

Practice responding with a friend!

To prepare for a scenario where the person you're negotiating with won't budge, create a package deal of other negotiables besides salary.

CHAPTER 7

LIVING A FINANCIAL FEMINIST LIFESTYLE

WHEW. WHAT A WILD RIDE.

I appreciate you sticking with me this entire time, and you deserve the world's biggest chocolate chip cookie, especially if you've already done some of the homework or put the advice into action.

You've already learned so much. You learned that our state of mind, emotions, and childhood impact how we manage our money—and how to work past our emotional hang-ups to start creating a more positive relationship with our finances.

You realize that budgeting does not mean deprivation; instead, you work to make thoughtful, mindful spending decisions to fill your life with things and experiences you love. You know the exact steps in the Financial Game Plan to take care of yourself—including how to save money, pay off debt, and invest in the stock market. Finally, you're equipped with the strategies and mind-set to get paid fairly for work that you're passionate about. What an incredible accomplishment.

But I've also given you a bunch of bleak information and stats about how our economic system is rooted in inequality. Yuck. Once you learn about wealth inequality, as with any injustice in the world, you immediately want to help as many people as you can. You realize how many people are financially struggling—your friends, family, coworkers, random people on the internet—and you feel the intense need to help, whether monetarily or emotionally.

But here's the thing: financial feminism works only if you take care of yourself first. No, that's not selfish. No, that's not greedy. A reminder that, yet again, these are shaming narratives from the patriarchy that weaponize your beautiful altruism, trying to convince you that finding solutions to systemic problems is your responsibility alone rather than the responsibility of powerful decision-makers.

You know how just before takeoff, airplane flight attendants give the safety briefing about how to fasten your seat belt and where your emergency exits are? (Note: they may be behind you.) When they get to the part about oxygen masks, they always remind you: "Put your own mask on before assisting others." Why? Well, if you don't put on your own mask first, you will die trying to help someone else. You both suffer. We want to be able to show up for others, but we can only do that if we're healthy and stable first. We practice Oxygen Mask Finances in this house.

For many, especially women of color, you might have family members who are financially dependent on you. You may have children's college educations to pay for or parents who need caretaking. And when you think about the sacrifices your family made to give you a good life, you want to repay them, take care of them. (Sometimes it's less "want to" than "have to.") I've worked with thousands of women who are their parents' 401(k)s, whose older family members need financial support.

You may feel an intense weight on your heart when you see a global tragedy, when you think about our climate warming at an alarming rate, when a natural disaster strikes. Your impulse to help others is capital-B Beautiful and capital-G Good. However, I need you to make sure you're taking care of yourself first. You can't pour from an empty cup. I promise that sacrificing your own needs for someone else's, even a loved one, will cause bitterness and stress. Sacrificing your retirement funds to pay for your kids' college will only lead to them paying for your retirement later. Sacrificing your emergency savings to help build someone else's only ends up leaving you strapped. You *must* put on your own oxygen mask before helping others.

I want you to take a deep breath. Seriously, it's cheesy, but please do it. I'll wait. I kindly remind you that there's only so much we can control. I kindly remind you that you've got lots of time to improve your financial situation, and if you're feeling overwhelmed, go back to the start of the book and try again.

It's going to be tempting to try to do everything all at once, and while that's beautifully optimistic, and I love the enthusiasm, I don't want you to sabotage yourself. It's like trying to put together a morning routine when you've never had one: it's hard enough to start waking up early, let alone adding yoga, drinking sixteen ounces of water, journaling, and making a healthy breakfast. Trying to do too much can overwhelm you to the point where you do nothing at all. Get started by working on just one thing. Do one activity from this book, then another, and another. Slowly and steadily work through the homework assignments one at a time.

I wrote this chapter especially as a place to turn to when you need some encouragement or guidance. I taught you the basic steps, and now this chapter will teach you how to practice those steps in your everyday life for the rest of your life.

Managing personal finance is a skill we'll need for forever—I mean, it's not like this book magically solves the Global Inequality Also Capitalism Sucks Crisis. So, what's next? Where do you go from here? How do you not only set financial goals but also stay the course in order to achieve them? How do you use your money as a source for good? When shit hits the fan, how do you keep going? How do you turn financial feminism from a concept into a lifestyle? Answer: a sustainable financial self-care practice.

Now, *self-care* has become a bit of a buzzword. There's nothing wrong with relaxing with a face mask and a glass of wine, but that version of self-care is a commodified, commercialized one. "Treat yo' self" is not actual self-care. It's self-soothing. The difference is that such activities help us feel better *in the moment*—like a bandage, they're temporary fixes to smaller problems.

Self-care, on the other hand, is the hard shit: the habits that must be repeated consistently over time in order to see change. It's the thing that Present You does, often begrudgingly, in order for Future You to feel better. Things such as meditating, eating a salad when you don't want to eat a motherfucking salad (Pity Salad, babyyyyy), having a hard conversation with a friend, working out, and, yes—you knew this was coming—looking after your money. I love the bubble baths and the face masks as much as the next person, but true self-care (going to therapy, setting boundaries, saving money) is hard and valuable work. *This* is the kind of self-care that makes you a less stressed, more self-assured person.

Every time I go on a trip, the day before is utter chaos. I'm checking my travel information, running last-minute errands, and asking the travel gods to allow me to fit everything I need into my carry-on (it never works). How many pairs of underwear do I need? Did I remember my phone charger? Where can I hide my vibrator so that the TSA agents won't see it? And every single time, I have an internal battle as I run around my house: whether to clean the kitchen before I leave. For whatever reason, asking myself to clean the kitchen on top of all the travel stress feels like the fucking worst thing in the world. I'd rather pluck my eyelashes than clean that goddamn kitchen. But I do it. I grab my sponge, and I fucking do it. And you know what happens? When my trip is over, when I'm exhausted from traveling, and I unlock the door to my house, I come home to a clean kitchen, and it's the best. I am most thankful ever to Past Me for having taken twenty minutes to wipe down the counters.

The financial self-care practice I use in my own life and with clients is what I like to call a Money Date.

THE MONEY DATE

MY BEST FRIEND, Kristine, and her boyfriend have scheduled times to discuss their relationship: instead of opening a can of emotional worms five minutes before one of them leaves for work or allowing things to fester unresolved, they sit down during their designated time and chat about how their relationship is going. It's like a (loving) performance review, discussing what they want to continue doing and how they can also better support each other. It's an amazing practice in being a fully present and caring partner. They work together to solve any conflict and to celebrate their relationship. Just the mere fact that the two of them schedule this time in the first place shows that they are committed to bettering their relationship through open communication.

This is what we're going to do with our money.

The Money Date is a nonnegotiable period of time where you practice some financial self-care. My money and I sit down, and we have a conversation, just like in any relationship. I ask my money, "What can I do better in this relationship? What am

I doing well to reach my financial goals, and what could be improved? Am I making thoughtful, mindful spending decisions? Am I working hard at my job and making a fair wage in order to set myself up for success (and a raise)? Am I investing in Future Me as much as Present Me? Do my current habits support the lifestyle I want?"

And I demand the same of my money. Is my money working hard for me? Could it be generating profits in a Roth IRA instead of earning no interest in a checking account? Is there a great credit card sign-up offer to take advantage of? Is there a bill I can negotiate down or a subscription I can cancel?

We use the Money Date to make sure we hit our goals and sometimes to recalibrate those goals. We also make time for intimate moments with our money to see progress toward those goals: to applaud ourselves and say, "I paid off a thousand-dollar debt last month!" or "My investments increased by five hundred bucks!"

Getting your financial shit together once is a *huge* accomplishment, but staying consistent is the thing that *keeps* your financial shit together for the long term. Just like you can't go on one run or eat one head of broccoli and suddenly be healthy for the rest of time, being financially healthy works only if you're committed to it.

If the idea of reviewing your finances critically terrifies you, you're definitely not alone. So, we're going to make this as comfortable for you as possible. Make your Money Date something you can look forward to. I pour myself a whiskey, wrap myself in a down comforter cocoon, and bribe myself with my favorite Indian takeout. Like all self-care, it's an act of love for yourself, and it should feel as "date-y" as you're comfortable with. Yes, I often light candles. Let's make it *sexyyyyy*.

If you are managing money with a partner, make this a literal date. This is your time to sit down, reflect, and set goals. We want to use money as a tool to build the life that you want together.

When my wife, Nicole, and I got married, we both made a decent income combined (a little over six figures), and we were spending all of it. We were in our late twenties, having a lot of fun and enjoying ourselves—and that's what you're supposed to do anyway. Then we learned that we were going to bring Zoey into the world, and something shifted in my brain. I started thinking, *What can I do to give my daughter a great life, and have her enjoy some of the pleasures we've been able to enjoy?* For me, that question became financial: "What can I do to help us get into a better financial position so she doesn't see Mom and Dad fighting about money as much as we saw our parents do? So that she doesn't worry as much about big student loans like we had to deal with?" That's really when we started to pay more attention to our money.

Originally, I was numbers driven: interested in paying off debt, growing our net worth, and becoming a millionaire—because wouldn't that be cool? That didn't mean a lot to Nicole. The conversation that inspired her was about owning more of her time. She wasn't excited about her job and wanted to eventually become a stay-at-home mom. Those conversations around owning our time became conversations around owning and controlling our money. Nicole was more about the emotional benefits of owning your time and being able to define who you want to be as an individual and as a parent. That's what inspired her and eventually inspired me.

The emotional side of what money can do became very important to us. What do we care about as a couple? What do we stand for? How do we allow our money to help drive us toward those values and goals? That was the process of crafting our budget. Are our expenditures helping us move toward goals and values that we're excited about? Or are they distractions, things we don't care about that much?

We're not about deprivation in our family—we love having fun, and we put vacations at the top of the list. But we also want to help our kids have a great life. We put a lot of our money toward kids' activities, as well as helping them get a good leg up on college when it's time. These became our family values, so we set our budget as a couple to make those goals happen.

As a household money nerd, of course I wanted to look at our finances weekly, but monthly was what we stuck to. I tried to make it fun when we got together: calling it a "budget party," ordering a pizza, having some wine. We wouldn't just talk about the numbers; we would talk about our life goals, the things that excited both of us, like "Wouldn't it be great if you're able to work twenty hours on that job? How about zero hours in the next few years after that?"

But eventually, after Nicole had been a stay-at-home mom for a while, she was like, "Get me out of this situation. I want to work part-time again." Right now she's finding that balance, and it's really because we've set those intentional times to sit down and talk about what we care about now and what we care about in our short-term future. Those goals can change all the time. That's life, and that's okay.

Our kids have chores because we want them to have some contribution in the house. We give them $1 for every year that they've lived, so ten-year-old Zoey gets $10 a week for her hard work, and my seven-year-old son, Calvin, gets $7 a week.

We split up that money among fun, saving, investing, and giving. Those four categories are really important to us, and we have conversations about them once a quarter, after the money's piled up in their electronic jars. We talk about what's going on in the world and about how they can help. The Russian invasion of Ukraine is a high topic in our house right now. Calvin and I recently discussed him donating his "give" money to help the children fleeing their homes. He's really inspired by giving. Zoey is definitely coming along on the giving side, but her heart leans more toward "I want to have some fun today with this money. What can I use it for?"

Learning the investing side of things is going to take a little bit longer to happen, but over time the kids are going to understand the power of compounding and how that can work in their favor. They can use their money for college, or maybe a big adventure or something like that when they're in their early twenties. They're going to be happy that Mom and Dad started those things early, and when they turn eighteen or nineteen or twenty, they can decide how much they want to adopt all the things that we advised them to do.

Wanting to increase your net worth and become debt free are all great, tangible ways for you to track your progress, but it really needs to come back to what you want out of life. Maybe when you're in your teens or early twenties, you don't know what you want, but having space, time, and freedom to make those choices and learn who you want to be is when you make those discoveries—and you can do that only when you control your money. By controlling your money, you can control your time.

We're going to do a few things during this Money Date.

First up: you're going to look at your spending, so pull up those credit/debit card statements. Here's what you're looking for: forgotten subscriptions that you almost never use anymore, fraud, unrecognized charges, and double charges. Part of your Money Date will be devoted to canceling those unused subscriptions, reporting any fraud, and making plans to return unused items.

You'll also use this time to audit your purchases. Remember the money diary, in which we analyze whether our purchases bring us joy as well as reflect our lifestyle and our financial goals? We're also going to keep a mini-money diary, but this time, in retrospect. As you go through the charges, ask yourself how you feel about the purchases you made in hindsight. It could be along the lines of "Hell, yeah, I loved eating at that restaurant," or "I bought this coat, and I've worn it almost every day since." On the other hand, you might come across a charge on your statement and think, *I don't even* remember *what this was for!* or *I don't love that Sephora spending spree when I had a bad day.* As always, this should be done without judgment or shame. Just analyze your spending, applaud yourself for thoughtful spending decisions, and learn from regrets if necessary.

The second practice for your Money Date is to check on your progress with your goals. In chapter 1, I asked you to picture how your life would be different if you achieved everything you wanted financially; then in chapter 3, you set specific money goals you felt good about, using the Financial Priority List as a guide.

1. **Starter emergency fund (three months of living expenses in a high-yield savings account).**

1.5. *Only if applicable:* **Contribute as much as needed to your 401(k) or 403(b) retirement savings account so that your employer matches that contribution.**

2. **Pay down high-interest debt (anything with interest over 7 percent).**

3. **Invest for retirement, while simultaneously paying down low-interest debt (anything with interest less than 7 percent).**

4. **Save for the Big Life Stuff.**

Now you're going to look at your account balances as a whole to see where you are with your goals. Pull up your checking accounts, savings accounts, debt accounts, and so on. If you're on a company 401(k) or 403(b), you might also want to look at your pay stubs for a clearer look at your retirement account contributions.

If you're working on filling up your emergency fund, have you made the monthly contributions that you set out to do? If you've filled up your emergency fund and have a 401(k) or 403(b) match, are you contributing enough to get the match? How about your high-interest debt? Do you have a plan to pay it off? And what about other big life goals, such as buying a house or having kids or starting a business?

That first part of checking in on your goals is metrics driven: you're looking at how much money went toward these goals. But this is also a time to *emotionally* reconnect with your goals. Maybe you're feeling motivated and excited—how do you keep that feeling going? Or, more than likely, you may be disconnected from your goals. Maybe you're feeling defeated by how much debt you still have, and the stock market is down, so are these contributions even worth it? Maybe you're not sure why you even need an emergency fund, and why can't you just skip ahead and save for Paris instead?

My goal of having $100,000 at age twenty-five was, yes, about seeing the $100K number. I'm a very numbers-driven person. But when I had to quit my toxic job without another lined up, I thought about giving up. Not only was I not earning any money, but also I was depleting my emergency fund and not saving anything. But I thought about what that $100K meant for me, for my life, for what I wanted. It meant the financial flexibility to make what felt like a risky decision: quit my corporate job to take my business full-time and do work that I was passionate about and that had a direct impact on my success rather than some corporation's bottom line. I could travel when I wanted and where I wanted. I could change lives and give people jobs and start a global movement. And I cared about all of that *way* more than I cared about the numbers.

Connecting with your Why is something you'll need when it's getting tough and you're feeling stressed or anxious, down or defeated. You'll come back to your goals—and more important, why you created them—and use that as motivation to move forward. (Go back to chapter 3 if you need a refresher.)

So, if you're currently on step "put $300 in an HYSA every month," and you hate it there, think about why you're doing it (flexibility, being able to grow wealth, etc.). Why do you want to pay down debt, or save an emergency fund, or get paid more? Will it help you be able to buy a house? Allow you to save for that vacation you've always wanted to take? Give you the salary you need to fund your own business?

It's okay if you missed your monthly target. There are going to be days when you overspend and months where you can't save any money. There are going to be times when you have to take on debt. And there are going to be periods of your life where you're cursing my name and wondering if you can keep going. That is normal and completely okay. We're not aiming for perfection, we're aiming for progress. The goal is not constant, upward movement but consistency. The goal is that you offer yourself grace and understanding for when things don't go your way, that you learn what you can and then keep going.

Even if you are on track, it's still a good idea to reflect honestly about how you're feeling about your goals. If you decided you wanted to pay off your credit card debt within the year, and you're finding you're depriving yourself too much, maybe it's time to ease off. I'd rather it took you three extra months than a shorter, miserable amount of time where you're more likely to burn out and give up. If you're on track, and you're comfortable with your daily spending, how about challenging yourself and increasing your Bucket #2 contributions?

The third and final part of this Money Date involves planning and optimization. Now that you've reflected on and reconnected with your goals, what do you need to tweak? Maybe you've decided you can put more money toward your financial goals, and it's time to increase your automated HYSA deposits, credit card payments, or investments. Maybe you discovered recently that a coworker with the same experience earns more than you, and it's time to do some salary range research. Maybe you just crossed something off the Financial Priority List, and it's time to move on to the next challenge.

This is also the time to take care of some financial tasks that you've been putting off but that you just need to suck it up and do, like taking the twenty minutes to finally open up a high-yield savings or retirement account, or filing your taxes (yuck).

Then it's time to optimize. Would another bank account be better suited to your needs? Do you need to raise your freelancer rates? Can you increase your retirement contributions by a few percentage points?

Finish off with a clear plan for next month. Based on insights from this Money Date, what are you planning to change? What's your new budget? What is your intention with regard to spending? Give yourself three action items that you can implement in between dates.

Once we've concluded our Money Date, it's important to schedule the next one. I like to do my Money Dates on a Sunday night. Seriously, put it on your calendar—make it nonnegotiable. These should happen monthly at a minimum, but more frequently if you're chasing a particular goal or if you're in a hard spot financially. For me, as a business owner who needs to be on top of my shit, I look at both my personal and business finances every week and then have larger, goal-setting Money Dates (again, both personal and professional) once a month.

Life gets so crazy. Whether you're single or partnered, it can feel like you just don't have time to sit down and look at money. Set a specific time and date to combat this. Make it a commitment.

MONEY DATE STEPS

1. Look at your spending: pull your statements and conduct an audit.

2. Set or check in on your goals. What's your Why behind them? What do your account balances say about your progress?

3. Create a plan to achieve your goals. What kinds of systems do you need to set up? Any optimization needed?

Remember that when it comes to money, it's not a mere diet but a full lifestyle change. When you are just trying to stay afloat, it can be stressful to figure out how to keep going, especially when you run into roadblocks such as losing your job, an emergency cropping up, or if you're not on track to your goals anymore. There might be times when you aren't able to save any money or pay down debt.

Emotionally and psychologically, this is where offering yourself grace becomes an absolute nonnegotiable. Shame and judgment have no place in personal finance *ever*, but especially not when you're struggling. Speak to yourself kindly. When I have the temptation to be hard on myself, I force myself to do a full 180 and make my internal voice ridiculously comforting. (It typically manifests itself as Paddington, because I cannot bear—*OMG, that pun came out of nowhere!*—to make him say something rude to me. It just isn't right.) Surround yourself with love, support, and understanding. It may be bad now, but it won't be bad forever.

Like most things worth doing, getting good with money is a lifelong practice that requires patience and a deep amount of grace for yourself. It's a habit that you build over time, through accountability and consistency. It's about maintenance.

Debt Free Guys (John and David)

HOSTS OF THE *Queer Money Podcast*

JOHN: We started Debt Free Guys because we found ourselves in $51,000 of credit card debt.

DAVID: When we were just starting to get out of debt, we had a combined thirteen years working in financial services.

JOHN: We had all the theoretical knowledge, and we were telling people how to apply it to their lives, but we weren't applying it to our own lives. I would argue that for much of our adult lives, we were living in blissful ignorance. We knew how much credit card debt we had, but we continued to ignore it until we were in Winter Park, Colorado, one weekend and started talking about buying land and building a modern home to vacation in up there. We finally got honest about our finances, and it hit us that we couldn't even afford to go up there for the weekend, let alone buy land and build a house. Then we're like, "Why can't we do the things we want to do?" We realized that if we were going to continue on the path we were on, we would never get to a different destination than the one already projected for us.

DAVID: Getting out of debt for us was just the first part of making financial progress, but we knew that still wasn't going to get us to where our true financial goals were. Even after we got rid of our $51,000 in credit card debt, about a year later, we had $6,000 in credit card debt again.

JOHN: Paying off the debt was our destination, but we didn't realize that's actually not the real destination, because this is a lifelong journey.

DAVID: A lot of people will make changes to their lives to get out of debt, hoping that they can go back to the life that they had before. But in reality, if they go back to the life they had before, they're going to go back to the debt they had before. It was during that discovery process of why we got into credit card debt that we truly landed on *why* we wanted to go where we wanted to go. We wanted a safe and comfortable retirement. We wanted to spend more time together, and we wanted to give back to the LGBTQ+ community.

JOHN: That's one of the first questions we try to tackle: "What is your goal, and why is that your goal?" It took us years to really peel back that onion and get to the truth. What we really wanted in life is what David said: to be able to live, have a comfortable retirement, give back to the community, and travel. But we also had to ask ourselves, "What got us to this particular point in time?" That was a whole other onion to peel. We realized that we were making up for pain and neglect from our childhoods, and the desperate need to fit into society. So we had to ask ourselves, "Do we want to fit in more than we want to spend more time together? Do we want to make up for past trauma with great jeans as opposed to having a secure retirement?"

The way you fight the Ostrich Effect is to figure out what it is that you *truly* want. If you truly want that, then you'll do whatever it takes to get there. If you're not willing to make the change to get where you think you want to go, then maybe that's not what you truly want. That might be a sign that you're letting society or your family or somebody else dictate what happiness means to you.

DAVID: Personal finances need to fit into who you are personally. Your personality and who you are really dictate how you spend your money. There are some people who are 100 percent comfortable staying at home and others who just have to go out. Some people don't like to travel. What drives *you* should be where you're spending your money.

JOHN: I think a lot of times when we start to consume personal finance content, we feel like we have to be perfect. It's not about how fast you can go or how far you can go. It's about that consistency. If you find yourself backsliding financially, give yourself some grace. The most financially astute people make the most egregious finance mistakes. I used to do compliance for financial services, and I can't tell you how many financial advisors had bankruptcies, delinquencies, and liens. We kind of think that everybody else has got it all figured out, and they don't. Even David and I today, we make all sorts of mistakes with our finances. Give yourself some grace to know that everybody else is making mistakes. The second step is to own the fact that you made the mistake and figure out what you need to do to correct it or to adapt. Then come up with whatever your plan B is.

In practicality, what happens when shit *does* hit the fan? What happens if you lose your job, or you get sick, or there's a global pandemic? How do you actually motivate yourself to invest money for Future You even though you won't see this money for another thirty years or so? How do you actively continue to be temporarily uncomfortable in the pursuit of a healthy relationship with money? And how do you keep this up for the rest of your life?!

Remember when we chatted about the Ostrich Effect? Guess what: this impulse doesn't just magically go away. This temptation to avoid, to numb, to ignore, to act like your money doesn't exist—this comes back full force when shit gets hard. But this is exactly when you can't afford to look away.

In times of crisis, we turn to the emergency fund. This is why we start with our savings first. It's there for a reason: to sustain you for a period of time until you're back on your feet. For example, if you were in the middle of paying off your credit card debt, then lost your job, you'll press Pause on the Game Plan. You'd rely on your emergency fund while you work to find employment again, with your Bucket #2 money going toward your living expenses (and eventually toward filling your emergency fund). If things are really doomsday—you've already used your emergency fund or you don't have one—and you're wondering what to do, a credit card with the lowest interest rate is your next best bet. (Many folks can qualify for zero percent interest for a period of time.)

Staying on track in an ever-changing, ever-developing world is hard—and, like we talked about, our finances, as personal as they are, are also subject to social factors. Sometimes, when other people get involved in our finances, we can veer off track. This can be as simple as your friends inviting you to an expensive dinner that you feel obligated to go to, or as serious as a family member falling ill and needing care. The ability to set boundaries—and again, put on our own oxygen mask first before running to help others—is an evergreen commitment and muscle that we build.

Making personal finance social and collaborative can also mean having a better relationship with money (and with one another). We can allow our relationships to give us accountability, support, and guidance when it comes to our financial goals.

Once oxygen is flowing through our masks—we're financially stable and on track to hit our goals—it's time for the other half of the bargain: helping others.

When I give live workshops, I often end them with a plea: you have the information now to put to use in your life, but you must then share it with someone who needs it. We sign an unseen contract when we take on the work to be financial feminists: we are obligated to pass on this information as well as to use it to change the world—or, at the very least, the piece of the world that's ours.

A word from
Simran Kaur
COHOST OF *Girls That Invest*

I've heard as women we learn through communication with each other. We will gauge something through "How does this thing work?" or "Did you like that pair of jeans that you bought? Do you trust that company? Okay, maybe I'll go look into it too." We really care about the views and opinions of the women around us.

In twenty years of friendship with Sonya Gupthan, my cohost for our podcast *Girls That Invest,* we never spoke about money, never spoke about income or how much we invested. We both loved personal finance, but I didn't realize how good she was with her money because she just walks around like a normal person. One day we spoke about money, and it really just opened the floodgates and made us realize that there was so much to learn from each other. In all honesty, talking with each other has helped elevate our finances. I think that's probably one of the actionable steps that I would want to give someone if they were starting out. It's uncomfortable, but ask your friends out for brunch and have a conversation. Say: "I want to share my goals around money, and I want to share that I started investing, and this is what I invest in."

There will be some friends (from my experience) that are a little bit uncomfortable. They're not there yet, and that's okay. They're allowed to walk away from that conversation. You'll find, though, that most people do engage, and they want to talk. That has helped me so much, because if someone sits down with me and goes, "This is how I bought a home," or "This is what a mortgage process is," then I know if she can do it, I can do it.

Make those conversations about money into long-term goals when you're speaking with your friends. "I want to retire early," "I want to do this with my life," and "I want to build generational wealth" are all the topics that we tend to see women talk about. If you share those types of goals, maybe you want to meet up in a monthly or quarterly fashion, where you sit down with your friends and review goals and what you've learned.

I think accountability buddies make it so much more fun, but also you realize that other people are human too. A friend would share that she ordered from Uber Eats, and it cost her a lot of money. I'd tell her, "You know what, I wasted a bit of money here and there too." It's like hearing your friend got a bad grade, and you say, "I got one too. It's not the end of the world. Let's just get back on track."

When I bring up the topic of money with a certain friend, I lead with vulnerability. If I go in and share what my goals and dreams are, I think that kind of gets them thinking, then they feel like, "Well, if she can share it, I'll happily share." If you go in with questions for them, then that can feel like a bit of an interrogation. You've got to be careful; you don't know what someone's been through. You might have a friend whose parents have secretly been bankrupt at one point, and they don't want to open up about that. It's about you leading with vulnerability and allowing them to have space to open up too, and then you can start sharing. It's a step-by-step process.

When you approach these conversations, it's helpful to accept that if this person wants to talk to you about it, they will open up. There have definitely been experiences where I've had a friend say to me point-blank, "I'm uncomfortable talking about money. This is not for me." That's totally fine—I'd rather them be honest about that. Still, I think it's important to ask your friends without being scared of them saying no, because it's not like we stop be friends afterward. It's just a no, and we can keep moving.

Talking to friends and family keeps me accountable. I tend to have those Money Dates with myself and review finances, then Sonya and I meet every quarter. It's just about finding what works for you.

In sharing your experiences, you're going to learn so much from each other, because friends are going to make mistakes, and you're going to make mistakes. If you learn from them, then maybe you won't make them as bad or as often. If you collaborate, you'll rise up so much faster together than if you're just trying to do this on your own. I really view managing money as like going to the gym. When you start off at the gym, it's the same concept as when you start caring about your money: it's intimidating, it's hard, and you don't want to do it. Sometimes you'll fall off and you won't go for a month, but it doesn't mean that you should never go back to the gym again; it just means you'll just start over. It's the same thing with money. I think it's naive for anyone to assume that from now on she's going to have a perfect money journey and a perfect experience. Allow yourself to make mistakes and be kind to your future self but also your past self. I think a lot of people that come into these communities say, "I used to have debt," or "I made that bad job mistake." It's okay that you did that. Forgive yourself. You're allowed to have a better future, even if the past wasn't so good.

Normalize talking about money. Make it as simple as sharing your skin-care routine. That's the kind of world I'd like to live in. In many places, money means the ability to have choices. It's your ability to choose the life you want, and if you can do that, if your friends can do that, and if your family can do that, what better way is there to live?

Her First $100K has been a small part in that change. Every five minutes, we get a message from a woman somewhere in the world, sharing her money win with us—"I negotiated a twenty-thousand-dollar raise!" "I paid off my student loans!" "I opened my Roth IRA!"—and how our advice made a difference for her. "I'm so much more confident in every aspect of my life now" is my favorite kind of DM.

Yet at the same time, whenever I consider systemic oppression, I think about how big and overwhelming the system is, and how I'm just one person. For every person I've helped negotiate salary, pay off debt, and start investing, there's someone who has fallen victim to predatory financial practices. There's someone living paycheck to paycheck, someone (especially those of color) who has been unsupported and fucked over by a country that is supposedly "the best in the world."

As just one person with her own challenges (yet who has buckets and buckets of privilege), I wonder: How can I possibly do anything to change something that is so much bigger than me?

But isn't that all we can do? Acknowledge our own privilege, take care of ourselves, and fight against injustice? Either we become paralyzed or we act. "I alone cannot change the world," Mother Teresa said, "but I can cast a stone across the waters to create many ripples." And one of my favorite quotes, from anthropologist Margaret Mead: "Never doubt that a small group of thoughtful, committed citizens can change the world; indeed, it's the only thing that ever has."

I hope you feel the same obligation, and that you see your ability to practice financial self-care and get your shit together as part of that bigger quest to improve our world a little bit at a time, because here's the thing: money runs the world. When we consider our current societal and political climate, money means power. Money means influence. Elections are bought by corporations and m(b)illionaires, who are overwhelmingly straight, cisgender white men and can force political issues dismissing women, people of color, disabled individuals, and LGBTQ+ folks. In a 2018 New York Times piece entitled "Money Is Power. And Women Need More of Both," New York City's deputy mayor for housing and economic development pointed out: "Political power is ephemeral. People can just wait you out. But if you're the richest person on the planet, there's no waiting you out." On the individual level, men are donating the most money to political campaigns, despite a record number of women donors for the Hillary Clinton presidential campaign in 2016.

Yes, these issues are often bigger than us as individuals. But a group of individuals coming together is what sparks change. Getting more money into more women's hands is the key to bridging the inequality gap. I've said it a million times, and I'll say it a million more: a financial education is a woman's best form of protest. Having money means having options—the option to live our lives abundantly, restfully, and fruitfully. And when we're financially stable, we then get to use our money as a force for change.

A word from
Tanja Hester

FINANCIAL EXPERT AND AUTHOR OF *Wallet Activism: How to Use Every Dollar You Spend, Earn, and Save as a Force for Change*

I wrote *Wallet Activism* because I wanted to read *Wallet Activism*. I wanted to take a more complicated look at the economy and our choices and how they manifest. Everything else I read was dumbed down out of fear of telling the whole and complex truth and thinking that people would just run away when faced with that truth. I don't see that. I believe millennials and Gen Z want to engage with substance. They *want* to know the whole picture and then make an informed decision. I think you can trust people to handle the whole truth, and that was really my point of view on it—even if it is complicated.

When writing the book, I focused on how we tell that truth and, at the same time, created a system for readers to make choices that feel doable. In the book, when I'm talking about making more ethical purchasing decisions, I offer these four framing questions:

1. **WHAT IS THE PRICE OF THIS ITEM TELLING YOU?** Is it too cheap? When it comes to getting a good deal, we rarely think, *If that price is really low, does that tell me that people were absolutely exploited? If it's a physical product, is the*

low price telling me that the workers could not possibly be paid a living wage? I'm trying to retrain your mind to think differently about deals.

2. WHO IS THIS FOR? I have a line in the book, "If your activism has an aesthetic, it's probably performative." Activism doesn't have an aesthetic. A solution like going completely zero waste or 100 percent vegan isn't likely to be impactful because few people can do it. Solutions like these feel so strict because they often imply perfection or nothing.

3. WHAT OR WHOM AM I FUNDING? It's important to keep perspective here. Eating at Chick-fil-A two times a year, even though it supports bad causes, is not as impactful as buying a Tesla or the thousands of dollars we spend at Amazon. Look at the political donations companies make, learn where they source their materials and labor—do they use conflict minerals? Do they use forced labor?

4. CAN EVERYONE DO THIS? Are the solutions we're proposing accessible to people beyond just those who have a lot of extra money to spend? Assuming that the Patagonia clothing company is perfect—which it's not—does it make sense to tell everyone that the solution is to buy only Patagonia clothes and other brands with extremely high ethical standards? Absolutely not, because Patagonia is expensive and will never be accessible to most people. We need to focus on solutions that are accessible, and often the most accessible solution is simply to buy less. That's good for your finances, good for the climate, and good for the exploited workers who make most of the things we buy.

Wallet activism goes beyond purchasing—it's how you earn money, how you conduct yourself in the workplace, where you choose to live, how you save and invest, how you give money away—all of it.

So much advice out there is so privileged and privilege blind, it doesn't recognize that most people can afford to shop only at Amazon and Walmart. If you need to shop at Amazon or Walmart, you can make a difference by refusing to shop at peak periods, like Black Friday or around Prime Day. On days around these "big sale events," employee injuries go through the roof, both in stores and warehouses, because people are under pressure and stressed. So much of the workforce abuse happens around these times. You'll even see workers being refused bathroom breaks.

When you're practicing wallet activism, it's easy to get discouraged and think, *No big corporation is even going to miss my purchases—how can I make a difference?* People forget that if corporate profits dip 3 percent, companies pay big attention and start asking why. If a particular product that's been doing well starts selling less, by even a tiny percent—a single digit— they listen.

This is important specifically to women because we control small finance. On the purchasing level, I know the stat is that women control 55 percent, but it's closer to 80 to 90 percent in terms of day-to-day purchases. The idea that you have to have some massive market swing, and everyone has to change her ways to get anyone to notice, is completely the wrong way to look at it, which makes me hopeful. We could make these marginal changes and have companies start to change their practices.

Changing your spending is not a diet, it's a lifestyle. If it feels like you're giving up all the stuff you love to try to do the right thing, you're not going to stick with that long term. When confronted with changing spending, I start people with a values exercise. I ask them to figure out the missions and the values they care about most, then we put together a money mission statement. This gives them a framework to say, "I don't buy XYZ anymore because _____."

Giving yourself a system makes these changes more sustainable, and it doesn't use any additional willpower. I don't want people going to the store and feeling frozen because capitalism compromises everything. Instead, how do you create a system that you can actually do?

I think about that with my own savings journey. It was built on always hiding money from myself, because if I have money, I will spend it. However, if it's not visible, I don't spend it. I started this habit with $50 out of every paycheck and then grew that amount. Everything is progressive: the more you make a habit of your goals in a small way, the easier it is to build up to it being something big. People tend to learn a lot and very quickly, and then they think, *Oh my God, this is so horrible—I have to do everything*! It's not a sustainable way to go.

It's important to start slow. "I'm going to not buy anything packaged in number five plastic because that's not recyclable," or "I'm going to do a lot of research and cut out anything that is produced with forced child labor" is a great place to start. Whatever that starting point is for you, start there, and then over time, once you feel comfortable with that, add something else.

Start small and build from there.

Take a deep breath. Remember that you don't have to take on all of this by yourself. You cannot consume every piece of media, have nuanced conversations with every single living person, or give the clothes off your back. Just commit to doing what you can, when you can, how you can. Just like when we follow the Financial Game Plan, where we start with one goal at a time, we have to do the same in life. You pick the thing you are sustainably able to do, then, hopefully, your financial situation changes such that you're able to do more things at once (like invest for retirement and save for more goals).

A word from
Debt Free Guys (John and David)

HOSTS OF THE *Queer Money Podcast*

JOHN: One of our biggest challenges in our business is that a lot of folks in our community feel a level of guilt if they have financial security. They feel like having abundance is immoral because the only way you can acquire that is if you step on other people's backs; you've done some evil deed to get there. We see so many people in the community who want to start or have already started a small business, but they're so focused on trying to be able to donate a certain percentage of their revenue or income to LGBTQ+ causes that they can lose traction in their business. Often, they're asking for a Kickstarter or GoFundMe campaign and trying to use that as their seed money to grow their business, while they use their own revenue donating to causes. We're trying to get out the message that you need to make your business secure and sustainable in order to have the overflow effect from your coffee cup.

I remember how we'd go to these beautiful charity galas with great music, food, people, and wine, looking fabulous in our fancy suits. Of course, there's the point in the evening where they ask you to donate money, and nobody wants to be the one that doesn't raise their hand. And if you're gonna raise your hand, you want to give a substantial amount.

We would give to these organizations and causes, but we couldn't actually afford it. We wanted to be helpful, but we also wanted to make sure people saw that we were giving so that we wouldn't be judged negatively. In the whole course of that experience, we weren't really helping the community, because we put ourselves in a worse financial position.

Now we're in a much better place where we can donate to causes and donate to them more consistently, so they can expect those donations and plan accordingly. We're not also hurting ourselves anymore.

THE FOUR *DS*

IN PONDERING HOW to actually practice financial feminism in our daily lives, I organized my thoughts into four main areas of action, or what I'm calling the Four *D*s: discussion, donation, decision, and development.

DISCUSSION

IF THIS BOOK has encouraged you to do anything, I hope it's challenged you to talk more openly about money. Talking about our financial situations is the only way we overcome the shame and fear that we've experienced our entire lives, and it allows us to create a better relationship with money and with one another.

In challenging the "talking about money is impolite" narrative, we turn something taboo into something typical. I've said it a billion times, but it is worth repeating: the narrative that "talking about money is gauche" is a story perpetuated by the patriarchy to keep us underpaid and overworked. It keeps us controllable and playing small. So, if we can start talking about our salaries, talking about our debt, talking about investing being intimidating, talking about our hopes and dreams and fears for the future—everything starts to change.

Talking about money also allows us to better understand the world around us: becoming aware of the experiences of others, making one another feel less alone, and holding space for stories and journeys that differ from our own. I'm beyond grateful for the times in my life that someone has felt brave enough to share their experience or thoughts with me—these different perspectives have changed my worldview more times than I can count.

So how do you go about broaching conversations about money in a world that treats them as taboo? My trick is offering vulnerability first. This can look like:

* "What was the first time you remember thinking about money?"

* "I'm really stressed about my debt; can I talk to you about it?"

* "I just paid off my student loans and want to celebrate. Want to grab dinner with me?"

* "I think I'm being underpaid, and I feel so disheartened. Has this ever happened to you?"

* "I have a goal of saving five thousand dollars this year. Do you have any tricks you've used to save money?"

* "I just read an article about the investing gap for Black women. Do you know about this?"

Naturally, if you put yourself out there, others feel comfortable to also be vulnerable. This may be easier if you're a more direct person, like I tend to be. I will often just ask specifically for what I need: "I'm trying to get better with money this year. Anyone else trying to do something similar? Can we talk about it?" Not everyone is going to be at the same stage as you in their financial journey, and that's okay—all of us will get there at our own pace.

But if you're not as direct, it can be harder to start these sorts of discussions. This is one of many reasons I created safe spaces online for women to talk about money, like my free Facebook group and my investing platform, Treasury. I can't tell you how many comments we get that say something to the effect of: "This is the only place I can talk about money openly," or "I get more support from strangers in this community than I receive in real life." It's been incredible to see the honesty, transparency, and support that we've cultivated among women who are total strangers. I remember us posting a discussion prompt a few years ago,

"What was the biggest financial decision you've ever made?" And the responses were incredible: being a caregiver for a dying parent, choosing to have a child as a single mom, bootstrapping a business. Something beautiful happens when people are vulnerable: it not only helps ourselves in building the muscle of transparency but also works as a permission slip for others.

DONATION

IF YOU'RE IN the financial place where you're able, sending money to organizations you believe in is the best way to create the change we want to see. We know that providing support in terms of actual dollars is the best way for us to show up for causes we believe in, and it allows us to give support to experts in various fields. For instance, I may know how to educate people about money, but I have no idea how to actually save the rain forests other than by not cutting them down.

Try to find organizations that have good scores from charity rating sites such as Charity Review and GiveWell, because many organizations don't use the donations very effectively, and we want our dollar to go the furthest it can. I personally find that supporting a few charities or causes is better than trying to give smaller amounts to a bunch of different things. For example, my main focus is women's rights. Some of my favorite places to give are Planned Parenthood, Equality Now, and Together Rising (founded by one of my idols, the incredible activist and author Glennon Doyle).

Can't donate money? Donate your time instead. Volunteer at a local organization, even if it's just an hour a month. My parents are pros at this: every Wednesday evening for seven years, they volunteered at their local food bank. They also sat on the boards of community theaters and supported my various school functions by coaching or chaperoning.

DECISION

WHEN I SAY *DECISION,* what I really mean is "deciding what you stand for." This book has shown you just how connected money and politics are—and we can make a direct impact on both by choosing to show up and fight for our rights. A woman's right to choose, for example, is not only a political issue but also a deeply rooted financial matter too. Forcing a person to have a child she does not want and often cannot afford leads to less financial power and significant monetary deprivation.

Decision includes being a voter, and an educated one at that—not just in national elections, but at the local and state levels too. It includes learning more about your community and becoming as involved as you're able. It includes protesting, picketing, and petitions. It includes calling or emailing lawmakers—both when you're pissed about some new law and when you're expressing support. These decisions should not only be informed but also have the weight of action behind them. Posting an infographic on Instagram and calling it a day is not activism.

Decision can also lead you to put part of your money in ESG investing (or any other form of socially responsible investing that Tim Nash talked about in chapter 5), putting some of your money in a credit union, or voting with your dollars. Beyond traditional politics and activism, "voting with your dollars" is one of the most impactful ways to create change. We have the opportunity to support entrepreneurs and causes we love by giving them our business. Like Tanja Hester mentioned, spending our money at businesses owned by people of color, LGBTQ+ folks, and women—or at the very least, local mom-and-pop shops—can make a massive impact. Frequenting your weekly farmers market. Shopping vintage or secondhand clothes (good for local businesses *and* the environment). Grabbing coffee from your local shop instead of Starbucks. (I'm currently writing this paragraph from a Black-owned café in Brooklyn.)

As the owner of a small business myself, I cannot tell you how much it means to have folks support your work. I still see every PayPal transaction that comes through. I see the names of people who are committed to supporting me, my business, and HFK's cause. (Maybe I've even seen your name come through!)

Just like when we are developing our Financial Game Plan and need to start with one goal at a time, we have to do the same in life. You're not going to be able to shop local for everything, and it will likely not be budget conscious to do it every time, so find a balance that works for you. You decide what you want to focus on—for example, sustainable fashion—then pick something you're sustainably able to do, like "I won't shop at Shein." Then hopefully one day, your financial situation changes such that you're able to do more, such as "shop only with sustainable/ethical retailers."

DEVELOPMENT

HAVE YOU EVER MET someone who just refuses to learn anything new? When you politely try to educate them on a new issue or tell them something they said was offensive, they scoff at you? Maybe it's your grandpa or your aunt. My God, is this attitude the worst! As we progress in our lives, we must not be this kind of person.

We want to live life being curious and contemplative, inquisitive and interested. Just because you've read this book doesn't mean you're automatically a financial feminist. You not only need to be an active learner (not just passively reading and not implementing) but also a lifelong learner. It must be a sustainable, long-term effort. We need to live outside our comfort zones. If we're going to actually change our financial foundations—and more important, the world around us—we must be committed to learning and growing for the rest of our lives.

Educating yourself about money, systemic oppression, and the world is a lifelong commitment. Whether it's dissecting a recent article about the racial wealth gap, watching a TED Talk, or creating a book club (maybe for this book: go to herfirst100k .com/book-resources for a book club guide! #shamelessplug), you can find ways to stay educated, informed, and challenged.

Committing to financial feminism as a lifestyle takes vulnerability, consistency, and grace. But this movement is so much bigger than us as individuals. When we make a commitment to bettering our own financial lives—as both a service to ourselves *and* to others—we start changing the equation. When we choose to take on uncomfortable situations, we can start to use money as a tool to create the life and the world we want to see. In good times and in bad, we make a commitment to taking care of ourselves so we can show up at our best for others.

HOMEWORK

1. **MONEY DATE**

Open up your Google Calendar or grab your agenda and establish your first (or next!) Money Date.

When it's time, pull up what you need for each step of the Money Date:

1. LOOKING AT YOUR SPENDING: Download your credit/debit card statements. If you've been keeping a money diary or otherwise tracking your spending, pull up those reports.

2. SETTING OR CHECKING IN ON YOUR GOALS: Find the goals you wrote before and pull up all your account statements (checking, savings, debts, investments, etc.) so you can track your progress.

3. CREATING A PLAN TO ACHIEVE YOUR GOALS: What kinds of systems do you need to set up? Any optimization needed? Do some research to figure out what you need.

2. DISCUSSION, DONATION, DECISION, AND DEVELOPMENT

DISCUSSION: Try igniting a vulnerable conversation around money with a friend, colleague, or family member this week.

_____

_____

_____

_____

_____

_____

_____

_____

_____

_____

_____

DONATION: If you're able, choose a charity you believe in and set up a monthly donation.

_____

_____

_____

_____

_____

_____

_____

_____

_____

_____

_____

DECISION: Decide what you stand for and how your finances will play a part.

_____

_____

_____

_____

_____

_____

_____

_____

_____

_____

_____

_____

DEVELOPMENT: Stay committed by watching a weekly TED Talk or starting a book club to stay informed.

_____

_____

_____

_____

_____

_____

_____

_____

_____

_____

_____

_____

_____

EPILOGUE

"WHEN YOU HAVE ALL YOU NEED, BUILD A LONGER TABLE—NOT A HIGHER FENCE."

This book has the nails and hammer you need to build a table—one with sturdy legs and a level top. It will be a place of abundance, full of blooming flowers, gleaming silverware, and endless fried chicken. Over time, when you're full and fed, you will add more planks and seats to the table. You'll invite others to share in your abundance, this joy, this ease. And when you're well nourished, you'll tear down the fences others have built.

Thank you for inviting me to your table. I can't wait to dig in.

ACKNOWLEDGMENTS

THESE ACKNOWLEDGMENTS AREN'T just for this book but for all the support I've received in my life and in the life of Her First $100K. If I missed you, my sincere apologies—I owe you a drink—but know that I appreciate your kindness and friendship so much.

To my editor at Dey Street/HarperCollins, Rosy Tahan. Thank you for championing the hell out of this book, for being patient when I made a million changes, and for pushing me to be better. This book is ours. And to everyone behind the scenes at Harper-Collins, who put their hard work and care into this book—Anna Montague, Danielle Finnegan, Julie Paulauski, Dale Rohrbaugh, Alison Bloomer, and Paul Miele-Herndon—thank you.

To my literary agent, friend, and mentor, Jess d'Arbonne. Thank you for always answering my panicked texts and for your depth of knowledge and guidance.

To everyone who worked on this book, but especially to my research assistant, Ariel Johnson; my sensitivity reader and DEI consultant, Victoria Bell; Sarah Wolfe, for a gorgeous-as-always book photoshoot; and Mary Stratton, for her cover advice and consultation. To every person I counseled with and interviewed for this book, thank you for your vulnerability, knowledge, and insight. A massive thanks as well to the supportive community of personal finance creators, especially the incredible women who have offered me perspective and guidance as I've grown my company. You inspire me deeply.

To my UTA team, especially Oren Rosenbaum and Shelby Schenkman. Thank you for believing in what we're building as much as I do. To the team at AdLarge, y'all are such a pleasure to work with. Thank you for supporting our mission of financial feminism.

To the Her First $100K team past and present: Ana Alexandra, Sophia Cohen, Jack Coning, Olivia Coning, Austin Fields, Kristen Fields, Caela Gray, Brie Haro, Alena Helzer, Paulina Isaac, Ariel Johnson, Zoe Major-McDowall, Valerie Oresko, Karina Patel, and Cherise Wade. In my wildest dreams, I never thought I would find people who cared as much about my life's work as you do. I am forever grateful. Look at what we've built!!!! And to KP especially, thank you for co-parenting this company with me. I cannot tell you how much it means to have a friend and leader like you.

To the HFK community and Financial Feminists everywhere, your support of me, my team, and HFK are beyond humbling. This is my life's work, and I'm grateful for every second I've gotten to realize that work. I'm so honored to play a small part in making your life better. Everything I do, I do for you.

To my teachers, coaches, and mentors, past and present. To Kahlil Dumas and Nicole Booz, who championed HFK and my work from the beginning. For everyone who offered their advice, guidance, and perspective on my manuscript, especially Dan Sutter. (I thought of your mom with every single word I wrote.)

To Ivar Vong and Elias Rothblatt, true manifestations of the word *ally*. The professional and personal relationships I have with you make my life so much better. You are the kind of men I hope every single woman has in her life.

To all the Hype Squad members, your friendship, support, care, and bottomless champagne are such a gift. Emily and Strom, I love you both so much. You take such good care of me. Rodman: Who would have thought that a hopeless teenage crush would turn into one of the most important relationships of my life? Thank you for six-hour conversations about Nothing and Everything. Peppa: My mind still replays you saying, "This is going to change your life," when I first told you about HFK. It meant more to me than you'll ever know. I'll never stop putting my feet in. And to Rachel Lind, who celebrates my wins like they're hers: So lucky to have you in my life.

Jonah, still my number one draft pick. You showed me what unconditional love looks like and changed my life in the process.

To my dear friends and collaborators Alexis Rockley and Mallory Rowan, I love the shit out of you.

To Cindi, my undying gratitude. I cannot imagine my life without you. You've made me into the woman I am today and constantly push me into the woman I'm becoming.

To Nana and John, for your love and support. I'll always wave back when I'm onstage, even when I'm not supposed to. To my extended family—my uncles, aunts, and cousins—thank you for your love and cheerleading.

Kristine, my favorite person on Earth. I've never loved anyone like I love you. Of all the universes and timelines and alternate dimensions, I cannot believe I got lucky enough to be in the same one as you. Grow up; I'll see you at midnight.

And finally, as always, to Mom and Dad. What a cool life I have because you gave so much.

GLOSSARY

NOTE: *The number in the parenthetical is the chapter where you will find this term discussed in depth.*

401(K): A retirement investing account offered by your employer (5).

403(B): The public sector's equivalent to a 401(k) (5).

APY: Annual percentage yield is the rate of return for your investment, which also includes your expected earning in compound interest (5).

BAIL BOND: Many defendants cannot afford to pay bail, which allows them to not have to sit in jail as they await their trial. So, they seek out a bail bondsman, who helps them pay bail but then charges them a fee of usually 10 to 20 percent of the initial bond, which is used as collateral so that the defendant shows up to trial (4).

BALANCE TRANSFER: Taking your debt from one place (typically a credit card) and moving it to another place that oftentimes has a lower interest rate (4).

BOND: The debt of a company or government. When you buy a bond, you are giving a company/government a loan and earning money on the interest (5).

BROKERAGE ACCOUNT: An investing account at a brokerage firm. Brokerage firms buy and sell stocks, bonds, options, and other financial products on behalf of clients (5).

BUDGETING: Instead of feeling guilt about spending money, it allows you to focus on spending money on the things you love, without explanation or justification. It's a permission slip. It also helps you avoid the guilt of not taking care of yourself financially. It makes sure that you're factoring in your financial well-being, in addition to your wants (3).

CASH BAIL: If you get arrested, you can be held in jail until your court date. Studies show that judges place higher bail amounts on people of color, which means the whole system relies on racism—from the arrests and the policing of communities to the economic state of the communities most affected. The alternative is sitting in jail for six months or sometimes years awaiting trial (4).

CERTIFICATE OF DEPOSIT (CD): A savings account with a higher interest rate, but in exchange, you cannot access your money for a certain period of time (3).

CHECK CASHING: A way for those who are unbanked or underbanked to get access to their money. They can cash checks in exchange for a fee rather than using a bank (4).

COMPOUND INTEREST: Compounding means that the interest isn't just on the principal—it's also on any interest accumulated in the compounding period (4, 5).

CONSUMER FINANCIAL PROTECTION BUREAU (CFPB): A government agency charged with helping to ensure that banks, lenders, and financial institutions are playing fair (4).

CREDIT CARD: A way for people to purchase items on credit, meaning they are expected to pay back the lender, and if they don't, the purchases will accrue interest. You're basically "borrowing" the money until you are able to pay it off (4).

CREDIT HISTORY: The age of your oldest line of credit (4).

CREDIT SCORE: Think of it as your adult financial GPA (4).

CREDIT UTILIZATION RATE: The percentage of credit you're using (4).

DEBT: Something that is owed, usually money (4).

DEBT CONSOLIDATION: Taking multiple debts and putting them together with only one interest rate (often a lower rate than you were paying before) (4).

DIRECT DEPOSIT: A payment made electronically from one person to another.

DISCRETIONARY MONEY: Money you can spend on things you want, not on things you have to buy. This is your "fun money."

DO-IT-YOURSELF (DIY) INVESTING: You're the one choosing the stocks and bonds you're buying (5).

EMERGENCY FUND: Three to six months of living expenses saved, in a high-yield savings account (3).

EMPLOYEE MATCH: If you contribute a percentage of your salary to your retirement account, your workplace will match it (for example, a 3 percent match means that if you contribute 3 percent of your salary, your employer will as well) (5).

EXPENSES: Everything that costs you money in order to eat, sleep, and live (3).

FIDUCIARY: A type of financial advisor that is legally bound to make decisions in your best interest (5).

FINANCIAL ADVISOR: A money manager or a broker who provides services to a client. If you're reading this book, you probably don't need one yet. But please make sure that the person is a *fiduciary* (defined below) (5).

FINANCIAL FEMINISM: The act of embracing the power you already possess in order to help yourself—and those around you—reach financial equality.

HIGH-YIELD SAVINGS ACCOUNT: An HYSA is most likely hosted on an online platform, which means it has less overhead cost than a traditional brick and mortar and gives some of those savings back to the customer (3).

INDEX FUND: A mutual fund or an exchange-traded fund (ETF) designed to track a particular financial market index—for example, the S&P 500, which follows the five hundred biggest companies on the stock market (5).

INDIVIDUAL RETIREMENT ACCOUNT (IRA): As you might guess from the word *individual,* an IRA is not tied to your employer. The annual maximum contribution is usually $6,000 (5).

INFLATION RATE: The rate at which the price of goods and services in the economy is increasing (5).

INTEREST: The money that accrues on top of the money that was lent to you (4).

INTEREST RATE: The percentage of money that accrues and you are responsible for paying on top of the money that was lent to you (4).

LINE OF CREDIT: The amount of credit you have available to use (4).

MARKET RATE: Market research tells you what you should be getting paid relative to other people in your industry with the same experience level (6).

OVERDRAFT FEES: When you withdraw more money than you have in your account, the bank or other financial institution imposes an overdraft fee (3).

PAID TIME OFF (PTO): A work benefit where you take time off but still get paid for the time (6).

PAYDAY LOANS: Short-term loans designed (in theory!) to cover the individual until his or her next payday, with insanely high interest rates (4).

PERSONAL LOAN: Borrowed money that you use for personal reasons, you receive one based on your credit history and income.

PINK TAX: A term used to describe the fact that items marketed toward women are often more expensive than the same items sold to men (2).

PLEDGING SHARES: Borrowing against a company's stock to avoid paying taxes.

PRINCIPAL: The original sum of money you borrow on a loan (4).

PROFIT SHARE: A system in which employees of a company receive a direct share of the profits (6).

RATE OF RETURN (ROR): Rate of return is how much your investments have either lost or gained over a specific period of time (5).

RETIREMENT ACCOUNT: Investment accounts that are specifically for retirement. They are tax advantaged (5).

RETIREMENT INVESTING: Strategically investing with the goal of being able to retire and live off the money you invested (5).

RETURN ON INVESTMENT (ROI): Return on investment is a way to make sure your investments are doing what they're supposed to do—earn you money!

ROBO-ADVISOR: A company that invests for you but takes a percentage of the money (usually 0.25 to 0.5 percent on top of any fund-specific fees) (5).

ROTH IRA: A tax-advantaged retirement account that is not tied to your employer, meaning just about anyone can open one. That's exactly what the *I* in IRA stands for: *individual* retirement account. You can open a Roth IRA at any age as long as you have a job, and unlike a traditional IRA, there are no required minimum distributions. You also pay the taxes now and receive the tax benefits later.

SAVINGS ACCOUNT: A type of bank account that usually accrues some sort of interest (3).

SIMPLE INTEREST: Interest based on the principal amount of a loan or the first deposit in a savings account (4).

SIMPLIFIED EMPLOYEE PENSION PLAN (SEP-IRA): Another kind of IRA. As with a traditional IRA, you pay the taxes you owe when you withdraw money—for instance, at retirement age. It's designed for solopreneurs or companies with a few people. Maximum contribution to a SEP is $56,000/year or up to 25 percent of your income (whichever comes first) (5).

SOLO 401(k): Similar to the employer-sponsored 401(k) plan, except you're your own sponsor (5)!

STOCK: Slivers of companies, so owning a stock means you're a part owner in a company (5).

STOCK OPTIONS: When a company gives you the chance to invest in that company at a discounted rate or a fixed price (6).

TRADITIONAL IRA: Like the Roth IRA, this is an individual retirement account, meaning it's not tied to an employer. You won't pay any taxes on this money until you withdraw it at retirement, so you receive benefits now rather than later (5).

UNBANKED: An individual who does not have a bank account.

UNDERBANKED: People who live in areas where financial services are not easily accessible.

VALUE-BASED SPENDING: The act of spending a majority of your discretionary money on what brings you true value and joy (2).

W-2: A type of tax form that you fill out when becoming an employee. It helps the IRS calculate how much of your income should be taxed (6).

NOTES

CHAPTER 1: THE EMOTIONS OF MONEY

5   *"If you don't name":* Bill Whitaker, "Brené Brown on Vulnerability and Courage" (transcript), *60 Minutes,* CBS News, last modified March 29, 2020, https://www.cbsnews.com/news/brene-brown-cope-coronavirus-pandemic -covid-19-60-minutes-2020-03-29/.

7   *shame is rooted:* Mary Lamia, *What Motivates Getting Things Done: Procrastination, Emotions, and Success* (Lanham, MD: Rowman & Littlefield, 2018), 52; Brené Brown, *Daring Greatly: How the Courage to Be Vulnerable Transforms the Way We Live, Love, Parent, and Lead* (New York: Gotham Books, 2012).

8   *shame is highly correlated:* Ronda L. Dearing, Jeffrey Stuewig, and June Price Tangney, "On the Importance of Distinguishing Shame from Guilt: Relations to Problematic Alcohol and Drug Use," *Addictive Behaviors* 30, no. 7 (2005): 1392-1404, https://doi.org/10.1016/j.addbeh.2005.02.002; Brown, *Daring Greatly.*

10   *"in part due to societal":* Vienna Miller-Prieve, "Women, Shame, and Mental Health: A Systematic Review of Approaches in Psychotherapy" (master of social work clinical research paper, St. Catherine University, May 2016), https://sophia.stkate.edu/msw_papers/630.

10   *"haven't earned it":* Ulrich Orth, Richard W. Robins, and Christopher J. Soto, "Tracking the Trajectory of Shame, Guilt, and Pride Across the Life Span," *Journal of Personality and Social Psychology* 99, no. 6 (December 2010): 1061-71, https://doi.org/10.1037/a0021342.

12   *"No one breaks their leg":* Tori Dunlap, "Breaking Down the Racial Wealth Gap & Minority Appraisal Crisis with Tiffany Aliche, aka The Budgetnista," *Financial Feminist* (podcast), May 24, 2021, 1:19.56, https://podcasts.apple .com/lv/podcast/breaking-down-racial-wealth-gap-minority-appraisal /id1566054936?i=1000523373031.

12   *Men are taught about:* "Adolescent Income and Financial Literacy," Giftcards.com, accessed March 24, 2022, https://www.giftcards.com /adolescent-income-and-financial-literacy?utm_source=rakuten&utm _medium=affiliate&utm_campaign=2116208&utm_content=686295&ra nMID=44432&ranEAID=TnL5HPStwNw&ranSiteID=TnL5HPStwNw -tv3XzBdJ3eUYQPzH8QXjeQ; Michael D. Newcomb and Jerome Rabow, "Gender, Socialization, and Money," *Journal of Applied Social Psychology* 29, no. 4 (1999): 852-69, https://doi.org/10.1111/j.1559-1816.1999.tb02029.x.

12 **credit card in their own name:** Jessica Hill, "Fact Check: Post Detailing 9 Things Women Couldn't Do Before 1971 Is Mostly Right," *USA Today,* October 28, 2020, https://www.usatoday.com/story/news /factcheck/2020/10/28/fact-check-9-things-women-couldnt-do-1971-mostly -right/3677101001/.

12 **a business loan:** Melissa Wylie, "28 Years Ago, Women Gained Control of Their Finances. Here's How," Bizwomen, last modified October 25, 2016, https://www.bizjournals.com/bizwomen/news/latest-news/2016/10/28-years -ago-you-couldnt-get-a-loan-without-a-man.html?page=all.

12 **majority of the wealth-building:** Michael S. Fischer, "Men Still Make the Financial Decisions in Most Couples: UBS," ThinkAdvisor, last modified May 10, 2021, https://www.thinkadvisor.com/2021/05/10/men-still-make-the -financial-decisions-in-most-couples-ubs/.

13 **fear of seeming:** Steve Rhode, "Why Are Women So Afraid to Talk About Money?," HuffPost, last modified June 23, 2015, https://www.huffpost.com /entry/why-are-women-so-afraid-t_b_7126686.

13 **On her show:** Emma Pattee and Stefanie O'Connell, "Personal Finance Advice Relies on Shame; What If We Tried Empathy?" CNBC, last modified October 13, 2020, https://www.cnbc.com/2020/10/13/a-new-approach-to -personal-finance-advice-empathy-instead-of-shame.html.

13 **"Feeling unsure and uncertain":** Nicole Peeler, "Brené Brown's Advice for When You Feel Like Shutting Down," Medium, last modified March 25, 2020, https://forge.medium.com/bren%C3%A9-browns-advice-for-when -you-feel-like-shutting-down-e809b94fcb40.

14 **We are more likely to talk:** Kevin Voigt, "Breaking the Last Taboo: Talking Money with Our Partners," NerdWallet, last modified January 7, 2018, https://www.nerdwallet.com/article/finance/breaking-last-taboo-talking -money-partners.

14 **"Your value as a human being":** Joe Pinsker, "Why So Many Americans Don't Talk About Money," *The Atlantic,* last modified March 2, 2020, https://www .theatlantic.com/family/archive/2020/03/americans-dont-talk-about-money -taboo/607273/.

15 **those who worked hard:** John Winthrop, "A Model of Christian Charity," in *A Library of American Literature: Early Colonial Literature, 1607–1675,* vol. 2, eds. Edmund Clarence Stedman and Ellen Mackay Hutchinson (New York: Charles L. Webster, 1891), 304–7.

15 **mastery over the "lazier races":** Ethan S. Rafuse, "John C. Calhoun: He Started the Civil War," HistoryNet, last modified October 29, 2021, https:// www.historynet.com/john-c-calhoun-the-man-who-started-the-civil-war/.

15   *financed through the GI Bill:* Bruce Lesh, "Post-War Suburbanization: Homogenization or the American Dream" (lesson plan, Franklin High School, Baltimore County Public Schools, n.d.), accessed March 26, 2022, https://www.umbc.edu/che/tahlessons/pdf/Post-War_Suburbanization _Homogenization(PrinterFriendly).pdf; Oliver Burkeman, "This Column Will Change Your Life: The Protestant Work Ethic," *Guardian* (U.S. edition), last modified September 10, 2010, https://www.theguardian.com /lifeandstyle/2010/sep/11/pain-gain-work-ethic-burkeman.

15   *"If you're working on":* Dave Ramsey (@DaveRamsey), "If you're working on paying off debt, the only time you should see the inside of a restaurant is if you're working there," Twitter, February 17, 2020, 10:22 A.M., https://twitter .com/daveramsey/status/1229425772546449409.

16   *women feel it:* "Two Reasons Women Feel Guilty as High Achievers," Fundid, last modified March 16, 2022, https://www.getfundid.com/learn/wo-reasons -we-feel-guilty-as-high-achievers.

16   *We feel guilty:* Ibid.

17   *women's brains exhibited:* Susan Scutti, "Men's and Women's Brains React Differently When Helping Others, Study Says," CNN, last modified October 9, 2017, https://www.cnn.com/2017/10/09/health/gender -differences-giving-receiving-study/index.html.

17   *default nature of giving:* Nicola K. S. Davis, "Stereotype That Women Are Kinder and Less Selfish Is True, Claim Neuroscientists," *Guardian* (U.S. edition), last modified October 9, 2017, https://www.theguardian.com /science/2017/oct/09/stereotype-that-women-are-kinder-and-less-selfish-is -true-claim-neuroscientists.

18   *"girls' toys were associated":* Judith E. Blakemore and Renee E. Centers, "Characteristics of Boys' and Girls' Toys," *Sex Roles* 53, nos. 9-10 (November 2005): 619-33, https://doi.org/10.1007/s11199-005-7729-0.

18   *"Girls, as they":* Susan Chira, "Money Is Power. And Women Need More of Both," *New York Times,* March 10, 2018, https://www .nytimes.com/2018/03/10/sunday-review/women-money-politics-power .html.

18   *women are overrepresented:* Claire Cain Miller, "As Women Take Over a Male-Dominated Field, the Pay Drops," *New York Times,* March 18, 2016, https://www.nytimes.com/2016/03/20/upshot/as-women-take-over-a-male -dominated-field-the-pay-drops.html.

18   *roles to specific kinds:* David Graeber, "Why Do We as a Society Not Object to the Growth of Pointless Employment?," chap. 6 in *Bullshit Jobs* (New York: Simon & Schuster Paperbacks, 2019), 232-39.

19   ***women are expected to:*** David G. Rand et al., "Social Heuristics and Social Roles: Intuition Favors Altruism for Women but Not for Men," *Journal of Experimental Psychology General* 145, no. 4 (April 2016): 389–96, doi:10.1037/xge0000154.

20   ***Anxiety regarding money-related issues:*** American Psychological Association, "Stress in America: Money, Inflation, War Pile On to Nation Stuck in COVID-19 Survival Mode," press release, March 2022, https://www .apa.org/news/press/releases/stress/2022/march-2022-survival-mode, and "American Psychological Association Survey Shows Money Stress Weighing on Americans' Health Nationwide," press release, February 2015, https:// www.apa.org/news/press/releases/2015/02/money-stress.

21   ***giving poor mothers:*** Jennifer Schmidt et al., "Too Little, Too Much: How Poverty and Wealth Affect Our Minds" (50:23), *Hidden Brain*, NPR, last modified October 4, 2018, https://www.npr.org/2018/10/04/651468312 /too-little-too-much-how-poverty-and-wealth-affect-our-minds; Jason Deparle, "Cash Aid to Poor Mothers Increases Brain Activity in Babies, Study Finds," *New York Times*, January 24, 2022, https://www.nytimes.com/2022/01/24 /us/politics/child-tax-credit-brain-function.html.

21 . ***higher incomes are correlated:*** Matthew A. Killingsworth, "Experienced Well-Being Rises with Income, Even Above $75,000 per Year," *Proceedings of the National Academy of Sciences of the United States of America* 118, no. 4 (2021), https://doi.org/10.1073/pnas.2016976118.

22   ***by age seven:*** Rob Phelan, "4 Ways to Teach Kids About Money Before Their Habits Are Set at Age 9," *Business Insider*, October 25, 2021, https://www .businessinsider.com/personal-finance/why-we-need-to-teach-kids-about -money-2021-10.

22   ***children as young as five:*** Craig E. Smith et al., "Spendthrifts and Tightwads in Childhood: Feelings About Spending Predict Children's Financial Decision Making," *Journal of Behavioral Decision Making* 31, no. 3 (July 2018): 446– 60, https://doi.org/10.1002/bdm.2071.

26   ***"money imprint"*** Michael F. Kay, "How Your Childhood Affects Your Money Today," *Forbes*, last modified May 31, 2016, https://www.forbes.com /sites/michaelkay/2016/05/31/how-your-childhood-affects-your-money -today/?sh=393799922c72.

26   ***we have to start:*** Julie Andrews, vocalist, "Do-Re-Mi," by Richard Rodgers and Oscar Hammerstein II, track 11 on *The Sound of Music Original Soundtrack Recording* (RCA Victor, 1965), 33 1/3 rpm.

CHAPTER 2: SPENDING

44 **women as excessive spenders:** Kristin Wong, "The Myth of the Frivolous Female Spender," *New York Times*, October 4, 2019, https://www.nytimes.com/2019/10/04/us/myth-frivolous-female-spender.html.

44 **spending power of women:** "Women's Spending Habits: 99 Must-Know Facts," Lexington Law, last modified March 19, 2021, https://www.lexingtonlaw.com/blog/finance/women-spending-habits.html.

44 **We've been marketed to:** Anup Shah, "Children as Consumers," Global Issues, last modified November 21, 2010, https://www.globalissues.org/article/237/children-as-consumers.

44 **the most marketed to:** Wong, "Myth of the Frivolous Female Spender."

45 **higher-interest mortgages:** Justin P. Steil et al., "The Social Structure of Mortgage Discrimination," *Housing Studies* 33, no. 5 (March 2017): 759–76, https://doi.org/10.1080/02673037.2017.1390076.

47 **show explicit bias:** "The 'Good Hair' Study Results," Perception Institute, accessed June 19, 2020, https://perception.org/goodhair/results/.

47 **women may pay 20 percent more:** Julia Menin, *From Cradle to Cane: The Cost of Being a Female Consumer—A Study of Gender Pricing in New York City* (New York: New York City Department of Consumer Affairs, December 2015), https://www1.nyc.gov/assets/dca/downloads/pdf/partners/Study-of-Gender-Pricing-in-NYC.pdf.

50 **"you are peeing":** Emmie Martin, "Suze Orman: If You Waste Money on Coffee, It's Like 'Peeing $1 Million Down the Drain,'" CNBC, last modified March 18, 2019, cnbc.com/2019/03/28/suze-orman-spending-money-on-coffee-is-like-throwing-1-million-down-the-drain.html.

50 **the reason you can't afford:** Sam Levin, "Millionaire Tells Millennials: If You Want a House, Stop Buying Avocado Toast," *Guardian* (U.S. edition), last modified May 15, 2017, https://www.theguardian.com/lifeandstyle/2017/may/15/australian-millionaire-millennials-avocado-toast-house.

50 **98 percent of diets fail:** Michael Hobbes, "Everything You Know About Obesity Is Wrong," HuffPost, last modified September 19, 2018, https://highline.huffingtonpost.com/articles/en/everything-you-know-about-obesity-is-wrong/.

64 **almost half reported:** Erin El Issa, "Survey: About Half of Americans Emotionally Overspend," NerdWallet, last modified January 31, 2017, https://www.nerdwallet.com/article/credit-cards/credit-card-debt-stigma-2017.

CHAPTER 3: THE FINANCIAL GAME PLAN

82   *women handle the grocery shopping:* "Own Your Worth—ubs.com,"
      UBS, accessed March 28, 2022, https://www.ubs.com/content/dam
      /WealthManagementAmericas/documents/2018-37666-UBS-Own-Your
      -Worth-report-R32.pdf?source=post_page; Katherine Schaeffer, "Among U.S.
      Couples, Women Do More Cooking and Grocery Shopping Than Men,"
      Pew Research Center, last modified September 24, 2019, https://www
      .pewresearch.org/fact-tank/2019/09/24/among-u-s-couples-women-do-more
      -cooking-and-grocery-shopping-than-men/.

86   *getting incredibly specific:* John B. Miner, "Theories of Motivation." Essay. In
      Organizational Behavior 1: Essential Theories of Motivation and Leadership
      (Armonk, NY: M. E. Sharpe, 2005), 155–67.

88   *"'Cause if I know":* "Winners Circle," YouTube, 3:29, Anderson .Paak, https://
      www.youtube.com/watch?v=3tcbxVU6inM.

93   *contributing 20 percent:* Investopedia Team, "Your 401(k): What's the Ideal
      Contribution?," Investopedia, last modified February 8, 2022, https://
      www.investopedia.com/articles/retirement/082716/your-401k-whats-ideal
      -contribution.asp.

CHAPTER 4: DEBT

118   *The first recorded debt systems:* David Graeber, *Debt: The First 5,000 Years*
       (Brooklyn, NY: Melville House, 2011).

118   *President Thomas Jefferson:* Ramsey Badawi, "7 Presidents Who Were Way
       Poorer Than You Realize," Ranker, last modified January 25, 2017, https://
       www.ranker.com/list/poor-us-presidents/ramsey-badawi.

118   *Nicolas Cage found himself:* Zack Sharf, "Nicolas Cage Paid Off Debts with
       VOD Films, but He Stands by Every Role: 'I Never Phoned It In,'" *Variety,* last
       modified March 22, 2022, https://variety.com/2022/film/news/nicolas-cage
       -defends-vod-films-debt-1235211377/.

118   *$90,000 in debt:* Bill Fay, "Demographics of America," debt.org, last
       modified February 23, 2022, https://www.debt.org/faqs/americans-in-debt
       /demographics/.

118   *total U.S. consumer debt:* Jeff Cox, "Consumer Debt Totals $15.6 Trillion in
       2021, a Record-Breaking Increase," CNBC, last modified February 8, 2022,
       https://www.cnbc.com/2022/02/08/consumer-debt-totals-15point6-trillion
       -after-a-record-breaking-increase-in-2021.html.

121   *women were more likely:* Jessica Dickler, "Fewer Women Now Pay Their
       Credit Card Balances in Full," CNBC, last modified September 3, 2019,
       https://www.cnbc.com/2019/09/03/fewer-women-now-pay-their-credit-card
       -balances-in-full.html.

121 **Women hold more than:** Abigail Johnson Hess, "American Women Hold Two-Thirds of All Student Debt—Here's Why," CNBC, last modified July 12, 2019, https://www.cnbc.com/2018/03/13/american-women-hold-two-thirds-of-all-student-debt-heres-why.html; Rajashri Chakrabarti, Ruchi Avtar, and Kasey Chatterji-Len, "Uneven Distribution of Household Debt by Gender, Race, and Education," *Liberty Street Economics* (blog), Federal Reserve Bank of New York, January 3, 2022, https://libertystreeteconomics.newyorkfed.org/2021/11/uneven-distribution-of-household-debt-by-gender-race-and-education/.

121 **open a credit card:** Hill, "Fact Check: Post Detailing 9 Things Women Couldn't Do Before 1971 Is Mostly Right."

121 **Black and white college graduates:** Judith Scott-Clayton and Jing Li, "Black-White Disparity in Student Loan Debt More Than Triples After Graduation," Brookings Institution, last modified March 9, 2022, https://www.brookings.edu/research/black-white-disparity-in-student-loan-debt-more-than-triples-after-graduation/.

122 **more expensive for almost every type:** Ibid.

122 **have lower credit scores:** Michelle Black, "Does Being a Woman Hurt Your Credit? Here's Why Men Typically Have Higher Credit Scores," Bankrate, last modified May 8, 2018, https://www.bankrate.com/finance/credit-cards/credit-score-gender-pay-gap/.

122 **the algorithm continued:** Karen Hao, "There's an Easy Way to Make Lending Fairer for Women. Trouble Is, It's Illegal," *MIT Technology Review*, last modified November 15, 2019, https://www.technologyreview.com/2019/11/15/131935/theres-an-easy-way-to-make-lending-fairer-for-women-trouble-is-its-illegal/.

123 **"participating in stupidity":** "Stupidity Is Alive and Well—Dave Ramsey Rant," YouTube, 6:54, The Ramsey Show—Highlights, https://www.youtube.com/watch?v=_xx4sUT2Hs0&ab_channel=TheRamseyShow-Highlights.

123 **"Not understanding how":** Hess, "American Women Hold Two-Thirds of All Student Debt."

123 **colleges still signed:** Melanie Hickman, "Credit Card Issuers Still Cashing in on College Students, Alumni," CNNMoney, last modified December 17, 2013, https://money.cnn.com/2013/12/17/pf/college-credit-cards/index.html; Megan Leonhardt, "Over a Third of College Students Already Have Credit Card Debt," CNBC, last modified June 3, 2019, https://www.cnbc.com/2019/05/31/over-a-third-of-college-students-have-credit-card-debt.html; Michelle Black, "What Is the Card Act of 2009?," *Forbes*, last modified February 27, 2022, https://www.forbes.com/advisor/credit-cards/what-is-the-card-act-of-2009/.

124 **class action law firm:** Melanie Hicken, "Attention Comenity Card Holders: Labaton Sucharow Pursuing Claims for Customers Deceived by Store-Brand

Credit Cards; Shoppers Strapped with Unexpected High Interest Charges Are Encouraged to Contact the Firm," Yahoo! Finance, last modified December 17, 2013, https://www.yahoo.com/now/attention-comenity-card -holders-labaton-120000496.html.

124 **_higher than the national average:_** Kate Gibson, "Average Retail Credit Card's Interest Rate Surges to 26%–Despite Fed Cuts," CBS News, last modified October 10, 2019, https://www.cbsnews.com/news/average-retail-card-card -apr-surges-to-26-new-study-finds/.

130 **_Creditors intentionally make:_** Claire Tsosie, "How Credit Card Issuers Calculate Minimum Payments," NerdWallet, last modified March 24, 2022, https://www.nerdwallet.com/article/credit-cards/credit-card-issuer-minimum -payment.

142 **_Consumer Financial Protection Bureau:_** U.S. Consumer Financial Protection Bureau, https://www.consumerfinance.gov.

142 **_"Cigarettes don't kill everyone":_** "Financial Cigarettes–Dave Ramsey Rant," YouTube, 9:25, The Ramsey Show–Highlights, https://www.youtube.com /watch?v=fYvE6fygZoI.

143 **_a long history of exerting power:_** Justin P. Steil et al., "The Social Structure of Mortgage Discrimination," _Housing Studies_ 33, no. 5 (March 2017): 759– 76, https://doi.org/10.1080/02673037.2017.1390076; "The Pink Tax: How Gender-Based Pricing Hurts Women's Buying Power," Joint Economic Committee Democrats, last modified December 31, 2016, https://www .jec.senate.gov/public/_cache/files/8a42df04-8b6d-4949-b20b-6f40 326db9e/the-pink-tax---how-gender-based-pricing-hurts-women-s-buying -power.pdf.

CHAPTER 5: INVESTING

152 **_the investing gap leads:_** Aditi Shrikant, "'It's Important for Everybody, but Especially Women, to Get Started Investing, Says Money Educator: Here's Why," Grow from Acorns + CNBC, last modified October 14, 2021, https:// grow.acorns.com/tori-dunlap-wise-for-everyone-especially-women-to-start -investing/?utm_content=Main&utm_medium=Social&utm_source=Facebook&f bclid=IwAR1DVi6KxJTvA7wYz7-1a9Si4C8EMMAhOW-U_Iyt3kJRzoLlLRWT FzOcPic#Echobox=1628781142.

152 **_median wealth for single women:_** Dedrick Asante-Muhammad, "Racial Wealth Snapshot: Women, Men, and Racial Wealth Divide," National Community Reinvestment Coalition (NCRC), last modified March 8, 2022, https://ncrc.org/racial-wealth-snapshot-women-men-and-the-racial-wealth -divide/.

152 **median wealth for Black women:** *Examining the Racial and Gender Wealth Gap in America,* Hearing Before the Subcommittee on Diversity and Inclusion of the Committee on Financial Services, U.S. House of Representatives, One Hundred Sixteenth Congress, First Session, September 24, 2019 (Washington, D.C.: U.S. Government Publishing Office, 2020), https://www.congress .gov/116/chrg/CHRG-116hhrg42351/CHRG-116hhrg42351.pdf.

152 **women over sixty-five:** Monique Morrissey, "Women Over 65 Are More Likely to Be Poor Than Men, Regardless of Race, Educational Background, and Marital Status," Economic Policy Institute, last modified March 8, 2016, https://www.epi.org/publication/women-over-65-are-more-likely-to-in -poverty-than-men/.

152 **they have less money:** Stefanie O'Connell Rodriguez, "The Gender Investing Gap Isn't About Confidence, It's About Compensation," Too Ambitious, last modified October 7, 2021, https://ambition.bulletin.com /583016876076864.

152 **women saved higher percentages:** "Fidelity Investments 2021 Women and Investing Study," Fidelity Investments, accessed March 28, 2022, https:// www.fidelity.com/bin-public/060_www_fidelity_com/documents/about-fidelity /FidelityInvestmentsWomen&InvestingStudy2021.pdf.

153 **only 28 percent of women:** Ryan Ermey, "The Reasons for the $3.2 Trillion Gender Investing Gap, and How to Bridge It," Grow from Acorns + CNBC, last modified February 14, 2022, https://grow.acorns.com/gender-investing-gap/.

153 **Victoria Woodhull, a leader:** Mary Pilon, "Decades Before They Had the Vote, Women Launched Their Own Stock Exchange," History.com, last modified October 24, 2017, https://www.history.com/news/decades-before -they-had-the-vote-women-launched-their-own-stock-exchange.

154 **Today only 15 percent:** "Wall Street Wants More Female Traders, but Old Perceptions Die Hard," CNBC, June 14, 2018, https://www.cnbc .com/2018/06/14/wall-street-wants-more-female-traders-but-old-perceptions -die-hard.html.

154 **23 percent of financial advisors:** *Making More Room for Women in the Financial Planning Profession. Recommendations to Increase the Number of Women CFP Professionals from CFP Board's Women's Initiative (WIN)* (Washington, D.C.: Certified Financial Planner Board of Standards, 2014), https://www.cfp.net/-/media/files/cfp-board/knowledge/reports-and -research/womens-initiative/cfp-board_win_web.pdf?la=en&hash=614591F508 4FDE519B27B7A2D3CA3AC6.

154 **Women were pressured:** Tabea Bucher-Koenen et al., "How Financially Literate Are Women? An Overview and New Insights" (working paper

20793, National Bureau of Economic Research, December 2014), doi:10.3386/w20793.

155 **the national average:** Matthew Goldberg, "What Is the Average Interest Rate for Savings Accounts?," Bankrate, last modified March 24, 2022, https://www.bankrate.com/banking/savings/average-savings-interest-rates/.

156 **a record high 6.8 percent:** Reade Pickert, "U.S. Inflation Hits 39-Year High of 7%, Sets Stage for Fed Hike," Bloomberg (U.S. edition), last modified January 12, 2022, https://www.bloomberg.com/news/articles/2022-01-12/inflation-in-u-s-registers-biggest-annual-gain-since-1982.

157 **your likelihood of profiting:** Morgan Housel, "Reasonable > Rational," chap. 11 in *The Psychology of Money: Timeless Lessons on Wealth, Greed, and Happiness* (Petersfield, UK: Harriman House, 2021), 111–20.

160 **gatekeep wealth building:** Whitney Morrison, "Why Fewer Women Invest in the Financial Market—and How to Change That," Wellness, Goop, accessed March 28, 2022, https://goop.com/wellness/career-money/why-fewer-women-invest-in-the-financial-market-and-how-to-change-that/.

162 **the number one financial regret:** Jessica Dickler, "Not Saving for Retirement Tops Americans' Greatest Regrets," CNBC, last modified May 23, 2017, https://www.cnbc.com/2017/05/23/not-saving-for-retirement-tops-americans-greatest-regrets.html.

162 **twice as likely to be in poverty:** John B. Williamson and Sara E. Rix, "Social Security Reform: Implications for Women" (working paper 1999-07, Boston College, Boston, December 1999), https://doi.org/10.2139/ssrn.252051.

171 **"a coin flip":** Bob Pisani, "In One of the Most Volatile Markets in Decades, Active Fund Managers Underperformed Again," CNBC, last modified November 1, 2021, https://www.cnbc.com/2021/11/01/in-one-of-the-most-volatile-markets-in-decades-active-fund-managers-underperformed-again.html.

172 **the cat chooses stocks:** Frederick E. Allen, "Cat Beats Professionals at Stock Picking," *Forbes,* last modified January 16, 2013, https://www.forbes.com/sites/frederickallen/2013/01/15/cat-beats-professionals-at-stock-picking/?sh=6afde688621a.

175 **such as target-date funds:** Kevin Voigt, "What Is a Target-Date Fund and When Should You Invest in One?," NerdWallet, last modified January 20, 2022, https://www.nerdwallet.com/article/investing/what-is-a-target-date-fund-and-when-should-you-invest-in-one#:~:text=The%20average%20target%2Ddate%20fund,there's%20room%20to%20shop%20around.

177 **withdraw 4 percent of your money:** Philip L. Cooley, Carl M. Hubbard, and Daniel T. Walz, "Sustainable Withdrawal Rates from Your Retirement

Portfolio," *JFCP Research Journal* 10, no. 1 (1999): 41–50, https://www.afcpe
.org/news-and-publications/journal-of-financial-counseling-and-planning
/volume-10-1/sustainable-withdrawal-rates-from-your-retirement-portfolio/.

182 **which hasn't performed well:** Lewis Krauskopf and Jessica Resnick-Ault,
"U.S. Energy Shareholders Seek to Leave Behind a Lost Decade," Reuters,
last modified December 27, 2019, https://www.reuters.com/article/us-global
-markets-decade-energy/u-s-energy-shareholders-seek-to-leave-behind-a
-lost-decade-idUSKBN1YV0CM.

CHAPTER 6: EARNING

195 **women make 82 cents:** Amy Stewart, "The Gender Pay Gap Is Real. To Close
It, Pay Equity Needs to Be a Continuous Practice," Payscale, last modified
April 30, 2021, https://www.payscale.com/compensation-trends/the-gender
-pay-gap-is-real-to-close-it-pay-equity-needs-to-be-a-continuous-practice/.

196 **being denied their requests:** Benjamin Arzt, Andrew J. Oswald, and
Amanda Goodall, "Research: Women Ask for Raises as Often as Men,
but Are Less Likely to Get Them," *Harvard Business Review*, last
modified June 25, 2018, https://hbr.org/2018/06/research-women-ask-for
-raises-as-often-as-men-but-are-less-likely-to-get-them.

196 **the bulk of lower-paid workers:** Courtney Connley, "The Coronavirus
Pandemic Further Highlights Why Women Workers Need Equal Pay,"
CNBC, last modified March 31, 2020, https://www.cnbc.com/2020/03/31
/how-the-pay-gap-hurts-low-wage-women-workers-impacted-by-the
-coronavirus.html.

196 **"fatherhood premium":** Shelley J. Correll, Stephen Benard, and In Paik,
"Getting a Job: Is There a Motherhood Penalty?," chap. 60 in *Inequality in
the 21st Century: A Reader*, eds. David B. Grusky and Jasmine Hill (New York:
Routledge, 2018), 391–99, https://doi.org/10.4324/9780429499821-67.

197 **majority of COVID-related job losses:** Titan Alon et al., "From Mancession
to Shecession: Women's Employment in Regular and Pandemic Recessions"
(working paper, National Bureau of Economic Research, April 9, 2021,
https://www.nber.org/books-and-chapters/nber-macroeconomics-annual
-2021-volume-36/mancession-shecession-womens-employment-regular-and
-pandemic-recessions); Julia B. Bear and Peter Glick, "Breadwinner Bonus
and Caregiver Penalty in Workplace Rewards for Men and Women," *Social
Psychological and Personality Science* 8, no. 7 (2016): 780–88, https://doi
.org/10.1177/1948550616683016.

204 **her incredible book:** Elizabeth Gilbert, *Big Magic: Creative Living Beyond
Fear* (New York: Riverhead Books, 2015).

204 *our brains don't know the difference:* Ibid.

205 *91 percent said:* Jeanne Meister, "The Future of Work: Job Hopping Is the 'New Normal' for Millennials," *Forbes*, last modified January 3, 2017, https://www.forbes.com/sites/jeannemeister/2012/08/14/the-future-of-work-job-hopping-is-the-new-normal-for-millennials/?sh=501f436113b8.

210 *100 percent of the requirements:* Mei Ibrahim, "Men Apply for a Job When They Meet Only 60% of the Qualifications, but Women Apply Only if They Meet 100% of Them. Here's Why," LinkedIn, October 28, 2019, https://www.linkedin.com/pulse/men-apply-job-when-meet-only-60-qualifications-women-100-mei-ibrahim/.

211 *more than $1 million:* Jeff Haden, "Research Shows Not Negotiating Your Salary Could Cost You $1 Million (Especially Women)," Inc.com, last modified December 19, 2016, https://www.inc.com/jeff-haden/research-shows-not-negotiating-your-salary-could-cost-you-1-million-especially-.html.

215 *"Choosing the right number":* Kitty, "How Not to Determine Your Salary," Bitches Get Riches (blog), last modified March 14, 2021, https://www.bitchesgetriches.com/how-not-to-determine-your-salary/.

215 *your market rate:* Ibid.

216 *containing anonymous salary information:* Monica Torres, "Salary-Sharing Spreadsheets Are So Hot Right Now. But Are They Safe?," HuffPost, last modified January 17, 2020, https://www.huffpost.com/entry/salary-spreadsheet-what-to-know1_5e1e2c6ac5b650c621e70856.

221 *proven to undercut themselves:* Morela Hernandez and Derek R. Avery, "Getting the Short End of the Stick: Racial Bias in Salary Negotiations," *MIT Sloan Management Review*, last modified June 15, 2016, https://sloanreview.mit.edu/article/getting-the-short-end-of-the-stick-racial-bias-in-salary-negotiations/.

223 *Companies expect you to negotiate:* Andreas Leibbrandt and John List, "Do Women Avoid Salary Negotiations?," *National Bureau of Economic Research Digest*, no. 4 (April 2013): 1–2, https://www.nber.org/digest/apr13/do-women-avoid-salary-negotiations.

223 *the gender gap disappears:* Ibid.

235 *69 (ayyyeeee) percent:* Zoë B. Cullen, "The Salary Taboo: Privacy Norms and the Diffusion of Information" (working paper 25145, National Bureau of Economic Research, October 2018), https://www.nber.org/system/files/working_papers/w25145/w25145.pdf.

237 *unionization of Starbucks stores:* Rani Molla, "How a Bunch of Starbucks Baristas Built a Labor Movement," Vox, last modified April 2, 2022, https://www.vox.com/recode/22993509/starbucks-successful-union-drive.

CHAPTER 7: LIVING A FINANCIAL FEMINIST LIFESTYLE

264 *"Political power is ephemeral":* Susan Chira, "Money Is Power. And Women Need More of Both," *New York Times,* March 10, 2018, https://www.nytimes.com/2018/03/10/sunday-review/women-money-politics-power.html.

264 *On the individual level:* Will Tucker, "Hillary Clinton Raised More from Women Than Any Recent Candidate. Donald Trump Raised Less," Yahoo! News, last modified June 10, 2016, https://www.yahoo.com/news/hillary-clinton-raised-more-women-211806168.html.

ABOUT THE AUTHOR

TORI DUNLAP is an internationally recognized money expert and podcast host. After saving $100,000 at age twenty-five, Tori quit her corporate job in marketing and founded Her First $100K to fight financial inequality by giving women actionable resources to better their money.

Host of the number one business podcast *Financial Feminist*, Tori has been featured on *Good Morning America*, the *Today* show, the *New York Times*, *Entrepreneur*, BuzzFeed, CNN, and more. Called "the voice of financial confidence for women" by CNBC, she has helped more than 3 million women negotiate their salaries, pay off debt, build savings, and invest.

Tori now travels the world writing and speaking about personal finance, entrepreneurship, and confidence for women. Based in Seattle, right now she's probably eating fried chicken and watching a Timothée Chalamet YouTube compilation.